Art for All the Children

Art for All the Children

A CREATIVE SOURCEBOOK
FOR THE IMPAIRED CHILD

By

FRANCES E. ANDERSON, Ed.D., ATR

Department of Art
Illinois State University
Normal, Illinois

With a Foreword by

Sandra Packard, Ed.D., ATR

Department of Art
Miami University
Oxford, Ohio

CHARLES C THOMAS · PUBLISHER
Springfield · Illinois · U.S.A.

Published and Distributed Throughout the World by
CHARLES C THOMAS • PUBLISHER
Bannerstone House
301-327 East Lawrence Avenue, Springfield, Illinois, U.S.A.

© 1978, by CHARLES C THOMAS • PUBLISHER
ISBN 0-398-03737-X
Library of Congress Catalog Card Number: 77-13602

*With THOMAS BOOKS careful attention is given to all details of
manufacturing and design. It is the Publisher's desire to present books that are
satisfactory as to their physical qualities and artistic possibilities and
appropriate for their particular use. THOMAS BOOKS will be true to those
laws of quality that assure a good name and good will.*

Library of Congress Cataloging in Publication Data

Anderson, Frances Elisabeth, 1941-
    Art for all the children.

    Bibliography: p.
    Includes index.
    1. Exceptional children—Education—Art. I. Title.
LC3970.A53   371.9′044   77-13602
ISBN 0-398-03737-X

Printed in the United States of America
C-2

Many of us have had at least one profoundly influential teacher in our lives. I have been fortunate in having many. In this work I gratefully acknowledge the influence of a truly gifted teacher, Larry S. Barnfield. It is to him and to the very special children at Metcalf Laboratory School, Illinois State University (who have taught me far more than I could ever teach them) that I dedicate this sourcebook. I praise God for the influence of these exceptional teachers and for the Creative Spirit which makes all artistic endeavor possible.

F. E. A.

FOREWORD

TODAY, WE ARE WITNESSING an unprecedented interest in impaired children. Activist parents, concerned educators, and responsive legislators are working together to demand and provide adequate education for them. In 1976, one out of ten, or approximately eight million school-aged children were handicapped, yet only about 40 percent of these children were enrolled in public or special schools. Now, with federal legislation mandating states to provide handicapped children access to a free, appropriate, and the least restrictive possible education, and with the concurrent outpouring of federal and state funds to achieve this goal, we are seeing a significant increase in the number of impaired children in the schools.

More is occurring than just an increase in school attendance, however. As this book reflects, our perspective on impaired children is shifting, as are our goals for them. The emphasis is on the child and his or her potential, not on the roadblock to reaching it. Doctor Anderson points out that these "children may have strange sounding labels like osteogenesis imperfecta, perceptually handicapped, athetoid cerebral palsied, multiply handicapped, hearing impaired, socially maladjusted, and on and on and on, but mostly they are children."

This book is most timely then. It comes at a period when there is a new belief in these children and in the potential of education for them. It is a multipurpose text, designed to serve the needs of several audiences. For the art teacher and therapist, it provides a treasure chest of art activities and ideas, with guidelines on adapting them for specific impairments. For the layperson and student, a concise explanation of each impairment and benefits of art activity for children with these impairments is provided. Also, most helpful are guidelines for using behavioral objectives and growth evaluation charts, ideas for mainstreaming art into the regular school program, and everything one needs to know about art materials and where to get them. This book is both text and sourcebook. It can be read from cover to cover for an introduction to the topic, or it can be entered at any point for guidance on what to do with a specific child.

Last but perhaps most important is that this book is a successful gestalt of art education knowledge and theory and art therapy insight and practice, both of which are forged in reality. In writing this book, Doctor Anderson drew upon her years of art teaching and art therapy with handi-

capped and nonhandicapped children, university students, and older
adults. It is a book of love and commitment to the value of art, of children, and of life.

SANDRA PACKARD, Ed.D., ATR
Miami University

INTRODUCTION

Art Is for All the Children

IN THIS LAST QUARTER of the century, a growing concern and interest is being focused on all kinds of impaired children. These are children who are mentally retarded, physically disabled, emotionally disturbed, or, as is more usually the case, a combination of these disabilities. In statistical terms, I am talking about a large part of our population, about eight million children (Public Law 94-142).

Parents of these handicapped children are demanding that their offspring have the same educational opportunities that other children have and sometimes take for granted. State and federal legislatures have and are continuing to respond to these demands (Absen, 1972; Public Law 92-424; Public Law 93-516, Sec. 504; Public Law 94-142).

It is especially important now when attention is centering on the educational needs of impaired children that we also focus on their artistic needs. Do the visual arts have meaning and value for the handicapped child? Indeed, yes. In some ways, the visual arts have far greater meaning and value for the atypical child. The values of arts programming for impaired children are legion. I shall mention only a few of these values here.

Initially, I cannot underscore too emphatically that the arts have *intrinsic value* in and of themselves. The arts are important for their own sake. They enrich and enhance our lives because they *are*. The arts are necessary requisites for what philosophers have called the "good life."

The arts provide vocational opportunities as well as life enrichments and embellishments. The artist, either amateur or professional, never retires. He has a lifelong activity requiring a minimal amount of equipment and a maximum amount of independence. Moreover, considering the implications of the concept of Art for Life's Sake, we may begin to realize how meaningful art can be for a handicapped child.

The need for man to create, to make images, is one of his basic drives. This is especially true of the impaired child who has fewer opportunities for creative expression. As such, this child may have more of a need for such expressive outlets. It is my belief, one shared by other writers in the arts (Langer, 1957; Lowenfeld, 1957; Stolnitz, 1960; Kramer, 1958), that there is a cathartic and therapeutic aspect to all artistic endeavor.

This sourcebook has emerged as the result of my frustrations in finding suitable materials and experiences for preparing special education teachers and for art teachers faced with the problem of teaching handicapped children who have been mainstreamed into the art room. Rarely is the art teacher prepared for this task which has been thrust upon him.

With the typical child, an art program focuses primarily on the structure and content of art; however, with the impaired child, the focus must be more on the child. Therefore, in this sourcebook, I focus on the *special child* and the ways that the arts can facilitate his total educational, emotional and physical development.

Art can enhance the impaired child's communication and cooperation skills. Art can also assist in building a positive self-concept which is crucial for a handicapped person. Throughout this book I discuss these skills, and I devote a chapter to "Developing a Sense of Self Through Art."

One of the very special child's needs is to express, create, and affirm himself as a creative, productive *human being*. This principle underlies every art activity I discuss, and I give special attention to these aspects of the arts in the chapter entitled "Being, Becoming, and Expressing Through Art."

One of the realities of the special education curriculum is the insufficient time for academic learning. Art can play an important role as a vehicle for and reinforcer of such academic skills. Art can be at the core of the curriculum. My dream of an art-centered curriculum is reality in some special education classes. It is my hope that the art-centered curriculum will become the norm instead of the exception. In the chapter entitled "Mainstreaming Art," I demonstrate for parents and classroom teachers implications of an integrated art approach for instruction in mathematics, science, and social studies.

The art learning situations I describe in the pages that follow may be remedial, therapeutic, educational, or all of these. Above all, they are *art* activities. They deal with the materials of art and are organized around the structure and principles of design. The goal of these activities is to provide aesthetic experiences which can occur either in the artistic process or in perceiving the outcomes of the process.

The art program I conceptualize in these pages is based on art activities I have found to be most effective in my own work with a variety of exceptional children. Adaptations are crucial to planning arts programming for impaired children. Therefore, I have suggested adaptations as a part of every art situation I discuss.

This sourcebook is not a visionary text. I have focused on pragmatic applications as opposed to theoretical constructs. My aim is to provide basic information necessary to arts programming for special children. For this reason, I have included a section on the artistic development of typical children and a brief description of the major categories of impairments which children may have.

It takes time, thought, and materials to launch an art program. Therefore, I also briefly discuss art materials and include a bare-bones art survival kit for the novice who needs to know the "what, where, when, and how much" of art supplies.

Such information is necessary in providing a foundation for what *could be*. We cannot dream or imagine what *could* be unless we know what is.

Some empirical research has been and is being done in the area of art and special education, but many more investigations are needed. However, carefully controlled empirical research takes time. Meanwhile, the handicapped child waits. I do not want to have this child wait much longer for an art program that is rightfully his.

The art experiences which I suggest in this sourcebook are just that: *suggestions*. A simple prescription for an art program is not the goal. This is in fact an impossibility. The goal, rather, is for the reader to learn from these examples and to *go forward* from them to develop *his own* series of appropriate creative endeavors.

In sum, I have noted the profound need of getting art into the lives of all handicapped children. That happy day when competently trained arts professionals are present in every typical and *atypical* situation is not yet upon us. Realistically, such an utopia is not immediately within grasp, in part because of the dearth of literature that might facilitate this goal. With the penning of this sourcebook, I hope and trust that some of the needs of special children and of adults who have formal and informal contact with these children will be met. We cannot deprive impaired children any longer.

REFERENCES

Absen, A. (Ed.) *A continuing summary of pending and completed litigation regarding the education of handicapped children.* Reston, Va.: Council for Exceptional Children, (5), 1972.

Kramer, E. *Art therapy in a children's community.* Springfield: Thomas, 1958.

Langer, S. *Problems of art.* New York: Scribner's, 1957.

Lowenfeld, V. *Creative and mental growth* (3rd ed.). New York: Macmillan, 1957.

Public Law 92-424, 1972.

Public Law 93-516, 1974.

Public Law 94-142, 1975.

Stolnitz, J. *Aesthetics and philosophy of art criticism.* Boston: Houghton Mifflin, 1960.

ACKNOWLEDGEMENTS

IN SO MANY, MANY WAYS large and small this writing has been a collective effort. I am grateful to Illinois State University for providing the situations, experiences and raw data out of which this work has been formed. A university sabbatical gave me the precious gift of time for reflection and for idea syntheses. The Center for Instructional Research and Curriculum Evaluation at the University of Illinois and the Art Department at the University of Arizona provided the supportive scholarly environs so essential for writing, and I am indebted to both institutions and their staffs.

Special thanks go to the families of the very special children for permitting me to include photographs of their children and their art in this book. I also wish to thank Samuel Kirk and Houghton Mifflin Publishing Company for permitting me to paraphrase some parts of *Educating Exceptional Children* (2nd ed.), 1972, and W. Lambert Brittain and the Macmillan Company for permitting me to paraphrase material from W. L. Brittain and V. Lowenfeld's *Creative and Mental Growth* (6th ed.), 1975.

A special word of appreciation goes to Barry E. Moore, Ed.D., Curator, International Collection of Child Art, Ewing Museum of Nations, Illinois State University and his staff for offering wise counsel and examples of typical children's art work which appear in Chapter II.

Several colleagues have offered perceptive critical comments. I wish to particularly thank Richard A. Salome, Robert Cardinale, Betty Wilson and Marilyn Raybould.

Additionally, I want to acknowledge and thank E. J. Bronkema for her keen eye, patient proofreading, and insightful suggestions during the final phases of this work. Thanks also go to Mary L. Leone for her efforts in typing the several drafts of this work.

I also wish to credit my graduate training under the tutelage of Guy A. Hubbard and the late Mary J. Rouse. I hope this sourcebook reflects well on these mentors and on Indiana University and continues their fine tradition of scholarship, humanism, and pragmatism.

For the moral and spiritual support of family and friends, I am most grateful and appreciative. Finally, I gratefully acknowledge the Lord for His gifts of talent, energy, wisdom, and discernment, and I thank Him for bringing this endeavor to fruition. (I Chronicles, xxix:11-14).

F. E. A.

CONTENTS

Art for All the Children

Throughout the text of this book, the masculine form of pronouns has been used. This has been done for literary purposes and is not meant to imply prejudice of any kind.

F. E. A.

Chapter I

WHO ARE THEY? CHILDREN FIRST AND FOREMOST!

A Brief Discussion of Impairments

INTRODUCTION

IMPAIRED CHILDREN may have strange-sounding labels like osteogenesis imperfecta, perceptually handicapped, athetoid cerebral palsied, multiply handicapped, hearing impaired, socially maladjusted, and on and on, but mostly they are children. In fact, there is a trend (Kirk & Lord, 1974) now *not* to label or categorize special children because such labels can become stigmas and children often have more than one disability, i.e., they are multiply handicapped. However, some comprehension of these categories will be helpful in grasping a better understanding of various impairments. The special education student or teacher may already know what all these labels and descriptions mean. The student or teacher of the visual arts or the regular classroom teacher, however, may not understand all these categories. This section is primarily for those adults who may not know the meaning of the descriptive names.

Six areas of impairment are briefly discussed:* learning disabled, mentally retarded, hearing impaired, visually impaired, physically handicapped, and behaviorally disordered. Some information about ways art activities might be tailored for children having these impairments is also included. More specific information about adaptations for art are included as a part of every art activity discussed in the rest of the sourcebook. There is some conscious redundancy of information on adaptations so that readers do not have to continually refer back to this first chapter.

LEARNING DISABLED

Children with learning disabilities have a *specific* impairment in the development of their ability to speak, perceive, read, think, write, spell, and/or calculate. These impairments are not caused primarily by visual, auditory, physical, mental, or behavioral handicaps or by environmental disadvantages. Learning disabled children may appear normal in all but one area of information processing, communicating, or expressing. Thus, one particular child may not be able to read but can learn by listening. Another child may have problems following verbal instructions but have

---

* Some material in this section has been paraphrased by permission from Kirk, S. A., *Educating exceptional children.* Boston: Houghton Mifflin, 1972.

no problem following a visual demonstration. Every individual learns best through one of four learning modes: looking, listening, touching, or moving.

Children with learning disabilities may have problems with gross and fine motor development. They may need help with basic psychomotor skills such as hopping, running, or catching a ball. Eye-hand coordination may also be a problem area. The learning disabled child may easily grasp many cognitive concepts but may need extra help and practice with fundamental skills such as cutting and pounding nails. Art can provide some of the basic remediation in these areas.

Some children may have problems with sequencing and visual and/or auditory memory. Art can reinforce sequencing abilities because many art activities require following steps in a specific order. It may be helpful to use both verbal and visual demonstrations of the sequences involved (Lerner, 1972). At times it may be important to combine a kinesthetic experience with a tactile experience in presenting an art lesson. For example, in presenting a lesson on basic geometric shapes, the children can tactilely explore cardboard shapes and form these shapes with their bodies. Sometimes using several sensory channels for instruction may provide an overload of stimuli for some learning disabled.

Some children may have very short attention spans and be hyperactive; others may be hypoactive and very slow in their movements. Hypoactive children may need to do some active learning before getting down to the art task. Perhaps having these slower-moving children stand for awhile during the start of the lesson can help (*Insights*, 1976). Some of these children may be on a special behavior modification program which the entire treatment team should consistently use. Setting up a reward system in the art lesson for appropriate social as well as artistic behaviors may help. The special classroom teacher can assist in planning such a reward system.

The hyperactive child may need more active learning experiences and/or times when he can be moving around the art room. In this situation, establishing specific rules and maintaining a consistent structure will help. Hyperactive children are easily distracted, and a classroom environment that is free of a lot of distracting and changing stimuli may be necessary.

Other children may have problems in social development. Socially poor development in learning disabled children usually means that they have a negative self-image and their body-concepts are poorly developed (Harris, 1963). They may have trouble working independently and will need encouragement and situations in art where they must work on their own. Some may have problems with laterality; this means they shift hand preference by sometimes using the right hand, sometimes the left. A choice of handedness should be made and consistently reinforced by the teacher. Finally, children with social development problems need a clear distinction between the real world and the world of fantasy. It will help to continually underscore what things are imagined and what things are a part of the real world.

Some children may have a perseveration problem: they dwell ideationally, conceptually, or physically on one task or subject and cannot shift without help from the teacher. Perseveration needs to be stopped and the child's attention shifted to something else.

Art is especially helpful for children who have perceptual-learning disabilities because perception is a learned behavior (Lerner, 1972; McFee, 1972) and a great deal of art focuses on perceptual development. Children with perceptual-learning problems may see only total configurations (gestalts) and not parts of items. Other children may have trouble with part-whole perception and have problems seeing gestalts, seeing instead only parts of objects. Both abilities are necessary. A child who does not see total wholes may color parts of objects instead of the whole thing. For example, a shirt may have one sleeve at the fold colored green and the rest of the sleeve colored blue (Lerner, 1972).

Children also may have trouble with figure-ground differentiation and may not be able to distinguish an object from its background. In discussing art work, the teacher may need to emphasize those parts that are background and those parts that are figures. Some specific art activities which may help with this problem are the geoboard and the puzzle activities described in Chapter V.

When children have trouble with visual closure, they cannot identify an item when part of it is missing. Starter sheets described in Chapter IV and the geoboards and the puzzle activity already mentioned can also assist with this problem. Three-dimensional art work may help children who have problems with spatial relationships and with seeing an item surrounded by space. The abilities to visually identify an object (object recognition) and to distinguish one object from another by sight (visual discrimination) can be helped by many art activities. Examples of such art activities are the texture sequence described in Chapter IV and the shape search described in Chapter V.

Visualization is the capacity to remember what has been seen and touched and to see it with the mind's eye. Visualization is a very important and complex perceptual ability. Many basic drawing and painting activities based on memory of either immediate past events (this morning's field trip) or several months ago (last summer's activities) can help the child to visualize. Visually expressing what the child plans to do in the future also helps him visualize.

It is important to remember that learning disabled children may frustrate easily. It helps to provide some choices and limits within which the child can work in an art activity. Many learning disabled children have poor self-concepts and body-images. The activities in Chapter IV are all designed to assist the child with building his body-image; Chapter VI focuses on activities that foster positive self-attitudes.

There are many, many learning problems, and each must be treated on an individual basis. Only some of the learning problems have been discussed. The art teacher must be sensitively attuned to the specifics of each child's learning impairment. This will mean spending time consulting with the classroom or resource teacher and spending time looking in files before planning specific art experiences and adaptations.

BEHAVIORALLY DISORDERED

The socially maladjusted child and the emotionally disturbed child are included in the behaviorally disordered category. Socially maladjusted children can adapt in their own subculture (usually a peer group or a gang). However, they will probably be in conflict with those in authority, such as parents, teachers, or the police. They are usually behind academically and are destructive and immature socially. They may engage in malicious behavior, cheat, lie, steal, and rebel against rules and regulations. They may be very aggressive and use obscene, inappropriate language. The socially maladjusted child is not prone to trusting others.

Emotionally disturbed children may exhibit a great deal of anxiety and may be withdrawn and socially isolated. They may spend a lot of time in a fantasy world. They cry easily, complain about physical ailments, and exhibit other neurotic behaviors. They also can be very belligerent, aggressive, and distrustful and can display other psychotic behavior patterns.

Because the behaviorally disordered exhibit maladaptive-inappropriate behavior, they require a special educational program. It is probable that such children may be placed in an educational framework which utilizes either a behavior modification or a psychoeducational approach. Since it will be important to follow the educational strategy being used in the rest of the child's program, a brief discussion of these two approaches will be given.

In the behavior modification approach, the assumption is that all behavior is learned (Ullman and Krasner, 1969). There are two basic types of conditioning: respondent (classical) and operant. In classical conditioning, responses (respondents) are learned by their proceeding stimuli. For example, a child may be presented with a loud noise (something already causing a fright response in the child) paired with a red tulip. After doing this a number of times, the red tulip is presented without the noise and the child gives the same frightened response. The fear reaction can be changed by presenting the red tulip along with a pleasurable stimuli (something the child really likes). This is done a little at a time and at a distance at first. Gradually, the child is encouraged to move closer and closer until he is desensitized and no longer gives a frightened response.

Operant conditioning (learning) is based on the premise that a person's actions are a function of his consequences. For example, to get a child to stop talking without raising his hand, the child is not recognized or attended to unless his hand is raised. Therefore, his attempts at getting attention are not rewarded (reinforced) unless the behavior is appropriate (he raised his hand). This may require several steps, and it may be necessary to reward closer and closer approximations of the behavior. Behavior modification requires identifying the behavior that is malappropriate, analyzing the events that are rewarding this behavior, and reordering the environs so that the rewards are no longer affecting the child.

Sometimes the child is placed on a specific reward system called a token economy. In this arrangement, the child is given points or some other token for an appropriate response and behavior. At the end of the period or lesson, the child is told specifically when and how his behavior was appropriate, and his points are added up. These points can then be turned in for other rewards, such as toys or snacks at the end of the day.

A more-or-less eclectic approach to the education of the behaviorally disordered child is the strategy termed psychoeducational. It is concerned with why a child does something (similar to the psychodynamic strategy) and what the child is doing (similar to the behavior modification approach). The psychoeducational strategy aims at breaking the frustration/ failure cycle that a behaviorally disordered child may have as he fails to measure up to the school expectations. These are expectations in terms of classroom behavior and academic performance and the consequent non-acceptance the child receives from peers and teachers. To intervene, it is important to consider the expectations and pressures on the child and his coping skills in the situation. Key factors in the intervention program are also the child's relationships with peers and the teacher, his motivation for the inappropriate behavior, and his self-image.

The teacher has at least four ways of coping with the child's inappropriate behavior. The teacher can reorder the learning situation to prevent disruptions. Certain behaviors can be permitted at certain appropriate times, such as on the playground. The teacher can tolerate some of the inappropriate behavior until the child can gain self-control. It is important that the child be told after control is gained that his behavior is expected to improve. Finally, the teacher may also choose to interrupt a behavior when one or more children are endangered or the class totally disrupted (Long & Newman, 1965; Long et al., 1976).

In the art activities, it will be important to have a structured approach with clear explanations of acceptable behaviors and consequences for inappropriate behaviors. This will be true whether the child is alone or in a small group. A firm but not rigid approach is recommended. Of course, there must be consistency with the educational program in the classroom.

A consistent routine will be important in terms of getting ready, presenting the activity, working, sharing time, and cleaning up. It may be helpful to provide choices so that unnecessary power plays with authority are eliminated. Setting up specific limits may help the child know where he stands. Using a game format for some of the art activities can also help motivate children and set some of these limits (Morse, 1975). The classroom teacher can help in determining some of these boundaries. The learning encounter itself can provide structure. For example, the teacher may establish a working policy in which everyone tries the activity or picks one of several choices. Just sitting quietly and watching might be one of the choices. It will be important to accept the child's efforts and to provide, at least at the start of the term, brief lessons with a high success factor.

Good work habits and efforts should be encouraged and praised. Not reacting at all to poor efforts may be best. The focus should be on rewarding best efforts and withholding reinforcement of poorer efforts. This is a more constructive approach than punishing a child for poor use of materials or an apathetic response. Such negative attention can become a positive reinforcement to the child, who thus may continue the inappropriate behavior.

Teachers need to be aware of the low frustration tolerance and short attention spans that many children with behavior disorders have. A second activity can be planned for those with attention problems. For many, it will be important to provide a positive outlet for feelings, and such expression should be encouraged. Until the teacher knows the child's limits and abilities, whatever attempts are made should be accepted.

It will be important to encourage cooperation and the sharing of materials. Group work can build social skills. However, there may also be problems in having children working in groups. Groups need to be carefully chosen.

Other therapeutic approaches have not been included because they are the domain of the professional art therapist. The art therapist may use any of a number of treatments with a particular child in a counseling setting, such as psychodynamic, gestalt, or existential strategies. The very nature of the artistic process can be a source of therapy and healing. This happens in the classroom or wherever the child produces art. The teacher should be aware of this therapeutic aspect of art. He must also be aware that specific art therapeutic treatment is *not* his responsibility. Such responsibility rests with the professionally qualified art therapist. (The exception would be that unique individual who is trained and certified as both a teacher and a therapist.)

HEARING IMPAIRED

The hearing impaired include the deaf and hard-of-hearing children. The hard-of-hearing child will probably be integrated with regular classes, though he may have special work in speech correction and auditory training. Hard-of-hearing children may have some speech problems, but their language and communication development is similar to their nonimpaired classmates. For better communication, it may be necessary for the teacher to look directly at the hearing impaired child and to speak distinctly, sometimes at a close range. In other respects, hard-of-hearing children are no different from other children. Their artistic abilities will be as typical as others their own age and class level (Silver, 1966).

Deaf children are those who lost their hearing prior to the time they gained speech and language or who were born without hearing (Kirk, 1972). In many ways, it is a miracle to be able to reach and teach the deaf child because he does not have verbal language which is the most important stimulus to mental development (Telford & Sawrey, 1977). Concept development is an important part of language development. It is very difficult to teach language because there are many concepts which cannot be pointed to and acted out. For example, it may be relatively easy to teach the concept and word *ball* but extremely difficult to teach the concept and word for *love, God, patriot,* or other abstractions.

The deaf child may begin school as early as two years of age. In addition to the regular school program, emphasis is on reading, language, speech, and speech reading. The curriculum includes many concrete experiences and demonstrations and dramatizations. There is also a heavy reliance on visual learning and imitation.

The deaf child is usually three to five years behind in educational achievement, and as he grows, this gap grows. The average reading level for a deaf person is third grade, but 10 percent of the deaf can read at the ninth grade level or higher. There is less of a lag in arithmetic, spelling, and motor skills (Telford & Sawrey, 1977). These lags in academic skills do *not* mean that the deaf child is less intelligent than his hearing peer.

The current trend in communication with the deaf is for them to use a combination of speech reading, sign language, and finger spelling. If the art teacher does not have manual communication skills, he can use gestures, facial expressions, visual demonstrations, and simple written explanations to communicate. In talking with a deaf child, establish eye contact first.

If possible, having an interpreter can be a valuable help with two-way communication. This is especially true with younger children who do not have developed writing and reading skills. Students who use manual or total communication will greatly appreciate the teacher who learns and uses some signs. Such effort will be a concrete demonstration that the art teacher is really trying to communicate.

In planning art instruction, the teacher should be sensitive to the imitative way (learning by modeling) by which many deaf children learn. These children will probably be inclined to copy and imitate either the teacher's examples or another student's work. This is especially true when the child may not fully understand a lesson. Encourage the child to work independently and foster unique solutions to art problems.

Deaf children have difficulty learning abstract concepts, and these concepts must be carefully developed over a period of time. Sometimes children will too quickly generalize from one or two experiences. For example, if they once painted in trays, the children may erroneously assume that every time trays appear in the art class they will paint in them. This kind of behavior is called a deafism. Thus, for the child to make appropriate generalizations, it will help to provide many experiences in building concepts.

When possible, concrete examples should be used in instruction. Working closely with the classroom teacher will help in planning art instruction that reinforces or builds on concepts, especially vocabulary, already being developed in the classroom. Instructional language should be geared to the language level of the children. The teacher should use brief sentences and define all key words that the child may not know. Students should be encouraged to use full sentences.

At times, a deaf child may not have the words to express an experience, but he can visually draw that experience. The expressive channel of art is very important and necessary to healthy educational development. The artistic development of deaf children will be no different from that of hearing children, provided their environment is not deprived (Silver, 1966).

Art also can be an important potential vocation for deaf children. In fact, in a 1972 study of occupations of the deaf (Schien & Marcus, 1974), the second highest percentage (21.3%) made their living as craftspersons.

MENTALLY RETARDED

For the purposes of this sourcebook, retardation includes two groups of children, the educable mentally handicapped and the trainable mentally handicapped. These two groups of children will be discussed separately.

EDUCABLE MENTALLY HANDICAPPED

The educable mentally handicapped child is placed in special programs usually after several years in the regular classroom. His retardation does not become evident until he is retained or held back for a year or longer. Special classes usually do not begin until the educable mentally handicapped child is nine years or older. This child develops at a rate that is one half to three fourths that of an average child. He remains longer at each developmental stage and is slower in learning.

This means that the educable mentally handicapped child may not begin reading until he is eight years old (or older). For example, it takes about seventeen repetitions for a typical child to learn a word in a primer. It takes between twenty-five and thirty repetitions for the educable child to complete the same task (Telford & Sawrey, 1977). His formal schooling may end with the completion of the academic equivalent of between the second and sixth grades. This child is below the normal child in motor abilities, reading, and social development. However, the interests of the educable mentally handicapped child will be similar to normal children of comparable chronological age.

Behavior problems such as short attention span and easy frustration occur when too high expectations are placed on educable mentally handicapped children. This often occurs when they are in a regular class. When these children are placed in special classes (usually between nine and thirteen years), they seem to adjust better socially. Sometimes such classes are resource rooms, and the child will be integrated for special subjects such as art, home economics, and music.

The educational program for the educable mentally handicapped child focuses on helping him attain a minimal level of skill in reading, writing, and mathematics. Programs also emphasize social adaptability so that the child can function independently in the outside community. Occupational abilities are also developed so he can be at least partially economically independent as an adult. Although intelligence quotients are only one means of signifying mental abilities, educable mentally handicapped children have been classified as having a range of intelligence from between 50 and 55 to 75 or 79.

With respect to organizing the art learning, the art specialist should be aware that the retarded child learns at a slower rate. The educable mentally handicapped child has trouble abstracting and generalizing. This child does not pick up skills and concepts incidentally but needs to be taught specifically in each situation. The teacher should not assume that the child can carry over learning from prior experiences (*Insights*, 1976). It is important that the child have some success from each art experience and lesson.

It may be necessary to build longer involvement in art activities over time. Shorter art encounters which focus on one key skill and/or concept which the child can master with little frustration will be most meaningful for the child. The child needs a lot of feedback as he works on his art. This feedback should be encouraging and positively reinforcing to the child.

It also will be important to incorporate repetition of new words and skills through several art sessions. Artistic processes should be broken down into small step increments which allow the child to focus on only one step at a time. It is also very important to provide, over time, a sequence of activities that proceed from easier to more difficult tasks. Such a sequence should include repetition of processes and ideas so that concepts and generalizations can be built.

Providing a cafeteria selection of many different art materials and processes can do more to confuse the child than to improve his expressive abilities and his knowledge of art processes and skills. At the same time, some materials and situations in the art lesson need to be varied to provide maximum involvement and motivation. For example, a lot of time may be spent on developing body-concepts in art. The media and situations in which body-concepts are being accomplished may shift from completing drawings of figures to executing a personalized life-size portrait. The concepts of body awareness and naming body parts are the same throughout, but the materials may vary according to the child's interests and skills.

Finally, it will be important to discover a good match between skills and concepts being taught and the child's ability to grasp them. Additionally, working as a team with other teachers can provide a united educational effort for each child. Key academic concepts can then be integrated into art learnings, and consistent classroom management can be maintained. These basic guidelines will also be useful in work with the trainable mentally handicapped child.

TRAINABLE MENTALLY HANDICAPPED

The trainable mentally handicapped child does have learning potential. He can develop self-help abilities and the social adjustment necessary to be at home in his family environment and in the immediate neighborhood. In many cases, he can function in a sheltered workshop situation as an adult. Again, although intelligence cannot be determined by one or two indexes, the trainable mentally handicapped child generally has an intelligence quotient of between 30 to 35 and 50 to 55.

This child develops at between one fourth to one half of the rate of the normal child. The trainable mentally handicapped child reaches a final mental age of between three and seven years. He will not be able to read but will be able to recognize key words. These children will be able to count up to ten, and older students will be able to write numbers. Some will be able to tell time, understand the calendar, comprehend some money concepts, and recall some telephone numbers.

The educational program focuses on self-help skills (dressing, toileting, eating, hygiene) and socialization skills. The curriculum will include using drama to act out stories, singing songs to get across key ideas, discussing pictures, and listening to stories. Older students will also learn prevocational and vocational skills such as cooking, sewing and gardening.

One of the problems that the trainable mentally handicapped child has is his delayed and poor motor development. An art program should focus on basic art skills such as proper use and care of art media, tools, and materials. Once the child has mastered the basic use of artistic media, he can use these skills for expression. The art teacher must realize the developmental lag that these children have. Therefore, a child who is scribbling is probably only functioning at an artistic developmental stage of a typical two-year-old. Such a child cannot be expected to draw, paint, or use art media in the same way as his counterparts in the regular classroom who may be the same chronological age.

The art program will be similar to that of a preprimary art curriculum. Manipulative and sensory approaches would be part of the program's focus. Assuming they are beyond the scribbling stage, it would be important to allow time for children to develop their own expressive abilities with art materials. Time to work with drawing and painting media should be provided. Sometimes, some art media such as paint are too fluid and too hard for some children to control, and they get frustrated. The teacher must be sensitive to this and to a child's possible frustration resulting from being offered too many choices.

A limited choice of materials and activities is encouraged, but some choice should be a part of each activity. Simple (but not simplistic) activities that provide for lots of repetition of basic ideas and key concepts are helpful. It must be remembered that these children have a short attention span and limited recall.

The teacher will want to work closely with the other adults who are a part of the trainable mentally handicapped child's educational team. This cooperation will provide important carry-over of management programs and academic concepts. Integrating the art activities with classroom activities may be important means of emphasizing key concepts and motivating these children. All staff must respond consistently to each child.

Older trainable mentally handicapped students can be taught art skills that may be used in a sheltered workshop setting. The skills discussed in the textiles section in Chapter VI are being used in at least one such facility (the Arizona Training Program at Tucson).

VISUALLY IMPAIRED

Included in this category are the partially sighted and the blind. The partially sighted are children who can be taught to read print with the help of enlargements and the use of magnification. The blind are those children who must use braille to read and cannot rely on vision for learning. The very first special education programs were initiated for the blind. Although the blind are a small group, there are ten times more legal, social, and educational services for them than for any other group of impaired individuals (Telford & Sawrey, 1977). Thus, there seems to be a great empathy for the blind person.

About 85 percent of what is learned is through vision. The blind child must shift to learning via the other sensory channels of feeling, hearing, and body sensation. There is a great need to develop listening skills. Braille reading is from one fourth to one third slower than visual reading. The blind have difficulty developing spatial concepts. There is some evidence that they think in more concrete terms and use less abstraction than their sighted peers (Telford & Sawrey, 1977).

Because the blind do not have usual visual cues to help in learning through modeling, there is a need for training in social skills such as eating, dressing, and basic social interactions. Development in all areas of motor coordination, socialization, speech, and mobility will be slower in blind children than in sighted children unless special training is provided. There is no evidence of special musical abilities or greater sensitivity to sound or touch. The blind may just rely more on these other senses.

It is important for the blind to develop the ability to use a variety of types of imagery. This will help them to grasp concepts which cannot be presented concretely or with real models. One of the greatest needs is to have the blind and the partially sighted develop mobility which will increase their independence and build their self-respect.

There is a need for a combination of tactile experiences along with verbal explanations in instruction. Ideas must be presented as a totality. For example, the child must have a total idea of a store before discussing a story about shopping. Real and concrete experiences with actual objects and models will help. Finally, there is a continuing need for providing the visually impaired with many opportunities to work independently. The emphasis now is on programs to help the partially sighted child make full use of whatever sight he may have. The trend is to integrate the visually impaired for at least a part of the school day.

As in other parts of the educational program, the art program must be tailored to each individual child. Art activities can be an important avenue for expression. Not only partially sighted but also blind children can become deeply involved in art (Rubin & Klineman, 1974; Fukurai, 1974). Naturally, three-dimensional and textured media will be a major part of such a program. Blind children can also paint and draw. Their interests will parallel those of their sighted peers.

Some adaptations will be necessary in planning art activities. Adaptations might include the consistent setup of a work area, different sized containers for different paint colors, or consistent placement of paint in braille-marked, spill-resistant, weighted containers. Having the child paint or draw on a tray with shallow edges will provide working limits for him. Sometimes it may help to put a dab of glue or tear a piece out of the drawing paper to provide an orientation point. Both the tray and the paper should be secured to the work table with *C* clamps and/or tape. Sometimes it helps to place a sheet of window screen under the drawing paper. The screen will help produce a textured path as the child draws with a crayon. Specifically scented markers can be used in drawing. These will help the child to identify colors, since each has a different color-related aroma.

When new media are being introduced, have the child explore each material in a sequence. In presenting a new art activity, it can be very helpful to have some completed examples to enable the child to grasp the total concept tactilely before beginning his own work. The child may need encouragement to become involved in messy materials. The art environment should allow the child maximum mobility and enable his rapid orientation to materials and their location. Such materials should be consistently stored and easily accessible to the child so he can work as independently as possible.

PHYSICALLY HANDICAPPED

The physically handicapped are a large, heterogeneous group of children whose one common denominator is their below-average physical ability. One major division is determined by those impairments caused by damage to the central nervous system. Within this group of neurologically disabled, one large category is the cerebral palsied.

Cerebral palsied children have had early (sometimes prenatal) damage to the motor area of the brain. There are three basic types of cerebral palsy. Those with the spastic type exhibit sporadic and uncoordinated muscle movement and rigid and distorted reflexes. When a spastic concentrates on controlling a particular movement, this concentration often produces the reverse effect. Those with the athetoid type have slow, undulating, snakelike motions of their paralyzed limbs. These movements are involuntary. Often it is the arms and hands which are affected the most in athetoid cerebral palsy. (Children who have severe physical impairments are described as being severely involved.) Efforts made by the child to control a motion may result in greater spasticity. Those having ataxia act as though inebriated, with awkward motion and slurred language.

Another way of describing cerebral palsy and other physical disabilities is by classifying the limbs and parts of the body affected. The monoplegic has one limb involved. The hemiplegic has both limbs on one side affected, while the triplegic has three limbs affected. The quadriplegic or bilateral hemiplegic has other involvement in addition to affected arms and legs. The paraplegic has just the legs affected, and the symmetrical diplegic has all limbs paralyzed. In addition to problems of muscle control in the limbs, children with cerebral palsy may have vision and speech problems. Some children may also have hearing problems and mental retardation.

Epilepsy is caused by a functional disturbance to the brain cells and results in intermittent seizures. In grand mal epilepsy, sometimes there is a warning (aura) that a seizure is coming. This aura may be in the form of strange sounds, visual phenomena, or an internal feeling. Initially there is a tonic phase to the seizure in which muscles are rigid and then a clonic stage where there are jerky muscular convulsions. This clonic stage lasts about three minutes, and then the child falls into a deep sleep. Often grand mal epilepsy is controlled by medication. This medication can slow the child's other responses and thinking processes.

When a child has a seizure, it is important to remain calm and be sure that the child is on his side and that the tongue has not been swallowed. Sometimes it may help to hold the child so he does not injure his head or other parts of his body during the clonic phase. It will be important to explain to the other children in the class that the child is just temporarily ill. The child should rest after the seizure, and parents and medical staff should be notified.

In petit mal epilepsy, there is a brief unconscious seizure stage that lasts only a few seconds. The child's head may nod and eyes blink. Children who have petit mal attacks often outgrow them.

Spina bifida is a birth defect in which the bones do not close in the spinal area. In one form, a neurological impairment results in the paralysis of the legs and incontinence. This lack of sphincter and bowel control can present a problem if the child is integrated into regular classes.

The orthopedically handicapped child is either born or later crippled due to injury to bones, joints, or muscles. These impairments require a special education program. Examples of some of the birth defects are curvature of the spine, wryneck, hunched back, dislocated hips, spontaneous bone breakage (osteogenesis imperfecta), and hemophilia.

With children who have osteogenesis imperfecta or hemophilia, it will be important to plan activities and arrange the class environment so that they do not bump or bruise themselves. Materials that require a lot of pounding (clay, hammers and nails) and sharp tools should be avoided and adaptations developed. For example, glue may be used instead of nails in constructing activities. Children who have these diseases have a high rate of absenteeism due to medical treatment for broken bones and blood clotting.

Muscular dystrophy is a hereditary disease five or six times more prevalent in males than in females. It is discovered at about three years and results in gradual internal weakening of the voluntary muscles, usually in the arms and legs. As much as the child's condition permits, the muscles should be used and the child integrated into the regular classroom. Children with muscular dystrophy rarely live into adulthood because other internal muscles gradually atrophy.

Arthritis is a progressive chronic disease which results in swollen and painful joints. The childhood form is called rheumatoid arthritis, and with maturity some individuals outgrow the disease.

Other physical disabilities include heart defects, diabetes, and respiratory disorders such as asthma and cystic fibrosis (a chronic lung infection). Usually these disabilities do not require placement in a special education program, and most children with these problems are integrated into regular classes.

Individuals with physical handicaps may have some problems adjusting to them. The handicapped child may have a greater degree of shyness and be less extroverted and more self-conscious than other children. The child probably lives in a more restricted environment because of his handicap. In addition, many families may be overprotective of their physically handicapped members. The handicapped child may have problems accepting his limited abilities, and there may be a gap between what he desires to accomplish and what he is realistically able to do.

The physically handicapped child may also have a greater need for acceptance because he may be quite deformed. This is a vicious circle because the child may already have experienced a lot of rejection due to the deformity. He will need experiences which help build a positive self-image and body-image. He will also need experiences which build his feeling of independence and enable him to work on his own without a lot of help from others, especially from adults. His frustrations may reveal themselves in terms of verbally aggressive behaviors, regression to more childish modes of acting, and withdrawal into fantasy. It will be important to help the child to set realistic immediate and long-term goals.

Much of the educational programming for physically handicapped children is individualized. A lot of vicarious and first-hand experiences are important, as these children's impairments may have precluded such encounters outside of school. The physically handicapped child may be educationally behind his nonimpaired classmates simply because he has not been as able to personally experience much of the world. In the education programs, emphasis is on developing self-sufficiency and on language and speech remediation. As much as possible, physically handicapped children will be mainstreamed for at least part of their school day.

In the art program, working closely with the special teacher and with each child is essential. Often, the child is the best source of information about what can or cannot be accomplished and the best ways to arrange work areas. It will be important to develop an atmosphere of acceptance and a willingness to explore and try new processes. Unless the child has full use of his hands, art activities should be developed which do not require fine, detailed work.

Physical adaptations of art media may be required. For example, handles of drawing and painting tools may need to be thickened and shortened. A piece of foam rubber, rubber-banded to the handles, will probably thicken handles so they can be easily grasped. Paper should be taped down and water containers and paint containers weighted so that they will not spill.

If it is medically permissible, it may be best to move the child from his wheelchair and let him work on the floor. Children who cannot use their hands may use their feet or may be able to grasp art tools in their teeth. Sometimes art tools can be attached to a helmet for use. Many children need large working areas. If they cannot be moved from their wheelchairs, large drawing boards can be clamped on to their chairs. Other specific adaptations are discussed in the art activities sections of this sourcebook.

REFERENCES

Fukurai, Shiro. *How can I make what I cannot see?* New York: Van Nostrand Reinhold, 1974.

Harris, D. B. *Children's drawings as measures of intellectual maturity.* New York: Harcourt Brace Jovanovich, 1963.

Insights: Art in special education. Millburn, NJ: Art Educators of New Jersey, 1976.

Kirk, S. *Educating exceptional children* (2nd ed.). Boston: Houghton Mifflin, 1972.

Kirk, S., & Ford, F., (Eds.). *Exceptional Children: Educational resources and perspectives.* Boston: Houghton Mifflin, 1974.

Lerner, J. W. *Children with learning disabilities.* Boston: Houghton Mifflin, 1972.

Long, N. C., Morse, W. C. & Newman, R. G. (Eds.). *Conflict in the classroom* (3rd ed.). Belmont, Cal.: Wadsworth, 1976.

Long, N. C., & Newman, R. G. Managing surface behavior of children in school, in Long, N. C. In W. C. Morse & R. G. Newman (Eds.), *Conflict in the classroom.* Belmont, Cal.: Wadsworth, 1965.

Morse, W. G. The education of socially maladjusted and emotionally disturbed children. In W. M. Cruickshank & G. O. Johnson (Eds.), *Education of exceptional children and youth* (3rd ed.). Englewood Cliffs: Prentice-Hall, 1976.

Rubin, J. A., & Klineman, J. They opened our eyes: The story of an art program for multiply-handicapped, visually-impaired children. *Education of the visually handicapped*, 1974, *4*(4), 107-113.

Sarason, I. G. *Abnormal psychology*. New York: Appleton-Century-Crofts, 1972.

Schein, J. D., & Marcus, I. D., Jr. *The deaf population of the United States*. Silver Springs, Md.: National Association of the Deaf, 1974.

Silver, R. A. *The role of art in the conceptual thinking, adjustment and aptitudes of deaf and aphasic children*. Unpublished doctoral dissertation, Columbia University, 1966.

Telford, C. W., & Sawrey, J. M. *The exceptional individual* (3rd ed.). Englewood Cliffs: Prentice-Hall, 1977.

Ullman, L., & Krasner, L. P. *A psychological approach to abnormal behavior*. Englewood Cliffs: Prentice-Hall, 1969.

Chapter II

EVALUATION AND ASSESSMENT: MEASURING THE UNMEASURABLE

INTRODUCTION

How is an art activity or program to be evaluated? How are children to be assessed in their art endeavors? What constitutes success or failure of an activity or lesson? Against what criteria are the merits of an art experience for the special child judged? These can be difficult questions, and there are no easy, pat answers to them. There are some guidelines which the adult can follow. These are just that, however: guidelines. The reader may wish to expand on these and develop his own methods. In this section, some possibilities for evaluation are presented to provide some choices for the adults who have responsibility for the art programming for special children.

SPECIAL CHILDREN ARE CHILDREN

Most emphatically it should be underscored that special children are *more like* other children than anything else. Special children desire to be treated exactly like other typical school children. Generally, they should be received and handled like any other student. Of course, there will be differences and limitations. However, these should be discovered in the course of an art program and not preconceived of as barriers or hindrances.

Labels can do a great deal of damage and can inadvertently result in preconceptions about what the child can or cannot do. Therefore, it is especially important for adults encountering special children for the first time to view labels with benign neglect. Without relying on labels and making prejudgements, important discoveries have been made about the art abilities of special children (Rubin, 1975). This does not mean a total disregard for any specific handicap or direction which might be prescribed in a child's file. The special education teacher will, of course, be attuned to such information. The art teacher should also be informed, especially in the case of the physically handicapped child, the child under medication, or the child who has epilepsy. Therefore, files as well as the individual child's classroom teacher should be consulted by the art teacher. Mainly this should be done to check on medical issues and possible allergies.

The child should be assessed against his own best efforts. For some children, just getting glue on the correct spot may be a miraculous achievement. For other children, getting glue all over the page and not in one

20

specific place may suggest they are not seriously working. Each child must be considered individually before specific goals and behavioral objectives can be set. Some of the art programs will be, therefore, a voyage of exploration to determine the skills a child has, the amount of eye-hand coordination he possesses, and how much cognitive and perceptual information he now has or can grasp.

At the beginning of the school year, some assessment of basic art skills and concepts may be helpful. A collection of several examples of each child's paintings and drawings will also help. Some topics for these might be a family member, a pet, or a house. This data should also be collected at several intervals during the school year.

It is dangerous to base an evaluation on just one or two pieces of evidence because children have good and bad working days. Research has graphically demonstrated (Kellogg, 1969) that the same child can produce five quite different human figures during the course of just one week. Therefore, in collecting work, obtain several drawings from each session and do so at several time intervals. Some notes should be made about the conditions under which the art works were made and how motivated the child was during the activity.

A beginning checklist has been included as a *suggested* starting point. This checklist summarizes what a classroom or art teacher might need to know about a child before setting objectives or planning a series of art activities. This is *one* way of getting started. The list would vary depending on the age level and other abilities of the particular child. The teacher is encouraged, therefore, to modify this checklist as needed. The more experienced teacher probably already does this sort of assessing on a less formal basis. Nevertheless, formally or informally, some art assessment will be necessary.

GETTING STARTED IN ART
(A BEGINNING CHECKLIST)

Child		Yes	Sometimes	Not Yet
Knows	1. How to hold paint brush and use paint			
	2. How to hold scissors and cut paper with them			
Can	3. Spread glue evenly, using appropriate amount			
	4. Pick out the right colors when given their names			
	5. Name 3 colors			
	6. Identify 3 or more colors by name			
	7. Complete a starter sheet			
	8. Hold a crayon correctly			
Knows	9. How to clean up			
Can	10. Name 3 art activities he did last year and describe the processes.			
Comments:				

Two ways of evaluating the child's art work are to compare his work with his own best efforts and to look for growth over time by comparing drawing, painting, and other current work with work done earlier in the term. There is also another means of making some assessment. This is to compare the work done by the child with what is typically expected in the artistic development of normal children. This is a *general* bench mark and is *not* meant to be anything more.

All children, impaired or not, go through developmental stages. For example, the mentally handicapped child will go through artistic developmental stages, but his progress will be at a slower rate (Saunders, 1968). Thus, it would be erroneous to expect a ten-year-old mentally impaired child at the scribbling stage to accurately complete a starter sheet, execute a painting of the morning's visit to the zoo, or make a pinch pot.

Scribbling typically occurs between the ages of two and four years. This stage must be experienced before progressing to more advanced artistic development (Saunders, 1968; Lowenfeld & Brittain, 1975). Therefore, the mental age of the child should be considered in planning art activities. When this is considered, it has been found that familial retarded children draw figures which do not differ from those of normal children of the same mental age (Golomb, 1976).

Since many classroom teachers may not be familiar with children's typical artistic development, a brief summary will be included here. A synoptic evaluation chart for assessing growth at each level is also included. A detailed analysis of each level is not possible here, and the reader is urged to study other original sources (Harris, 1963; Kellogg, 1970; Lansing, 1969; Lowenfeld & Brittain, 1975).

SUMMARY OF CHILDREN'S TYPICAL ARTISTIC DEVELOPMENT

Perhaps the most widely utilized framework to explain children's normal artistic development is that research by Viktor Lowenfeld (Lowenfeld & Brittain, 1975). There are many others who have researched this basic area (Kellogg, 1969; Lindstrum, 1960; Lansing, 1970), but because Lowenfeld's chronologizing of the artistic stages of development is the most widely known, it is his work which will be discussed.* Some other recent work on the art abilities of normal children will also be included. Some suggestions about what should constitute drawing and painting activities at each level are also discussed.

In using the research of Lowenfeld, the reader must be aware that many children are now a part of the television generation and are developing

---

* Paraphrased by permission from V. Lowenfeld & W. L. Brittain, *Creative and mental growth* (6th ed.). New York: Macmillan, © 1975.

perceptually at an earlier rate. This acceleration may be reflected in their artistic development, and children may be progressing through the Lowenfeld developmental stages at a more rapid rate than would have been expected even a decade ago. More research is needed, and until it occurs, the artistic developmental stages documented by Lowenfeld should be viewed as *guidelines* and benchmarks of growth.

Scribbling Stage

(18 Months to 4 Years Typically)

The typical child has been learning about himself and the world around him from his first breath. However, the eye-hand coordination necessary to pick up a drawing instrument and the ability to make a mark on a page do not develop until about age two. These first marks are randomly placed and are relatively disordered sweeps across the paper. These are records of kinesthetic actions and are intrinsically pleasing to the child. There is no connection between these marks on the paper and any specific object in the real environs.

Next, the child moves into the controlled scribbling stage which occurs

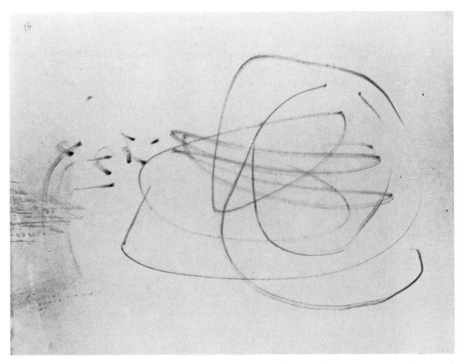

Figure 1. A scribble drawing done by a three-year-old boy. The repetition of several of the same lines and marks indicates that the child has gained some control over his drawing tool. This control was also evident during the creation of the drawing. The child watched what he was doing and did not go off the page with the marker. (*c.* 33 by 48 cm.)

about six months after his first disordered scribbles. These controlled scribbles are achieved as the child learns that there is a connection between his marks on the page and the movements which he has made. With this connection established, the child will repeat similar or same kinds of lines. One researcher (Kellogg, 1970) has identified twenty basic different scribbles which the child makes.

At around three and one-half years, the child moves from thinking kinesthetically to thinking imaginatively. He names his marks. These marks appear little changed from other controlled scribbles he has made. Naming his scribbles means that the child is relating to the world outside of himself.

At age three, the child can draw a circle, and at age four, he has mastered the square (Cratty, 1970). Color discrimination also begins at this developmental point, and by the time the child is four years old, he can correctly name five colors and two geometric shapes (Castrup et al., 1972).

At this level, a multisensory approach to art is recommended. Activities need to be chosen for their appeal to several senses, and part of the focus

GROWING CHART/SCRIBBLING STAGE
(TYPICALLY 1.5-4 YEARS)

	Yes	Sometimes	Not Yet
Random Scribbles			
1. Disordered marks			
2. Copies a straight line			
3. Random pounding of clay			
Controlled Scribbles			
1. Repeats marks			
A. Horizontal			
B. Vertical			
C. Circular			
2. Method of grasping, drawing, or painting instrument varies			
3. Copies a circle			
4. Makes coils and balls in clay			
Named Scribbles			
1. Gives names to scribbles and lumps of clay			
2. Can distinguish one color from another			
3. Can name 5 colors			
4. Can name 2 geometric shapes			
5. Matches shapes on the basis of color			
6. Copies a square			
7. Colors for painting picked randomly			
8. Increased attention span			
Other			
1. Can follow cleanup procedures			
2. Can share sometimes			
Comments:			

should be on discovery (Young, 1972). This does not mean a whole host of media is presented. It does mean a perceptive choice and presentation of art activities to assist in building the child's concepts of his environment (Young, 1972; Harms, 1972).

Preschematic Stage

(4 to 7 Years Typically)

The child begins to relate more to the environs and less to his own body movements, and his created images reflect this. Thus, his drawings become a concrete record of his thought processes. The first graphic symbol (schema) to emerge is that of a man. Usually this consists of a head and feet and indicates the commencement of logical thought process.

Figure 2. This crayon drawing is by a five-year-old boy. It shows his developing symbols for a man and for a house. The emerging man-symbol—head and feet and eye(s)—is drawn five times in the picture. The figures change each time so that one time the figure has no feet (left), another time it has arms and a hat and feet (top) or head, eyes, nose, and mouth (right). The large square near the center of the drawing is a television set. There is an orientation to the drawing in terms of top and bottom; however, there appears to be no meaningful visual relationship between the floating figures. These emerging symbols and floating placements suggest that the child is in the preschematic stage of artistic development. (c. 33 by 48 cm, from the collection of R. A. Salome.)

As the child develops in his drawing, he will typically at about five years produce some more-or-less representational drawings of other objects in his world. As he develops and refines his concepts of these items, these changes will be reflected in his drawing of them. Thus, many variations of a child's rendering of persons, houses, trees, or other items appear. The child experiments with his symbols for these objects until around age seven. At that time, these symbols become fairly well-established schemata and are relatively consistently repeated.

The child is also very much at the center of his world and is not fully ready to share and cooperate. He relates things and objects in the world mainly to his own body. This is reflected in his drawings where things may appear to float randomly in space. By the time he is seven, he can accurately judge right and left and visual space, using himself as the reference point (Cratty, 1970).

Although word recognition and counting abilities develop during this period, the child is not ready to read in the preschematic stage. Drawing also will reflect to some degree his level of intellectual functioning. Thus, the child who is still scribbling, albeit in an ordered fashion, will probably not be as developed intellectually as the child who is drawing representational objects such as men or houses (Harris, 1963).

As with other areas of development, artistic development cannot be accelerated until maturation occurs (Lowenfeld & Brittain, 1975). The child must have the development of eye-hand coordination before he can draw recognizable objects. Not only is skills development necessary, but the child must also have the concepts before he can draw representationally. He must have an active knowledge of his environment in order to produce a graphic record of it.

Some of the expected psychomotor skills (Castrup et al., 1972) are enumerated in the growing chart for this level. It is important for the teacher or adult who works with children at this or any other level to provide a supportive, encouraging atmosphere and an attitude of interest and flexibility. A program should provide sensory experiences and relate directly to the child and his world; suggesting topics such as "my family" or "my house" can help to motivate the child in his art work. The most motivating situations will be those in which the child is directly involved and in which there is little time lapse between the experience and the art lesson.

The materials of art can be motivating as well. The child is involved in a trip of exploration of his world. Paint, glue, nature objects, and other art media are a part of that world. Merely providing these various materials and having the child explore them does *not* constitute a total art program. An art program is much more than mere exploration.

GROWING CHART/PRESCHEMATIC STAGE
(TYPICALLY 4-7 YEARS)

	Yes	Sometimes	Not Yet

Two-Dimensional Work
1. Form for man emerges
   a. Head, feet depicted (*c.* 5 years)
   b. Details of arms, face, and others included in figure drawings (*c.* 6 years)
   c. Body parts drawn with greater accuracy than ability to name or recognize them
   d. Now child can name all parts of face and rest of body
2. Schemata for trees, persons, houses, etc. constantly being altered as concepts are being built
3. Colors picked for their intrinsic, subjective appeal rarely relate to actual color of object in world
4. Spatial Representation
   a. Objects float in space
   b. Appear randomly placed

Three-Dimensional Work
1. Can make a ball of clay
2. Can make a flat clay form
3. Can join 2 pieces of clay
4. Can make a construction that stands on its own

Art Skills Achieved (*c.* 5 years)
1. Correctly holds crayons
2. Correctly holds brush
3. Correctly holds scissors
4. Tears paper in straight line
5. Mixes 2 colors correctly
6. Can glue objects but may
   a. have trouble using right amount
   b. have trouble applying even coat
   c. place glue on wrong side of object
7. Can identify most colors except
   a. grey
   b. bright and dull colors
8. Will also have trouble identifying smooth textures, thick/thin, and light lines

Other
1. Can cooperate with other children on an art task (*c.* 4 years)
2. Can identify own work
3. Can follow directions in sequence
4. Can clean up without prodding
5. Can cut paper with scissors
6. Can cut some cloth with scissors

Comments:

An art program focuses on developing expressive skills, aesthetic awareness, and conceptual learning. Care should be taken to insure that the child goes beyond his discoveries of materials to the development of expressive skills using these materials. The child needs time and repeated experiences with the same media to develop in-depth artistic expression (Saunders, 1977).

The main thrust of the art program should be on the creative process—the doing, the creating, rather than the end product. Adults should be aware of this and not expect functional finished products. In fact, children at this level of development may not have any interest in the finished art work (Lowenfeld & Brittain, 1975).

Schematic Stage

(7 to 9 Years)

During the preschematic stage the child experiments with his graphic symbols as he attempts to develop his own schemata. (A schema is an individual's own unique visual concept of an object, such as a person, house, tree, or flower. A schema is consistently drawn unless specific instruction in a particular lesson alters this image.) Schemata are not stereotypes but are, rather, the child's own visual vocabulary; they reflect what he knows about an object represented.

Now in the schematic stage, the child begins to order objects in his drawings along a baseline. The child is representing only the flat (two-dimensional) aspects of objects. A strip of sky appears at the top of the page. On occasion, the child may use two baselines in the same drawing. Objects on these baselines are always perpendicular to the baselines, even if the baseline is a curved one.

There are three things the child does to represent space during this stage. He may use baselines, foldovers, and/or x-ray drawings. In a foldover (or foldup) picture, part of the drawing appears upside-down or sideways to the viewer. If the picture were folded (up or over, depending on the placement of the objects), all items would appear right-side up. In this way, the child may draw both sides of a street in the same picture.

Sometimes it is only a part of an object that is folded or tilted up. The child does this because a particular object has special significance and importance in a drawing. Thus, in a picture of the family eating Thanksgiving dinner, the table top may be tilted up so that the viewer gets a bird's eye view of it and all the dishes on it. This mixture of plane and elevation in the same picture may also be done to show several activities or to indicate several different time segments in the same drawing. The child seems to desire to be inclusive of one important event which may have several parts to it. He wants to come to closure on the total experience and thus includes all parts in the same picture.

Additionally in this stage, children typically may draw x-ray pictures to depict both the inside and outside of an object. These spatial representations follow a child's logic and what he knows about the subject rather than laws of perspective or representation from an adult point of view.

The child may vary his developed schemata intentionally in three ways. He may emphasize and enlarge important parts, he may omit seemingly unimportant parts of objects, or he may ignore (deny) some parts for emotional or psychological reasons. These variations depend on the child's experiences and the significance which such experiences have for him. For example, if the child just went to the dentist and had a tooth filled, he might enlarge his mouth and his teeth in a drawing or painting of the experience. The proportions which a child may use in a picture, therefore, may shift from time to time.

The child also develops a schema for color. His concepts of colors of objects will depend on the particular experiences he has had with these objects. The child's ability to generalize and develop color schemata for objects represents an important development in his ability to think abstractly. As the child generalizes from "this leaf is green" to "trees are green," his color schema for trees is being established.

The child in this period moves from a predominately ego-centered perspective to a more other-centered perspective on the world. As the child perceives himself along with others in his environs, he becomes more of a social being and is able to cooperate with others. The inclusion of a baseline in pictures and the placement of other objects on it suggests that the child is also ready to begin a full-fledged program of reading (Lowenfeld & Brittain, 1975).

There is a danger of the child's schemata becoming rigid and stereotyped unless many varied experiences with these objects are provided. By offering these varied experiences, the teacher can help the child expand his concepts and alter his schemata from time to time as the situation dictates. It is important to focus on expanding the child's personal awareness of aspects of his world rather than imposing information on him. This fostering of personal awareness of the environs can be enhanced by asking the child careful and discerning questions about his experiences and by relating these experiences to what the child records in paint and crayon or marker.

For example, a child may have a specific schema for a flower. During the spring the teacher may want to bring in several different kinds of flowers or take the class to a greenhouse. As they draw spring pictures or the field trip experience, the teacher can show them the different colors and smells and shapes that each plant has. This will encourage a variety of drawn symbols for flowers.

Toward the close of the schematic stage, the child begins to draw more of what he sees of objects and relies less and less on what he knows of

Figure 3. This crayon drawing, entitled "My Friends at Church," is by a seven-year-old girl. The repetition of the stick figures indicates that the artist's schema for figures has been established. Although the figures and cars seem to float in space, the child has used the edge of the paper as a baseline for the church. Although the girl has not actually drawn in either a skyline or a baseline, she has shown an x-ray view of the interior of the church with all the chairs lined up. The work is an early schematic drawing. (*c.* 33 by 48 cm, © International Collection of Child Art, Ewing Museum of Nations, Illinois State University, Normal, Illinois.)

Figure 4. This painting, "Girl with Braids in the Spring," is by a five-year-old girl. The artist's work is typical of the schematic stage, and she may be artistically advanced. The child may be reflecting an early exposure to complex visual images via television which may accelerate development. A skyline is painted across the top of the picture. A schema for flowers is developed and repeated along the bottom. The exaggerated braids and bows illustrate how a child will enlarge those items which have a particular significance. This exaggeration, the skyline, and the flower schema are all typical of work in the schematic stage. (*c.* 48 by 64 cm, © International Collection of Child Art, Ewing Museum of Nations, Illinois State University, Normal, Illinois.)

Figure 5. "Jumping Rope on the Playground" is by a seven-year-old boy. The artist has painted two views of these rope jumpers. The figures appear to be lying down on either side of an invisible center line. If the painting were folded along this invisible line, the figures would be standing up. This means of depicting space is called a foldover and is typical of the schematic stage. (c. 48 by 64 cm, © International Collection of Child Art, Ewing Museum of Nations, Illinois State University, Normal, Illinois.)

Figure 6. "My Friends at Play" is a crayon drawing by a seven-year-old girl. The figures here have less of the sticklike quality and are fuller than those in "My Friends at Church" (Fig. 3). The figures here are placed along two distinct baselines. This double baseline is a way of ordering space in the schematic stage. Note the developed schemata for girls, boys, and birds. Note also that the schema for girls is specifically changed in the rendering of the two larger figures in the middle of the picture. This kind of conscious alteration in schema does occur when a specific individual or object is depicted. (c. 33 by 48 cm, © International Collection of Child Art, Ewing Museum of Nations, Illinois State University, Normal, Illinois.)

Figure 7. This painting, entitled "Friends Walking in the Rain," is by an eight-year-old boy. Here, the figures are full, though flat and stiff, and facial details such as eyelashes are shown. The figures are placed along the paper edge as though on a baseline. Some details of the raincoat are shown. The space between the top and bottom, though filled with raindrops, does not have depth to it. The two-dimensional nature of the picture, the stiff figures, facial details, the placement on a "paper" baseline, and the outlining with a continuous contour of the figures are all characteristic of work in the later phases of the schematic stage. (*c.* 48 by 61 cm, © International Collection of Child Art, Ewing Museum of Nations, Illinois State University, Normal, Illinois.)

Figure 8. The seven-year-old male artist of "My Mother Irons Clothes" has tilted up the ironing board because it is a particularly important part of the crayon drawing. In showing this view of the ironing board by drawing it from the top, the child can show all the important items on it. Tilting up a part of a drawing in this way to show two points of view in the same picture typically occurs during the schematic level of artistic development. Note that the child has begun to fill the space between the bottom and the top of the drawing, shown some action, and included a little intentional overlapping. This suggests more advanced work occurring late in the schematic stage. (*c.* 33 by 48 cm, © International Collection of Child Art, Ewing Museum of Nations, Illinois State University, Normal, Illinois.)

Figure 9. In this crayon drawing, entitled "My Town" by an eight-year-old girl, every part of the picture is organized and filled with objects. This filling of the page also occurs late in the schematic stage. The space, though ordered, remains flat and two-dimensional in spite of the child's attempt at showing depth by adding diagonal lines in the sidewalk. Two baselines have been used (one at the top of the picture with cars on it and one along the bottom of the buildings), yet the space between them is filled with numerous objects. An x-ray of one of the stores has also been used. The front of the department store on the right has been cut away to reveal all three of the interior floors (including clothing on the racks, a saleslady, a customer, and a lady buying shoes). The see-saws on the playground have been folded up by the artist. A schema for cars has been used. This schema includes four wheels and indicates the artist has represented what she knows about automobiles, not what is actually seen. (*c.* 46 by 61 cm, © International Collection of Child Art, Ewing Museum of Nations, Illinois State University, Normal, Illinois.)

these objects. Therefore, more activities which have direct experiences and observations may encourage this development in the child.

During this stage children should be encouraged to further develop their basic cutting, gluing, and construction abilities. As the child uses three-dimensional media such as wood, clay, and cardboard, he begins to expand his spatial concepts. In working with clay, the additive or add-on method of constructing is still valid, and it is not important to have a finished, kiln-fired ceramic work. In fact, in the add-on approach, most clay work will not survive the firing. For the child in this level, the artistic/creative process is still of primary importance to him.

GROWING CHART/SCHEMATIC STAGE
(TYPICALLY 7-9 YEARS)

	Yes	Sometimes	Not Yet

Human Schema (2-dimensional work)
   1. Clearly identifiable
   2. Includes body, arms, legs (or clothing)
      a. Head and facial parts
      b. Other details
   3. Frontal or side view or combination
   4. Human form depicted with ease in 3-dimensional
      as well as 2-dimensional media
Spatial Representation (2-dimensional work)
   1. Objects set along a baseline
   2. Sometimes 2 baselines in same picture
   3. Objects are flat
   4. Skyline appears
   5. Foldover or foldup pictures
   6. Several items from different points of view
   7. Different events or time sequences in same picture
   8. X-ray presentations
Color
   1. Schema for colors develops
   2. More accurate relationship of color to objects
Schemata vary at times
   1. Significant parts enlarged
   2. Unimportant items omitted
   3. Suppressed objects (ideas) also left out
Art Skills
   1. Full ability to use correctly
      a. paint
      b. drawing items
      c. scissors
   2. Can sculpt with clay using the additive method
   3. Better able to share work
   4. Better able to work with others on group projects
Comments:

Gang Age

(Typically 9-12 Years)

During this period the child discovers that he is a part of a larger world, a world that includes his peers. This is a period of group relationships and activities. Girls tend to prefer the company of other girls, and boys prefer all-male cliques. Each group develops some special interests that are reflected in their art work.

In the past, such interests coincided somewhat with externally imposed role expectations. For example, boys had a great interest in cars and machines; girls preferred animals, especially horses. With the current women's liberation movement, these sexually stereotyped interests may be shifting to more idiosyncratic ones.

In the child's two-dimensional work, he finds his schemata too limiting and he will expand these to include more details. Instead of geometric shapes, a more natural rendering of shapes and forms is used to depict facial parts, houses, trees, and other items. However, these drawings are not yet a totally representational view of the world as an adult would perceive it.

Also, during this period there is less inclusion of movement and action in figures. In fact, figures appear rather stiff. Folds in clothing usually are not included, and hemlines are usually drawn as straight lines. No longer do exaggeration and omissions of parts occur, nor foldover or x-ray pictures. Occasionally there may be enlargements or distortions of one segment of a drawing, but this only occurs as the result of a specific, emotionally significant event.

Color is freed now from its former strict adherence to objects, and subtler color differences are noted. The child is now aware that the green color of grass is a different green from the green of a leaf or a particular kind of tree. However, children still have not developed their color perceptions enough to note the differences between colors in sunlight and in shade or the changes which distance and atmosphere have on colors.

In terms of spatial representations, objects are now arranged on the page in a definite relationship to each other. This reflects the child's growing ability to handle several ideas at the same time. Objects are not now exclusively placed along the baseline. The space between the sky and the ground becomes important, and this space is consciously filled by the child. The child begins to more consciously overlap objects in his drawings and paintings.

Another aspect of the child's expanding awareness of the world is a developing curiosity of the man-made and natural environs. Children become collectors of all sorts of treasures from their environment. This can be a potent motivating force in their art. Additionally, now, children in rendering figures focus more on decoration and attention to details such as pattern on clothing.

Because of the greater awareness of peers and groups at this age, children enjoy working on group art projects. Additionally, topics focusing on community endeavors in which children might be involved are important themes for art. The key is to gear the art activity to what seems to be of greatest interest to the child.

Figure 10. This painting, entitled "My Friends," is by a nine-year-old boy. The picture is typical of work executed early in the Gang Age. Several repeated figures are shown and some attempt at showing action is made, yet the figures remain stiff and frozen. The artist has overlapped several objects in the picture and placed the fence above and behind the figures to create more depth to the picture. This illusion of some depth in the picture is characteristic at this developmental level. The figures have been turned to present a profile view. Clothing details such as belt tabs and cuffs are shown. (*c.* 48 by 64 cm, © International Collection of Child Art, Ewing Museum of Nations, Illinois State University, Normal, Illinois.)

Figure 11. During the Gang Age more attention is given to clothing details and patterns. In "The Carol Singers," the nine-year-old female artist has rendered the dresses with attention to details. The "baseline" has disappeared and has been replaced with a shallow plane on which the three figures stand. A beginning awareness of perspective is indicated by the way the music books are drawn and in the rendering of the front view of the feet in the figures on the right and in the middle. (*c.* 61 by 46 cm, © International Collection of Child Art, Ewing Museum of Nations, Illinois State University, Normal, Illinois.)

Figure 12. Both profile and frontal views of figures are included in this painting, entitled "Singing on the Corner," by a twelve-year-old girl. Although stiff, the figures are better proportioned in this work from the later phases of the Gang Age. Now, within the same drawing, changes appear from figure to figure in terms of clothing, size, placement, and position. The artist has considerable overlapping of figures and objects in the picture and has attempted one-point perspective in her rendering of the sidewalk which goes off the page at the right. The figures stand in a shallow plane in front of the building. (c. 48 by 64 cm, © International Collection of Child Art, Ewing Museum of Nations, Illinois State University, Normal, Illinois.)

CROWING CHART/GANG AGE
(TYPICALLY 9-12 YEARS)

	Yes	Sometimes	Not Yet

Human Schema (2-dimensional work)
1. Many more details appear
2. Fewer geometric shapes and more natural forms and shapes included for body parts
3. Many more details in the figure
4. Many more details in clothing (patterns, decoration)
5. Hemlines straight
6. Folds omitted
7. Figures stiff, little action portrayed
8. Schema appears in 3-dimensional media as well

Spatial Representation (2-dimensional work)
1. Space between sky and ground filled and ordered
2. Baseline disappears
3. Overlapping of objects
4. Still some exaggeration of objects due to emotional importance

Color
1. Less generalized schema
2. Variations in the object-color adherence

Art Skills
1. Can mix own colors
2. Uses wood tools appropriately
3. Can work 3 dimensionally with paper
4. Still uses additive method in clay

Works well with others
Comments:

Pseudo-Naturalistic Stage

(Typically 12-14 Years)

In this stage, there is a change to an adult point of view in artistic rendering and expression. No longer do students draw what they know about objects; rather, they draw what they perceive in the natural world. There is an increased critical awareness of the outcomes (product) of their own work. The focus is now much more on the end product and how it is accepted by the peer group as well as the creator himself.

Young persons entering adolescence are experiencing many emotional and physiological shifts. The individual student at this stage must decide whether to move into the realities of the adult world or to turn inwardly to his own fantasy world. There is great vacillation in these students as sometimes they act as children, other times as adults.

Schemata for human figures and other objects disappear and are replaced by a more representational depiction. The student includes joints in his figure drawings, and human forms move and appear more active and less *stiff* than in the gang age of development.

Sexual characteristics are included and often are exaggerated. Folds of clothing appear, and there is an awareness of the effect of light and shade on colors and form; this awareness is reflected in figure drawings. Also, some students depict figures in caricature and cartoon forms.

Spatial representation is more sophisticated now. However, unless the student discovers for himself rules of perspective, he will not make use of these artistic methods in his own work.

There is a greater awareness of design, color, and fantasy, and they begin to play an important part in the student's work. Often students doodle and draw outside of class in margins of notebook pages and other seemingly unlikely places. This reflects a continuous need for self-expression and a constructive outlet for feelings. There is a great empathy for naturally occurring designs in the real world.

Consideration should be given to the student as a future consumer and advocate of a well-designed environment. This is especially important since many students may never have another art class after junior high. Students should also be made aware of the vocational as well as avocational possibilities of the arts.

Figure 13. "My Friends Are Marketing," by a thirteen-year-old boy, shows an awareness of linear perspectives in the rendering of the cans on the shelves, the counter, and the floor tiles. Compared with "Singing on the Corner" (Fig. 12), this picture has greater depth, and the viewer is now actually looking into space. This depth and the more naturalistic proportioning and three-quarter view of the cashier are characteristic of the pseudo-naturalistic stage of artistic development. (c. 46 by 61 cm © International Collection of Child Art, Ewing Museum of Nations, Illinois State University, Normal Illinois.)

Figure 14. In the painting entitled "First Baptist Church," the twelve-year-old male artist indicates depth by using linear perspective in his rendering of the church building and the sidewalk on the right which narrows. The attention to detail and pattern in the building, along with the depth in the picture and use of perspective, is typical of the pseudo-naturalistic level of development in art. (c. 48 by 61 cm, © International Collection of Child Art, Ewing Museum of Nations, Illinois State University, Normal, Illinois.)

Figure 15. In the pseudo-naturalistic stage, figures become more realistic. In this painting, entitled "My Friends," by a fourteen-year-old boy, features are rendered in a naturalistic way which includes shading and considerable attention to facial details. The central figure has more volume and is less stiff and flat than figures drawn by a child in any of the earlier developmental stages. The arm bends at the elbow, showing the artist's awareness of joints. (c. 47 by 61 cm, © International Collection of Child Art, Ewing Museum of Nations, Illinois State University, Normal, Illinois.)

Figure 16. In the pseudo-naturalistic stage, the student sometimes is introspective and focuses on his own inner fantasy world. This painting, entitled "As I See Myself," by a thirteen-year-old female, reflects this introspectiveness. As the artist develops through this stage, she becomes more aware of the special effects that may be created with the medium. (c. 48 by 61 cm, © International Collection of Child Art, Ewing Museum of Nations, Illinois State University, Normal, Illinois.)

GROWING CHART/PSEUDO-NATURALISTIC STAGE
(TYPICALLY 12-14 YEARS)

	Yes	Sometimes	Not Yet

Human Figure (2-dimensional work)
  1. Schema disappears
  2. Joints indicated, figures active
  3. Color changes indicated
  4. Sexual characteristics
  5. Folds and wrinkles in clothes
  6. Age factors included in figures
  7. Cartoons/caricatures
  8. The above reflected in 3-dimensional media as well
Spatial Representation (2-dimensional work)
  1. Baseline disappears
  2. Horizon line included
  3. Discovery of perspective methods
     a. one point
     b. aerial (things smaller in distance)
Three-Dimensional Work
  1. Interest in making functional clay work
  2. Interest in making representational figures in clay,
     plaster, and wire
Other General Concerns
  1. Focus on decorative qualities in work
  2. Interest in fantasy topics
  3. Concern for various artistic techniques
  4. Concern for end product
  5. Heightened criticism of own work
Comments:

Postscript

During the final years of formal public schooling, the student's art work does not go through any major developmental transformation. Since many students do not go further in their formal studies of art and opportunities are not available, most individuals do not develop further. The art of high school students reflects their growing self-criticalness, self-awareness, and introspection. As would be expected of most adults, they are ready for in-depth study of the fundamental methods, materials, and tools of the artist. The history of man's artistic achievements and the aesthetic principles which have and do govern these achievements should also be a part of the art program (Lowenfeld & Brittain, 1975).

Figure 17. This drawing, entitled "SUE," by a seventeen-year-old girl, shows the artist's mastery of drawing techniques and sensitive use of line. This is an artistic statement by a high school student who has developed beyond the pseudo-naturalistic stage. (c. 46 by 61 cm, © International Collection of Child Art, Ewing Museum of Nations, Illinois State University, Normal, Illinois.)

Figure 18. This untitled collage is by a seventeen-year-old female student. It is a commentary on the reality and fantasy of love. The subject and the way the artist has handled the materials reflect her own growing maturity and adult view of the world. (c. 31 by 46 cm, © International Collection of Child Art, Ewing Museum of Nations, Illinois State University, Normal, Illinois.)

Figure 19. The careful rendering and execution of a sixteen-year-old high school student in the woodcut medium in "Old Man and His Dreams" indicate his concern for artistic skills and his successful mastery of them. He has gone beyond mastering skills to make an artistic interpretation of the subject. This kind of work may be expected by high school students who have matured beyond the pseudo-naturalistic stage and who have had opportunities for an in-depth artistic study. (*c.* 43 by 38 cm, © International Collection of Child Art, Ewing Museum of Nations, Illinois State University, Normal, Illinois.)

ACCOUNTABILITY AND ART

Behavior Objectives Are Here to Stay

As has already been noted, it is very important to evaluate the special child as an individual and compare his performance against his own best efforts. For this reason, it is difficult to set out specific behavioral objectives for the art activities that follow, without a specific child in mind.

There are some limits to behavioral objectives. They are not a panacea, and they should not be used as *the* means of evaluating a child's progress, the teacher's effectiveness, or the art program's success. The very nature of art and its focus on divergence and individualistic search for unique solutions does not easily lend itself to a series of specific behavioral or performance objectives.

Moreover, some behaviors, such as aesthetic response, cannot directly or overtly be measured easily (McAshan, 1970). Thus, covert and unobtrusive means must be sought to provide some index of aesthetic response (Webb et al., 1966). At best, these are gross indicators and do not really touch or explain or assess the tremendous complexity of aesthetic response. Such behaviors as facial expressions, long undistractable attention, verbal or written expressions such as *wow, fantastic,* or even dead silence in a class can give some clues about artistic response. Until more sophisticated measures are developed, these indirect means will have to be used.

Behavioral objectives do not often allow for the long-term effects of instruction. The assumption is that learning is a continuous cumulative process, and to determine that learning has occurred, some overt response must be made. However, incidental instruction occurs continually by observation, and it may be even years before a particular student behaviorally demonstrates what he has learned (Effland, 1974).

Yet, the reality that behavioral objectives are a part of the educational system must be accepted. About half of the states require the use of behavioral objectives in order to assess the normal student's progress through the educational system (Eisner, 1974). Not only are behavioral objectives being required in the general school curriculum but also in special education programs. The Education for All Handicapped Children Act of 1975 became law on July 1, 1975. This law (P.L. 94-142) states that each child receiving special education must have an individualized education program. A part of that program must be stated in instructional objectives (P.L. 94-142, Sec. 4:19). Many states interpret "instructional objectives" to mean behavioral objectives.

Thus, behavioral objectives may be necessary. However, it must be underscored that behavioral objectives are primarily a means of stating instructional goals or outcomes. An assessment of a total art program would require a broad multifaceted approach (Stake, 1975).

WRITING BEHAVIORAL OBJECTIVES IN ART

As many readers may know, there are three main requirements for an objective to be behaviorally stated (Mager, 1965). First, the final outcome of the behavior is specified by name. For example, a child prints a card, builds a pot, or mixes a secondary color. Second, the behavioral objective must describe conditions that are important and necessary for the performance to occur. Thus, the child will build a pot using water base (earth) clay in two half-hour art periods.

The third component of a behavioral objective is the criterion. Criterion statements may be cast in terms of quality, frequency, duration and/or a combination of these factors. The criterion-measure provides a means of assessing when the child has demonstrated the desired behavior and mastered the particular educational goal. To be complete, therefore, the behavioral objective for a child would be stated: Given earth clay and two half-hour art periods, the learner will pinch a pot having smooth concave sides, one-quarter to one-half inch thick, and having no holes.

One art lesson may have several intermeshed learning experiences. The learning outcome would depend on the child's need and developmental characteristics. For example, for a painting activity the intended outcome for one child might relate to controlling the dispersal of paint on the paper. For another child, the outcome might be the demonstration of cleaning-up skills, while for a third child the intended outcome might be engaging in an activity continuously for a period of time (i.e. expanding his attention span). These three outcomes would be stated behaviorally as follows:

Given paint, paper and a half-hour art period, the child will paint a picture without running colors of paint together on the paper.

Given a paint-spotted worktable, the child will wipe the table without prompting so that all paint spots are gone.

Given paint, paper and a half-hour art period, the child will paint for 20 minutes without engaging in a non-related activity.

Thus, there is a great need to write precise behavioral objectives for specific children. It is also necessary to define art words and activities more specifically. The definitions must include *action* verbs that incorporate knowledge of artistic processes and result in overt activity. Therefore, such statements as "the child learns how to paint" or "the child makes a sculpture or makes a pot" are inappropriate. It is more precise and appropriate to state: "The child *paints* a picture, *builds* a sculpture or *pinches* a pot." Moreover, the abstract concepts of explore, enjoy, appreciate, create and express need operational definitions such as:

To explore	Find by "accident" a different (new) way of doing an art activity; apply a media in two or more different ways.
To enjoy or *To appreciate*	Say words of pleasure; for example, *Wow, this is fun! I want to do this all afternoon.* Observe behavior such as totally undistractable attention being given for a longer than average period for this particular child.
To express	Fill the page with drawn figures, tell a story about one's art work, paint shapes and figures with colors that have never been used before by that child.
To create	Paint or draw a picture, build a sculpture or a pot, construct a puppet that is not copied and that includes something about the creator (a favorite color, a favorite topic, or an event that scared the child or made him happy). Select materials, subjects or page placement that differ from others in the class.

Because of divergent individual skills and developmental levels of handicapped children, it is difficult to specify in advance "exact" behavioral objectives for a handicapped population. Therefore, a section titled "Potential

Outcomes" has been included as a part of each art learning activity discussed in this sourcebook. These proposed *potential outcomes* are NOT behavioral objectives. They provide a flexible base for the development of behavioral objectives. Thus, the discussion of each art activity (and these potential outcomes) provides guidance around which specific behavioral objectives for a given handicapped learner can be written. Such specific behavioral objectives must include precise conditions, outcomes and criterion statements using action verbs. The teacher should also be aware that a task analysis may be necessary to insure a particular child's successful mastery of a specific behavioral objective.

TASK ANALYSIS

Task analysis or instructional sequencing may be relatively unfamiliar to the art teacher; however, task analysis may be a requisite for the instruction of an impaired child (Morreau, 1975), and it is a standard methodology in special education.

In a task analysis, all the steps necessary for achieving a particular behavioral objective are isolated, described and sequenced. Task analysis enables the teacher to quickly pinpoint any specific skill with which a specific child is having difficulty. Consequently, a high success factor is built into the instruction of the impaired child because complex operations are broken down into their simplest units.

A task analysis requires several steps. First, subskills or prerequisite skills necessary for each behavioral objective are identified and sequenced. In art programming it is *crucial* for the teacher to execute the art activities himself. Thus he can identify, list and then sequence in the most efficient manner the subskills which the child needs for a particular art task.

Second, the teacher must assess the entrance behaviors needed to complete these identified and sequenced subskills. With each prerequisite subskill (task), the teacher must ask whether the child has already mastered this skill. If not, then he must determine what needs to be taught so that the child can master that subskill. Using this procedure, the child's art skill repertoire will be established and time will not be spent on redundant instruction.

For example, the behavioral objective "Given paper, brush and three colors of tempera paint, the child will paint a picture of one identifiable object as indicated by teacher/peer review" would include these subskills necessary for painting with a brush:
1. Picks up brush with thumb and forefinger.
2. Holds brush two to four inches above bristles.
3. Puts brush into container of paint.
4. Covers bristles with paint.
5. Lifts brush one inch above paintline.

6. Strokes side of paint container upward two inches with paint covered bristles.
7. Repeats step 6.
8. Moves brush up and out of container.
9. Moves brush three to six inches in the air over to paper.
10. Lowers brush until bristles with color touch page.
11. Moves brush across page, left to right or top to bottom, or circularly to make lines and shapes.
12. Lifts brush, repeats steps 10 and 11 until paint no longer flows off the brush.
13. Lifts brush from paper.
14. Repeats steps 3 through 12, if same color is selected, or
15. Selects a different color.
16. Puts brush into clean water container.
17. Lowers brush into water so all bristles and any other paint covered part of brush are covered with water.
18. Moves brush back and forth in water five times.
19. Lifts brush out of water one inch.
20. Strokes side of water container upwards two inches.
21. Lowers brush in air two inches and repeats step 18.
22. Repeats step 21 four times.
23. Removes brush from water container completely.
24. Dabs bristles three times on pile of three paper towels.
25. Repeats steps 3 through 22 as needed to complete picture.

The following example illustrates the use of task analysis for identifying the entry point for a learner. A teacher assesses a child during a painting activity and finds that the child has all the skills listed above in his repertoire, but the child scrubs instead of strokes with his brush when he paints. Based on a task analysis, the steps to be followed in mastering painting with strokes include:

1. Lower brush until it *touches* paper.
2. Move brush two inches in one direction.
3. Move brush to one side one half inch (i.e. the thickness of the bristles).
4. Move brush two inches in a direction opposite to the first stroke.
5. Repeat steps 1 through 4 making strokes side by side, creating contiguous areas of paint until paint no longer flows off the brush.

Using sequential steps, the teacher can determine the exact skills the child needs to master. The entry point in this example will be teaching the child to hold his brush appropriately when making contact with the paper.

As the example indicates, task analysis is an important method for facilitating a child's successful performance on a particular behavioral objective. With more and more handicapped learners being integrated into regular art classes, the art teacher may need to utilize task analysis procedures in instruction. Task analysis can be a powerful tool in the instruction of any learner, handicapped or non-impaired.

Evaluation and Closure: Summing It All Up

The final part of the art lesson is as important as the beginning and sometimes more so. The final part can be a time when the teacher and the child can sum up what has been learned, and this is another important part of evaluating what just happened. The child needs to come to closure on his art experiences. He should be able to step back and assess what he has done and see what others have accomplished. The child should have a chance to see how others have solved artistic problems and to review key concepts.

This closure period can also be a time when decisions may be made about a new direction or related art experiences which might evolve out of the art activity which the child just experienced. For example, a child may be so involved in a wood construction that he decides he wants to paint it. Another child decides at the end of a period of making a salt clay animal that the animal needs an environment (a home, a cage, or a habitat). This moment of closure will be the time to discuss what and how such new activities can be accomplished during the next art period.

Closure may be something as simple as taking two or three minutes to share each child's work with each other. It can be as complicated as deciding to write a play to accompany puppets that have just been made. Children should not be left up in the air at the end of a lesson without any discussion because they may have key ideas to share. This is an optimal time to review and reinforce what has been learned. A display or an experience story about the art activity may emerge from the lesson. This is also a good time to encourage each child in his creative efforts and in his increasing ability to properly use and care for art materials.

The teacher is urged to plan for closure at the end of each art experience. It also must be realized that some closure events may emerge during a particular activity and may be spontaneous in nature. Nevertheless, a few moments at the end of the lesson should be set aside for both the child and the teacher to sum things up and to evaluate informally what has happened.

REFERENCES

Castrup, J., Ain, E., & Scott, R. Art skills of preschool children. *Studies in Art Education*, 1972, *13*(3), 62-69.

Cratty, B. J. *Perceptual and motor development in infants and children.* New York: Macmillan, 1970.

Effland, A. Evaluating goals for art education. *Art Education,* 1974, *27*(2), 8-10.

Eisner, E. Do behavioral objectives and accountability have a place in art education? *Art Education,* 1974, *27*(2), 2-5.

Golomb, C. The child is image-maker: The invention of representational models and the effects of the medium. *Studies in Art Education,* 1976, *17*(2), 19-27.

Harms, J. Presenting materials effectively. In H. P. Lewis (Ed.), *Art for the preprimary child.* Reston, Va.: The National Art Education Association, 1972.

Harris, D. B. *Children's drawings as measures of intellectual maturity.* New York: Harcourt Brace Jovanovich, 1963.

Kellogg, R. *Analyzing children's art.* Palo Alto, Calif.: National Press, 1970.

Lansing, K. M. *Art artists and art education.* New York: McGraw-Hill, 1969.

Lindstrom, M. *Children's Art.* Berkeley: University of California Press, 1964.

Lowenfeld, V., & W. L. Brittain. *Creative and Mental Growth* (6th ed.). New York: Macmillan, 1975.

Mager, R. F. *Preparing instructional objectives.* Palo Alto, Calif.: Fearon, 1962.

McAshan, H. H. *Writing behavioral objectives.* New York: Harper & Row, 1970.

McFee, J. K. *Preparation for art* (2nd ed.). Belmont, Calif.: Wadsworth, 1972.

Morreau, L. Objective-based task analysis. In J. Maestas Y Moores (Ed.), *Proceedings of the Minnesota special study institute on education of the deaf: some practical considerations.* Special Education Programs, Psychoeducational Studies. Minneapolis: University of Minnesota, August, 1975.

Public Law 94-142, 1975.

Rubin, J. Art is for all human beings, especially the handicapped. *Art Education,* 1975, *28*(8), 5-10.

Saunders, R. J. *The levels of development in child art.* Paper presented at the Institute for Teachers of Trainable Children, Southern Connecticut State College, July, 1968.

Saunders, R. J. *Relating art and humanities to the classroom.* Dubuque: William C. Brown, 1977.

Stake, R. *Evaluating the arts in education: A responsive approach.* Columbus: Charles Merrill, 1975.

Webb, E. J., Campbell, D. T., Schwartz, R. D., & Sechrest, L. *Unobtrusive measures.* Chicago: Rand McNally, 1966.

Young, E. Art in children's learning. In H. P. Lewis (Ed.), *Art for the preprimary child.* Reston, Va.: The National Art Education Association, 1972.

Chapter III

PLANNING ART FOR ALL THE CHILDREN

ART ACTIVITIES

IN ANY ATTEMPT at designing a series of art activities for adults to use, several pitfalls and problems occur. There will always be criticism. Some will be critical because the art activities are too structured; others will perceive these art suggestions as not nearly explicit enough. In the curriculum presented here, efforts have been made to find a *via media*, a middle ground. The guiding principle has been to give enough detail to enable any sensitive adult to proceed with the activity. When possible, these activities are accompanied by illustrations or photographs to assist in the explanations. The old adage about saving a thousand words with a picture is still very valid.

These art activities were accomplished with a variety of impaired children ranging in chronological age from two to sixteen years. The work was done in small groups of children and, at times, in a one-to-one situation. The major focus is on art activities for the primary level. When appropriate, suggestions are provided for changing the motivation and situation to tailor the activity for older students. Each art activity includes a listing of materials necessary, the procedures required, motivations, *suggested* adaptations for specific impairments, and an evaluation section including *suggested* potential outcomes and *suggested* closure experiences.

It is difficult to predict exactly how much time involvement each activity may require. Often, time is the enemy in an art activity. Some children work very slowly, and others seem to be functioning at unbelievably rapid speeds. Some suggestion about the time required to accomplish each art activity is given. However, with the various learning differences and abilities of the children involved, these time indications can only be *suggestions*. The children themselves should be allowed to set some of their own work paces.

How often should the child have art? Art should be integrated as much as possible into the rest of the curriculum. Thus, there should be an art-related activity going on in the special education classroom at least once a day. Additionally, the National Art Education Association (*Essentials*, n.d.) urges *at least* 100 minutes for art per week for the primary child. This should be organized in addition to art-related classroom experiences.

As with other areas of the curriculum, typical children in an art class differ in their abilities; they are very much on an art-learning continuum. Each child's emotional, conceptual, and perceptual level, as well as physical ability, may differ. One child may have a very sophisticated painting style, while another may not yet have learned how to use a paint brush. Typical children may already have a well-developed body-concept. Normal children may have a good sense of who they are psychologically and possess a fairly complete perception of their world. In such a situation, a teacher may focus more on encouraging the child to make aesthetic decisions per se and to learn about the structure of art and how to evaluate art. Such abilities are developed in children as they grow in their knowledge of art processes and their capacity to utilize these processes in making artistic statements.

An art program for impaired children, however, often differs. Any art activity must start with the child. If that child needs help in defining his body-concept or in language development or in eye-hand coordination, then this must be considered in the art program. These needs are the appropriate beginning point for art learning. The arts thus assist in developing the handicapped child's concepts about himself, his language, and his world and how to function in it. This does not diminish the activities as valid art experiences. It does mean that curriculum development for the special child must focus more on *his* individual needs.

Finally, every child, no matter what his condition or degree of impairment, must have opportunities to draw and paint at every level of development. Through these opportunities the child begins to refine concepts and build important eye-hand coordination skills which are necessary to other forms of development. The art activities enumerated in this sourcebook should be viewed as making up the other one third of any art program. They must be orchestrated with a regular program of drawing and painting.

As the reader becomes familiar with the rest of this sourcebook, he will realize that it is important to have some variety in activities and media. It is also important to reinforce key concepts through several art lessons. Some time should be spent developing artistic skills and concepts. Thus, it is not good to have a continuing smorgasbord of media but, instead, a steady diet of two- and three-dimensional activities where there is *some* variety yet *enough repetition* to enable good skill and concept development on the part of the child (Saunders, 1977; Young, 1972).

In the pages that follow, the art activities are organized with three main purposes. First, the activities are centered on the child's need—emotional, physical, and educational. Second, the art learning situations are sequenced, as opposed to isolated, unrelated types of lessons. They are grouped around specific content and arranged in a series. This has been done because like other learning, art occurs best when the experiences are interrelated, overlapped, and set into a progressively more difficult continuum. Whether a child starts at the beginning of each series, in the middle, or at some other point, however, must be determined by each teacher as he considers the interests and abilities of that child.

Third, throughout the art series presented, opportunities are provided to convey information about the content and processes of art. At times, this is done in a very direct and explicit manner, as in the activities focusing on texture or those directing the child to learn how to use new art media. At other times, this is accomplished in more subtle ways by limiting choices of materials for a lesson or by carefully choosing art media which create a more harmonious and aesthetically pleasing combination. For example, by making a mobile of varying sizes of the same geometric shape, harmony and unity will be one of the outcomes of the activity because of the repetition of shape which is accompanied by size variation. Or, by limiting the media in making a mural to only different types of papers, unity is automatically structured into the composition. In providing these kinds of design limitations, the art learning is more rigorous. The problems solved are more challenging, yet there is a built-in structure.

In using this methodology, children will learn about appropriate combinations of art materials as well as the content and structure of art. Such a methodology will explicitly and implicitly convey proven artistic values. For example, by using the principle of a limited combination of media, the child learns that a "limited palette" is more appropriate. He learns that art learning does not require incorporating *every* material in the art room into each art activity.

Thus, by implicitly ordering and structuring the outcomes via a judicious selection of materials as well as establishing limits through the instruction provided, the artistic outcomes will be more pleasing and more self-affirming. Children often have a very perceptive sense of the qualitative aspect of an art outcome. They know when the product is tastefully executed and when it is just a hodgepodge of many different materials. For this reason, great care has gone into the planning of the art activities in this volume so that there will be aesthetically pleasing outcomes. However, within this structure and framework there are no absolute *right answers* in terms of products or solutions to the artistic problems posed. Within the art learning situation there is a divergence of correct outcomes.

The outcomes of an art activity may not be primarily the product produced or the processes involved in making art. There may be some more appropriate responses or behaviors that are the desired outcomes. For example, one primary goal for an art activity might be the appropriate use and care of materials or the ability to set up and clean up work areas. Later, more complex goals in art may be attempted.

An important requirement of anyone who is leading a child through an art experience is that he be a doer of art himself. Nothing has been said about becoming an artist. All that is requested is that the adult "field test" the activity *first*. This suggestion holds for the artistically educated adult as well. It is hoped that these artistic *field tests* will be undertaken with a spirit of inquiry. This spirit will perhaps be contagious and will become a guiding force behind the activities when the children are making art also.

ADAPTATIONS: THE KEY CONCEPT

Often in bewilderment, parents, students, and teachers have stated that they are frantically searching for new art ideas and that they can find nothing written for a particular disability. In reality, these persons may be searching for a recipe or cookbook for art. There is no such thing!

There are many books that have been written on art and art education, but only a few on art for the handicapped child. These books are not all inclusive, nor should they be. In fact, it would be a sad state of affairs if the definitive book had been written on art. It is not possible in one short term or in one volume to cover the field of impaired children and their art. Moreover, more than one book or one source would be needed simply because the teacher eventually would end up repeating the same series of art activities (which is not necessarily an undesirable thing to do).

In many ways, teaching and working with exceptional children is the most challenging and taxing of one's creative abilities. Being able to solve the daily problems that occur in designing adaptations for special children's art is the most rewarding and intellectually stimulating of endeavors. Being able to creatively design individualized adaptations is the key to planning art situations for the impaired child. To do so, the adult must know both the child and the art materials.

An adaptation may mean developing special equipment for an art learning experience or shifting the order of a lesson presentation. It might require concentrating on special motivational considerations or changing the art materials themselves to make them more accessible or more easily used by the child. Or, it might mean physically moving the child so that he can more easily become involved in the activity.

Adaptations can also mean changing the art activity so that it requires greater cooperation between children. A careful analysis of the steps involved in an art activity so that the less mentally able child is able to participate in art, so that he *can* weave or draw or sculpt, may be necessary.

Adaptations might involve a careful integration and correlation of art activities with other aspects of the curriculum. In such a situation, the children are learning about art and reinforcing other concepts as well.

Some art adaptations have already been discussed in Chapter I under the sections dealing with the different impairments. In the art activities that

Figure 20. Sometimes it is easier for the handicapped child to work at an easel. The table easel may be preferable for the child who must sit and work. The paper is placed against a strong piece of cardboard and then taped to the easel.

Figure 21. For added security, the easel is anchored with a sandbag.

Figure 22. A ten-year-old physically handicapped girl completes her wood pieces by painting them. Note that the plastic bottle water container has been adapted. A window has been cut in the side, and the bottom is weighted with gravel (to prevent tipping). (This water container was designed by Larry S. Barnfield.)

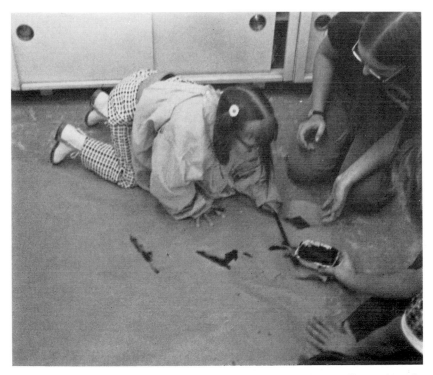

Figure 23. Sometimes it is easier to work on the floor. Here, a visually impaired, physically handicapped six-year-old begins painting with tempera.

Figure 24. If a child has limited control of her hands, a simple guide might help. A ten-year-old cerebral palsied child draws in a guide made by cutting out hand holes in a box. Note that the cut edges are taped and the drawing paper is taped inside the box. An aide is taping the drawing box to the work table. *C* clamps can also be used to secure the box to the work table.

25   26

Figure 25. Often it is better to let the child who is in a wheelchair draw or paint on a drawing or lap board. The paper probably will need to be weighted down. If there are no "extra hands" (as provided here), masking tape will hold the paper. Here, a nine-year-old cerebral palsied child wets down his paper before drawing with chalk.

Figure 26. A seven-year-old blind child explores drawing with chalk on wet paper. Notice how one hand holds the chalk while the other becomes a reference point. A reference point can also be created by taping down a small piece of textured paper to the drawing surface or by tearing a small hole in the drawing paper.

Figure 27. Finding the best working conditions takes time, patience, and team work. Often just asking the child what is best for her will provide the answer. Here, the child is drawing with markers, a medium which she prefers. She has decided her own working position. Sometimes when the child cannot easily move, the paper must be rotated.

Figure 28. The completed drawing by this ten-year-old cerebral palsied girl depicts a child playing ball outside.

29   30

Figures 29 and 30. An adaptation may also mean providing special motivation for the handicapped child. One of the best ways of drawing or painting motivation is by means of immediate, direct experience. The puppet drawing was done by an eight-year-old boy in a primary hearing impaired class right after his class had seen a puppet show presented by volunteers. The children were given a chance to "play" with their favorite puppet before drawing. The actual sock puppet was made by a college student.

follow, examples of adaptations are presented to tailor the art situation to fit the needs of the child and his handicap. These are *suggested* adaptations. The reader is urged to go beyond them to develop his own for specific children and art situations. It will help to peruse *every part* of each adaptation section because often the subsections build upon each other.

The illustrations in this chapter provide some visual examples of adapting, in order to help the reader think along these lines. These adaptations focus mainly on drawing and painting and ways to overcome any obstacles the impaired child may have that might prevent him from fully expressing himself.

REFERENCES

Essentials: The essentials of a quality school art program: A position statement. Reston, Va.: National Art Education Association, n.d.

Saunders, R. J. *Relating art and humanities to the classroom.* Dubuque: William C. Brown, 1977.

Young, E. Art in children's learning. In H. P. Lewis (Ed.), *Art for the preprimary child.* Reston, Va.: The National Art Education Association, 1972.

Chapter IV

DEVELOPING A SENSE OF SELF THROUGH ART

INTRODUCTION

A DEVELOPED BODY-CONCEPT is one of the impaired child's most basic needs. Normal children usually acquire this concept without special focus or learning. Such is not the case with the handicapped child. He simply docs not have the usual opportunities for the development of this concept, and it usually takes a good deal longer to be refined. This is especially true with a physically handicapped child. Additionally, many impaired children have some distorted concepts of themselves, both physically and emotionally. Developing a sense of self through art is a most appropriate beginning place in any discussion of art programming for special children.

This chapter is organized and written to assist both the classroom teacher and the art teacher who may not have a full knowledge of and/or experience with impaired children. The art teacher will probably focus on the way the sequence of activities builds to more and more complex learning and experiences. The classroom teacher will probably center more on the procedures, rationale, and motivation section of the art activities discussed.

It is always difficult to decide how much information to provide and to know what prior information a reader might have on the topic. Therefore, no assumptions have been made about previous knowledge. The guiding principle has been to present enough information so that a sensitive layman (either in art or special education) could proceed to develop an art program geared to the needs of his own very special children.

A SENSE OF SELF

Body-image and self-image are intimately related. The child's concept of his *self* (psychologically, socially, emotionally) is developed and fostered by means of an awareness and understanding of his body. Art has an important and valuable role to play in developing the child's body concept. Through art, the child will learn general body parts and how these relate and are integrated to form a total concept, i.e. a boy, a girl, a man, a woman.

Moreover, by engaging in the following activities, the artistic process itself will in turn be self-affirming. With the development of body awareness and positive attitudes toward the body via art experiences, the child transfers these affirmative feelings to his concept of self. As the child grows in his esteem of his body through art, so will he grow in his esteem of his self-concept.

PLEASE NOTE: There will be an illustration section *before* every chapter or major section. The reader is asked to examine the photographs before reading further. These photographs were taken over a five-year period and include several pictures of the same children at different ages.

Figure 31. A starter sheet can help a child get started in an art activity. It can also take the threat out of a drawing activity and out of confronting a blank page. A starter sheet may also help assess a child's schema for a person. Here, an aide shows a seven-year-old boy with muscular dystrophy how to make the letters of his name. He has just finished a starter sheet.

32

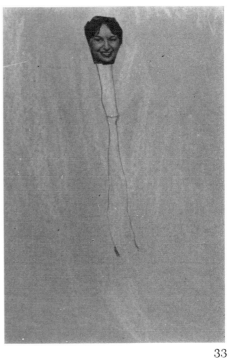

33

Figure 32. This completed starter sheet is by a fourteen-year-old trainable mentally retarded boy. He related the activity to bowling. After completing the figure, he added a bowling ball, then the bowling pins, and a second figure which was also a picture of himself about to throw a bowling ball.

Figure 33. A thirteen-year-old mongoloid (trainable mentally retarded) boy completed this starter sheet.

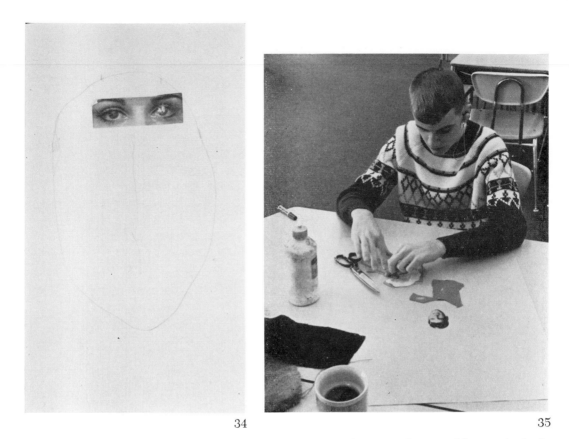

34

35

Figure 34. After the child has had several experiences with starter sheets and knows the body parts, he can try completing some variations. This modified starter sheet (with eyes only) was completed by an eleven-year-old boy in a learning disabilities class.

Figure 35. After doing a series of starter sheets using markers and crayons, this fourteen-year-old retarded boy tries his hand at "dressing" his figure using paper and cloth.

Figure 36. In this variation, the learning disabled eleven-year-old boy was given a sheet with only the four triangles drawn on it. He finished the drawing by turning the triangles into kites and adding two people to fly them.

Figure 37. This trainable mentally retarded/deaf teenager learns about printing and his hands at the same time.

Figure 38. A group of primary deaf children try some foot printing. This activity makes the child more aware of his feet and walking patterns.

Figure 39. A seven-year-old boy with muscular dystrophy explores the sand before making a sandcasting.

40
←

41

Figure 40. A five-year-old visually impaired child examines the marks she is making in her clay with her fingers. This activity increases the child's awareness of textures and her fingers.

Figure 41. A thirteen-year-old cerebral palsied girl holds up one of the clay medallions she is stringing with leather for a mobile. Another clay medallion is on the table in front of her. She made these by flattening balls of water base (earth) clay and texturing them with her fingers. The clay pieces were fired in a kiln and glazed by her before this final stringing and hanging operation.

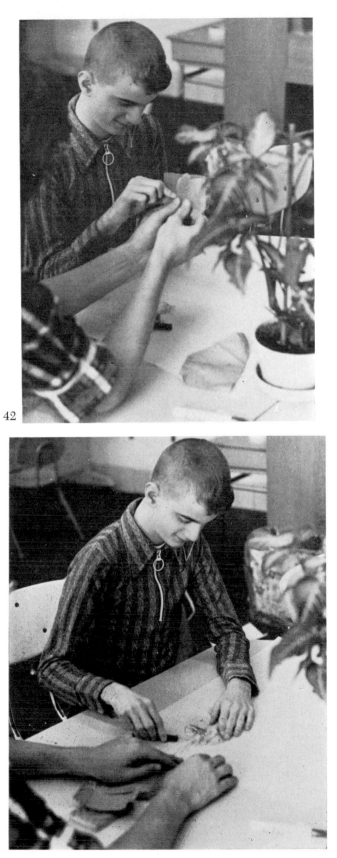

42

43

Figures 42 and 43. A trainable mentally retarded/deaf teenager explores texture with his fingers and then makes a rubbing.

Figure 44. A seven-year-old physically handicapped child makes a face with seeds. This activity helps reinforce what the child knows about facial parts.

Figure 45. A sixteen-year-old wears his sack mask. This trainable mentally handicapped boy has been learning about facial and body parts, and the sack mask is one of a series of art activities to help him gain a greater sense of himself.

Figure 46. An eight-year-old deaf child has her paper plate mask tied on. She has made a crown to go with her mask and has stepped into the regal realm.

Figure 47. A ten-year-old boy with cerebral palsy wears his space mask. He has transformed an ice cream carton by using paint and adding small cans.

Figure 48. It is most essential that children have a chance to play and act after making their masks. Two cerebral palsied children try "scaring" each other with their masks. The boy is ten years old and the girl is eleven.

Figure 49. If a physically handicapped child cannot use scissors, she can *tear*. Here, a cerebral palsied ten-year-old tears cloth for her life-size figure.

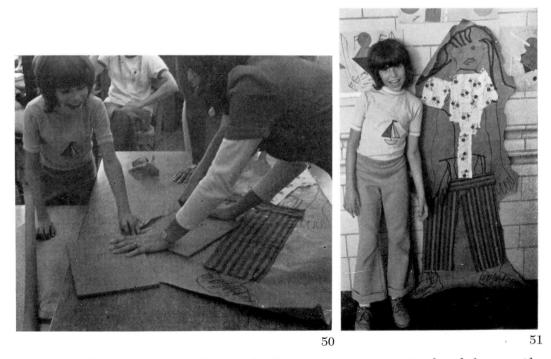

50   51

Figure 50. She then tears out the completed portrait, using a tearing board for a guide.

Figure 51. The artist has finished her self-portrait and stands beside it. She now has some concrete idea of how tall she is.

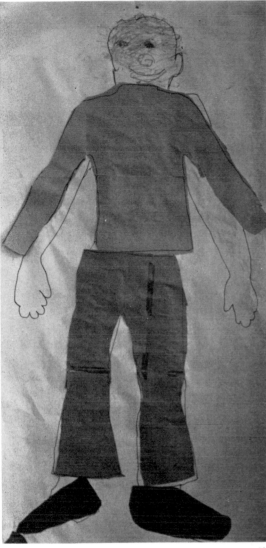

52

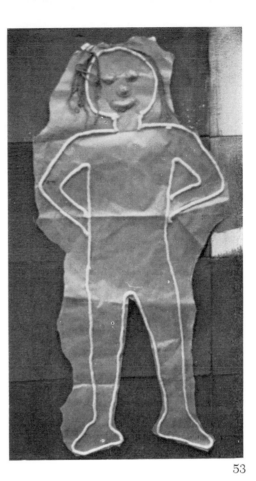

53

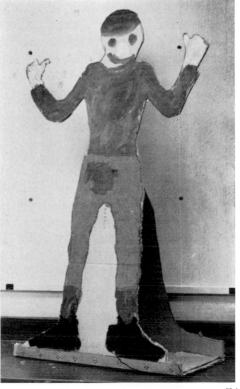

54

Figure 52. These are three variations of the life-size figure. A trainable mentally retarded teenager made his figure using crayons and construction paper.

Figure 53. A blind thirteen-year-old boy used yarn and followed a "line of glue" that had been "traced" around him.

Figure 54. The cardboard free-standing figure was made by an eight-year-old hearing impaired boy. He worked on a discarded bicycle box. An aide cut around it for him. Extra cardboard left at the bottom was later scored and folded up in back to support the figure.

THE GENESIS OR BEGINNING
How and where do I start? With a STARTER SHEET.

Purpose/Rationale

Sometimes it is hard to get started in an art activity. Sometimes a starting place can help, and a starter sheet can provide such a beginning point. By providing a hint (via a head), threat is taken out of the drawing situation and it is easier to initiate responses to tasks. It is important that the head be of the same sex as the child so that he can have a healthy identification with the drawing. The focus is on the particular child's development of his own body-concept. Starter sheets can also be *one* means of assessing the child's schema of a person.

Materials†

It is crucial that all art materials be nontoxic. Materials will have their nontoxicity stated on the label. If these is no such statement, check with the manufacturer.

Heads of boys, girls, men, and women from magazines or old pattern
    books
Newsprint or white drawing paper, 12 by 18 inches (*c.* 30 by 45 cm)
Watercolor markers or crayons
White glue

The outdated pattern books can be obtained from local fabric or sewing stores. The heads should be large and the same sex as the child who is to complete the picture. The heads should have no distracting elements such as cigarettes visible. One head per sheet is glued down. Other starter sheets can be made using bodies and omitting the heads.

Motivation

Hold up several of the starter sheets and ask the children what is missing. Discuss the missing parts, and name them or point them out to the child, using his own body as a reference. If the aim is to find out how much the child knows about his body, just give him one sheet at a time and ask him to finish the picture.

Procedure

When the child knows that he is to finish the picture, provide him with drawing tools. Give the child a choice of using watercolor markers or crayons. As the child finishes a picture, point out the various body parts

---

* The author wishes to acknowledge Larry S. Barnfield as the source for this concept.

† Metric equivalents are indicated in parentheses in this and all subsequent materials sections.

and ask him to name them. To enlarge the child's vocabulary, list the names of body parts and clothing on the chalkboard. The child can point out and name these parts on his completed picture.

If the child omits a part such as the hands, touch or point to his hands and ask him what they are. Or, ask him where the hands are in his picture. Depending on the child's ability level and his attention span, indicate (using him as the model) details such as fingernails and eyelashes. Whether this approach is used depends on the teacher's assessment of the child's abilities.

The school year's art activity can begin with several starter sheet exercises (some with only the heads missing and others with only the bodies missing). The child completes these without any specific instruction on body parts. These then may become important benchmarks of where the child began in his learning of body parts and his artistic schema for a person. Depending on the length of presentation, it will probably only take two or three minutes to complete one starter sheet.

Adaptations

LEARNING DISABLED. The hyperactive child will probably complete one in a very short amount of time (a matter of seconds), so several starter sheets will be needed. Stress some naming of body parts, and also ask which part is up, down, left, and right. Other materials can be used to complete the project, such as construction paper and glue, scrap materials, textured paper, or cloth. This depends on the child. For some, too many choices will be frustrating. Some materials such as construction paper and glue can slow the hyperactive child. Drawing materials can encourage swift completion of the project.

BEHAVIORALLY DISORDERED. If the child appears reluctant, do not force him into doing any art activity. It may just be that the child might need to watch for awhile before he becomes involved. The child can be given the option of watching others engaged in the activity. Children appreciate the security provided by the structure in this type of activity. Finally, some children will be bewildered if they are given too many materials choices.

HEARING IMPAIRED. Do not show completed examples at all. These children have a tendency to copy. Begin by explaining what they are to do and then demonstrate by partially completing the picture. Stress that the children are to do their own work. Suggest that they keep their pictures a secret until everyone has finished and then share what they have done.

RETARDED. Encourage the children to do their own work and not to copy. Try the "secret method" discussed above. For the severely retarded child, it is best to begin with starter sheets that have only the head missing. When he understands the procedure, go on to the sheets that have the body missing. Another variation would be to have photographs of each child made into starter sheets. This may assist the child in relating and identifying with the activity.

VISUALLY IMPAIRED. Begin with a sheet that has outlines of the head or body. To do this, use an outline of yarn or string or a "trail" of white glue that has dried. The child can complete this using either a glue outline or masking tape or some other substance that produces a raised surface. The sheet can also be placed on a window screen in a frame and taped down. The child then draws using a crayon, and he can feel where he has drawn. The child may also cut or tear the parts to be added from construction paper and either glue or tape them down.

PHYSICALLY HANDICAPPED. These children may prefer using felt-tipped markers. Whatever their choice of drawing material, the tool may need thickening by taping sponge rubber around it or by using a bulldog clip to hold the tool. The starter sheet should be taped down to the work surface. If the child cannot hold a drawing tool, he may be able to use his teeth, a helmet with a pencil attached, or his feet. If the child is too involved (very severely handicapped), a starter sheet with the body parts ready to assemble can be used. The child indicates when the parts are in the right place. Or, this involved child can work in a team with a more able classmate.

OTHER ADAPTATIONS. Starter sheets can also be used in the following manner. First, heads of several persons or a combination of a head and part of some everyday item (a car, for example) can be placed on the page. Half of a face may be used, and the child must finish the other half. A long mural can be made with several items from magazines pasted down to get the children started.

Other parts of the curriculum can be tied in by using a house starter sheet (windows only or doors only) or a nature starter sheet (leaves only or a mountain or clouds). The children can make starter sheets for each other from magazines. Finally, the same idea may be used by just tearing or cutting shapes from construction paper and gluing them down for the children to complete.

A *simple* pencil line on a page may also become a starter sheet. Try a straight line on one page, a circle on another, or a diagonal line on another. Using ink or paint blots as the starting stimulus can be another variation.

Getting started has many, many types of beginnings and endings. However, do not try the variations until it is established that the child understands the basic idea that a picture is to be completed. Try these variations after the child has worked through the series of art activities geared to foster body-concept.

Evaluation

POTENTIAL OUTCOMES. The child has completed one (or more) starter sheets using drawing materials. He has included appropriate body parts with over 75 percent accuracy.

CLOSURE. Display the finished drawing. Students can make starter sheets for fellow classmates. Classmates may then check one another's work for accuracy. For reinforcement, play a game with each student's finished drawing by covering one body part and having someone tell what is missing.

FEET AND HANDS, FINGERS AND TOES
Purpose/Rationale

This is a continuation of art activities designed to foster body awareness. Through these activities, the child becomes more aware of his extremities and identifies them as his own. This includes learning names of these parts. Mostly, the aim is for the child to delight in the discovery that feet and hands and fingers and toes are marvelous to have and can do many exciting, wondrous things. The child's own response and the teacher's evaluation of his capacities will determine how much of this sequence will be accomplished.

FOOTPRINTS, HANDPRINTS, FINGERPRINTS
Materials

Aluminum pie tins larger than the items to be printed
Brown wrapping paper or butcher paper in long sheet
Drawing paper and newsprint about 12 by 18 inches (*c.* 30 by 45 cm)

Masking tape to hold paper	Soap
Old newspapers	Sponge
Paint shirts or smocks	Tempera paint
Paper towels	Tub of water

Motivation

Bring in handprints of someone whose hand is much bigger or smaller than those of the children in the class. Play a detective game. Have each child place his hand on the print. None will match. Suggest that they make their own prints.

Or, put some fingerprints and handprints up. Point out that each child has his own unique print, one that is as unique as his own signature. If the class is at an intermediate level and they understand the concepts, police and detectives can be discussed. Then, have children make their own prints.

For younger children, just explain that they are going to make pictures using their hands and not anything else. Another alternative would be to tell them that "the brush thief stole all the paint brushes, so we will have to use our hands." Talk about prints and define them. Define *print* as a mark made by an object, a piece of type, a sponge spool, or other found object that has been coated with ink or paint and is pressed on a surface. Demonstrate the process as a part of the definition.

Procedure

Handprints

Take the hand and dip it into a shallow pan or tray of tempera paint that is not too thick. Press the hand several times in several places on the page. Have the children try several patterns or rows of handprints. Some math reinforcement can also be included by having the children "print" their hands a specific number of times. This can be done for both the left and right hands.

Another approach would be to start by having the children wiggle their fingers and play a game. Ask the class, for example, to "Show me your thumb"; "Show me your little finger." Then, demonstrate how to make a print, and start with fingerprints first. Next, make handprints, and have the child locate all of his thumbs, little fingers, etc., on his hand and then on the page. The child lifts his hand and presses, lifts, and presses, as opposed to using the paint like fingerpaint. Or, begin the entire activity by finger-painting and by showing how to make finger- and handprints. Variations such as "The Ten Little Handprint" song (similar to "The Ten Little Indian" song) can also be tried. This should take about one-half hour. Ample time should be provided for cleanup.

Footprints

Have the children take off their shoes and socks. Then, have everyone wiggle their toes and count them. Roll up pant legs. Have a roll of brown paper laid out in the room or on the playground. The playground may be the best place to do this activity, as the rain can do the cleaning up. Obtain permission to go out.

Have the children line up, step into the pan of tempera paint, and *walk* across the page. Label each row of footprints as the child finishes. Be sure to have a big tub of water to wash the children's feet when they are through. This activity should take about forty-five minutes for the children to do, allowing lots of time for cleanup.

It is suggested that only a few children at a time do the footprints and that classroom rules and procedures are carefully worked out before doing this. (Otherwise, footprints may end up in the wrong places—the halls, the walls, the bathrooms!)

Adaptations

LEARNING DISABLED. The left and right foot and hand can be color coded. Have the child use the same color exclusively for his right hand and right foot. Before footprinting, have the children practice small steps and giant steps. Have some of the more coordinated children try this on the paper, but watch out for possible slips and falls. Later, as a closure activity, cut out the feet and make them into a personalized hopscotch game. The children can learn about fingernails and toenails by drawing them in on their own prints.

BEHAVIORALLY DISORDERED. In addition to the above, limit the activity to only one or two children per session. Have the rest of the class help by holding the paper. A whole mural of hand- or footprints may be made for the room. When the completed prints are put up, be sure each child's name appears underneath his prints so that he identifies with them.

HEARING IMPAIRED. In addition to the above, the language involved in the whole process should be stressed. Think through the steps and the key action words. In addition to words such as *hand, thumb, finger, right,* and *left,* there are *foot, big toe, walk, hop, jump, lift,* and *press.* These are all key words which the child will learn from these printing activities. It may help to use the step-by-step method described below.

RETARDED. In addition to those suggestions under the hearing impaired section, a step-by-step method will probably be best. For example, tell the child to (1) dip his hand into the paint, (2) press once on the paper, and (3) if there is enough paint left, press on another *clean place* on the paper. Be sure that the child understands that he is to press rather than smear the paint, or the whole process becomes another fingerpainting exercise. Remember, however, that fingerpainting can be one of the goals for this activity.

VISUALLY IMPAIRED. Tempera paint that has some texture added, such as fine sand, can be used. By doing so, the child is able to feel the print where it dries. Emphasize that part of the activity is getting paint on the hands.

PHYSICALLY HANDICAPPED. Be sure that the paper is taped down for the prints. The tempera should be of cream consistency. Test the tempera before proceeding. Emphasize that getting paint on the hands is a very necessary part of the activity. For the footprints, a large roll of paper should be taped to the floor. Those children in wheelchairs can print in their chairs by rolling through some paint and then crossing the page. Make the most of the activity, and encourage the children to move their fingers and toes before beginning.

Evaluation

POTENTIAL OUTCOMES. The child has made at least one foot-, thumb-, or handprint with the art materials. He has shown he knows the printing process by lifting and pressing (and by not smearing the paint). He has named body parts with 75 percent or more accuracy.

CLOSURE. When finished, the prints can be displayed. Help the child cut his prints out, and use them for comparison or for identification. Prints can be used, for example, as arrows to direct children to some part of the room or building. Have the children make up stories about who made the hand- and footprints. The prints may be used as wallpaper in the room, or a class can choose one or two prints and draw a picture to go with them.

It is important that learning body parts is emphasized and that the child gets satisfaction in making prints using *his* hands and *his* feet. With older children and thinner paint, fingerprints and patterns may be made. Enlarge these prints using an opaque projector, and discuss the whorls and lines found in them. The children can go on to create imaginary fingerprints and footprints and make stories to go with them.

Build on class knowledge of printing, and do other printing activities using found objects, spools, sponges, etc. The finished prints may be used as folder covers; handprints and footprints made on cloth using textile paint instead of tempera can become gift items (for example, a handprinted hand towel).

Sandcasting

Purpose/Rationale

Sandcasting is another activity emphasizing learning about feet and hands and fingers and toes. It is a bit more involved activity and probably should be done in small groups or one at a time. Sandcasting does build on some of the skills learned in the printing activities, so it probably should be done after the printing activities.

Materials

Aluminum foil

A hand or a foot

Mixing stick or old spoon

Old newspapers

Paint shirts or smocks

Plaster of Paris in 10-pound bag
   (*c.* 4.5 kg)

Plastic bucket or old large plastic bottle
   with top cut off

Sand, about 2 pounds (*c.* 1 kg) per child

Shoe boxes for each child

Motivation

The activity itself may be enough motivation. Talk about animals leaving footprints in the forest, or take the class on a walk. (Check beforehand to be sure that there is a footprint or toeprint to be discovered by the class.)

Procedure

The mixing and proper disposal of the plaster are important in this activity. Never pour plaster down a sink. (Plaster will clog the sink, make an enemy of the janitor, and strain relations with the principal.) Plaster is to be mixed in an old can or plastic bottle (with the top cut off). The containers can then be thrown away along with any excess plaster which is mixed.

When mixing plaster, follow the directions on the box. Add plaster to the water by sifting, and then stir. When the mixture is the consistency of cream, it is ready to pour. Do not waste time after the plaster is mixed. Pour it immediately; otherwise, the plaster will harden and a new batch will have to be mixed. Remember to field test the plaster mixture before doing the activity with children.

Before mixing the plaster, mold the foil on the inside of the shoebox, covering every area. Then fill the box about two-thirds full of sand. (The school sandbox is a good source, but do not advertise that.) Wet the sand just enough so that it will stick together. Press the hand or foot (without shoe or sock) into the sand. Remove the limb, mix the plaster, and pour enough to just fill the imprint. Let the print mold dry for about a week, and brush off loose sand. (Remember to return the sand to the sandbox.)

The result is a footprint or handprint mold that can be painted with tempera and used as an instructional tool, as a paperweight, or whatever. This should take about forty-five minutes, with one or two children helping to mix the plaster. Allow another half-hour to paint the plaster.

Adaptations

LEARNING DISABLED. Some careful classroom management will help. Work in small groups, and assign several children to a plaster mixing team. Sand-casting can help the child who has problems with laterality (right/left orientation and use). Have each child do both his right and left hands. The contrast between the sand and the plaster will help emphasize the figure (the plaster) and the background (the sand) for those who need some work on this area. After learning the basic process, other kinds of things from the environment can become models for the plaster cast.

BEHAVIORALLY DISORDERED. Again, set some rules so that plaster ends up only in the imprint. Training one student to help in mixing and pouring the plaster may help. Other favorite objects can also be sandcasted in addition to hands. This can become a lesson in Pop Art as well.

HEARING IMPAIRED. It will help to demonstrate the entire process and to have some partially completed examples. Have plaster in several stages of drying to help define plaster for the children. Bring in some other examples of molds, and focus on teaching the concept of mold. Emphasize that learning to make a plaster cast is only one kind of artistic process. It should not be an end in itself. What is created after learning the process is much more important.

RETARDED. The child may be tempted to spend time exploring and playing in the sand. This is fine and may become a part of the lesson. Fully demonstrate the process. It also will help to break the activity into two parts. First, focus on making a good handprint in moist sand. Second, mix and pour the plaster. Finally, if there is still interest, the children can paint their plaster creations with tempera paint.

Visually Impaired. At least one example of a completed plaster cast will help the child grasp the total concept. It also will help to have plaster in its several states (dry, partly mixed, ready for pouring) to more fully communicate the concept of plaster.

Physically Handicapped. Some children will need help with pouring the plaster. By teaming children in pairs with a more able child in each team, this problem may be solved. Another alternative may be to have one child who is most able help pour all the plaster. If the children desire to paint their finished work, it may be easier to use sponges instead of brushes. Sponges are easier to hold for some children. By limiting the paint choices to one or two colors, children with fine motor coordination problems will not be frustrated by having the many colors of paint running together.

Evaluation

Potential Outcomes. The child has made a mold (impression) of one of his body parts (hand, foot, finger) in sand. He has learned how to mix plaster and to pour it. He has had the difference between his right and left hands or feet reinforced. The child has learned that other items can also be molded in sand by making molds with one or more other objects. He has cleaned up without being told more than once. He has learned the whole plaster casting process and can explain it with 80 percent or more accuracy to another classmate.

Closure. Have a display of everyone's work. Compare the plaster mold with the child's own hand or foot. Review the sandcasting process. Discuss other things that may be made with this process, and plan to do some of these also.

Awareness Through Clay: Finger and Foot Stamping

Purpose/Rationale

This activity is a continuation of the body awareness activities, with specific attention given to the fingers and toes and how they can create textures in clay. It is especially planned for those children who need hand and finger exercise. This would probably be a good logical follow-up of the printing activity and can be a lead into a series of activities based on texture. Texture is one of the elements of design and is a part of every artistic work.

Materials

For the first activity:
Oil base clay
Old cookie sheet with sides
Paint shirt or smock
Stick of wood with smooth side
Willing fingers

For the second activity:
Canvas squares approximately 16 by
    24 inches (*c.* 40 by 60 cm)
Old newspapers
Paint shirts or smocks
Paper towels
Water
Water base clay
Willing fingers

Salt and flour clay may be substituted for water base clay. The formula is equal parts of salt and flour, plus enough water to adhere and mix the dry ingredients, and a few drops of disinfectant. Remember that only water base clay will make a sound, so it should be used for the windchimes. Other heavy cloth scraps can be substituted for the canvas.

Motivation

The medium will probably be motivation in itself. Demonstrate and challenge the children to see how many different kinds of marks they can make with their fingers in the clay. The word *texture*, which can be defined as the way something feels, can also be emphasized. For older children, suggest that this activity leads into making a windchime or trivet out of clay.

Procedure

Have an old four-sided tray half-filled with oil base clay or earth clay. However, remember that water base (earth) clay will dry out. It will either have to be kept moist and covered with plastic between sessions or replaced with fresh moist clay for each session. Be sure it is smooth. Start by referring to the handprinting and sandcasting activity and the ways these processes were done. (They did this by pushing their fingers into the clay, paper, or sand.) Challenge the children to try and make as many different marks as they can in the clay with their fingers. Ask for a volunteer to show his clay marks. Talk about pattern, or count the marks. If the child does not like a mark, he can erase it with the straight edge of a piece of wood. This will be a brief, ten-minute activity.

With older children, the same idea can be used with water base (earth) clay. The class can mix it themselves in large garbage bags, following directions on the package. If clay is going to be mixed in the classroom, allow one forty-five-minute period for this. Start with a ball of clay. Have the children flatten the ball and then experiment with the various kinds of marks that their hands and fingers can make.

The next step for both processes is to start with another ball of clay, flatten it, and repeat some of the marks the child liked the most from his experimentation. Make a hole in the top about ⅛ to ¼ inch in diameter. The hole should not be less than one inch from any outer edge of the clay pancake. This hole will be used to hang the completed work. Set aside the clay to dry and fire. It then can be either painted with tempera paint or glazed (if there is a kiln available). The children will probably want to make several.

These clay pieces then can become windchimes, wall handings, or trivets. If the class does not have the attention span to make several clay pieces individually, they can add theirs to make one group windchime or wall hanging. Making the windchimes will take one half-hour session. If there is high interest, a second period can also be spent in this activity.

Adaptations

LEARNING DISABLED. Not only making textures but also letters and words in the clay tray can help the child to identify and learn these figures. It may also help the child to separate figures from the background. Some textures and letters can already be made beforehand in clay or on paper. The child then matches some of these by creating them in his own tray. This can become a game. Each child may create one texture and have a teammate try to match it. Part of the activity should be set aside for exploration and for the child to make his own unique textures.

BEHAVIORALLY DISORDERED. Be sure that a supportive atmosphere is established so that the child understands that a part of the activity is getting his hands in the clay. As with all art activities, if the child does not want to participate, do not force him. Provide an alternative for those children who are hesitant about putting their hands in messy art materials. Many will just wish to explore the clay by pounding it and poking it. This may be the primary goal. If the class is interested, have them do the windchimes and encourage them to contribute to a class windchime. Another alternative would be to decorate a whole wall with clay tiles. Each child can create a clay tile, and these can become part of the larger group project.

HEARING IMPAIRED. For older children, it may be best to talk about making a wall hanging or a hot plate (trivet). The children can also make smaller medallions. These can become necklaces, bracelets, or other kinds of jewelry (body adornment). Math concepts may be included by suggesting that the children put ten to fifteen marks on their clay pieces.

RETARDED. Depending on the child's ability level, the clay tray may be as involved or as simple as the teacher desires. Words such as *press, smooth, rough,* and *lift* should be reinforced. Math skills can be incorporated by counting how many marks the child makes in the tray. Also, writing skills can be reinforced by having the child make letters in the clay tray. The older children and some of the brighter ones may be quite capable of doing the wall hanging, windchimes, or jewelry out of the water base (earth) clay.

VISUALLY IMPAIRED. These children will want an established work area. Have the children work in a large tray that has shallow sides. This sets boundaries. Tape cloth to the tray and work on top of this so that the clay will not stick. Set several clay balls to the right of the tray. Tell the child where these are. Place one ball in the tray for the child. He may need help in making the hole for the string. If he is older and can grasp the concept, discuss the fact that different sizes of balls and different thicknesses will produce different sounds. Have a damp paper towel or sponge on the left so that the child can moisten his clay when he needs to. ·

PHYSICALLY HANDICAPPED. Follow the same basic procedure. Be prepared to let the children use their feet and toes instead of their hands. Tape down canvas pieces (on the floor, if this is appropriate) and work on top of them. Let the child determine the best work posture for himself. Be sure that the clay is soft enough for stamping.

It may be beneficial for the children to understand how clay is mixed. Some children may need this type of physical activity and experience, so let them mix their own clay. Such an experience also builds cooperation because the children will probably do this in groups. Having the children do as much of their own work as possible builds a greater sense of independence and accomplishment. This includes mixing their own clay. Put the clay powder and the right amount of water (following directions on the package) into large plastic garbage bags. Work in pairs, and mix by kneading the bag. Leave the bag loosely closed overnight if the clay is still a little wet. Roll the clay into balls for use, or have one of the less involved children help do this.

Evaluation

POTENTIAL OUTCOMES. The child has explored clay by making three or more different sets of marks in it using his hands. He has tried making repeated patterns by stamping in the clay with his hand, fingers, or found objects. The child has learned that different textures, i.e. more than one kind of stamped impression, can be made in moist clay. He has learned that texture is one of the basic art elements. The child has made at least one medallion which will be painted or glazed for a windchime or mobile, and he has learned how to mix clay (either water base clay, or salt and flour clay, or both).

CLOSURE. Have the children share their texture explorations in their clay tray and tell how each pattern was made. Those who are making windchimes or mobiles can do the same thing. The mobiles and windchimes will be finished by glazing, painting, or by using shoe polish, wood stain, or coffee and then displayed in the classroom. The concept of texture can be reinforced in many other class experiences. This concept will continue to grow as the teacher points out and describes textures in other art activities that the class will be doing.

Texture Here, There, and Everywhere

Purpose/Rationale

These three activities are designed to help the child discover that he has a sense of touch and can discriminate between different textures. Texture is an important part of the child's world. So is his sense of touch and the abilities to discover the varieties of textures at the tips of his fingers.

Materials

Crayons, large with paper peeled off
Drawing paper or newsprint about 9 by 12 inches (*c.* 22 by 30 cm)
Masking tape
Varieties of textures (burlap, cloth, corrugated cardboard, metal screen, sandpaper, etc.)

The textures should be flat items cut into various shapes. Small paper sacks and masking tape are also needed for the second activity.

Motivation

Bring in some obvious texture opposites, such as coarse sandpaper, grainy wood, cloth, metal screen, or other items. Make two piles of these, a rough and a smooth pile. Hold up the items, or better yet, pass them around asking for class reaction. Or, have one child come and place a texture shape on the rough or smooth pile.

Procedure

Rubbings

The children select textures (three or more, one at a time) and make rubbings with them. A rubbing is done by placing the object under a piece of newsprint or thin drawing paper and by rubbing across it with the long side of a peeled crayon. The pressure should be even, and the area rubbed should be at least one inch square so that the area can be easily seen. The item can be taped down for easier rubbing. The children should have a choice of crayons. Have the children try and match up their rubbings with the objects afterwards. This should take about one-half hour.

Texture Hunt

The same rubbing procedure is used, but the children are instructed to go on a texture hunt or safari in the room or outside. Give some guidelines about how many and what kinds of textures are to be hunted. This should take about one-half hour.

*Texture Game**

Texture bags are made for each class member and one for the teacher. Each bag (small sack) contains four or five different texture items—for example, a square of screen, a piece of sandpaper, corrugated cardboard, a piece of bark, a thick piece of yarn, and a thin string. As one texture is pulled out, pass it around the class. Without looking, each child is to feel in his bag and find the same textured item. Then he makes a rubbing of this. The procedure is repeated until the bag is empty. This game should take about one-half hour to play.

Adaptations

LEARNING DISABLED. Set down specific ground rules so that each child knows when it is his turn to match up textures. The children can cut out their own texture rubbings and make a collage from them. (A collage is a picture made with only different kinds of textured papers.) Some children may need some suggested topics for their collages.

BEHAVIORALLY DISORDERED. Set up ground rules, especially for the texture hunt. Otherwise, the children will collide. Perhaps have the children hunt one at a time or in teams of two. Allow only one group at a time on the hunting ground. The children can bring in a favorite object that has lots of texture and share it with the others. A texture hunt outside may reveal lots of unusual discoveries. A group texture mural can be made.

HEARING IMPAIRED. This activity is an excellent chance to build language. Among others, key words would be *touch, texture, feel, rough, smooth, press, rub, same,* and *different.*

RETARDED. The slower, younger, or less developed children may desire to stop with the first part of these texture activities. Again, it may be an important opportunity to reinforce vocabulary. Select a few key words, and use many examples and a lot of repetition.

VISUALLY IMPAIRED. A bulldog clip around the crayon will help the child to grasp it. Use a no-roll crayon (flat-sided). Tape the sack to the table so that the child can reach into it. On the texture hunt, it may help to set aside one part of the room for this purpose and *plant* some interesting textures. The children may want to work in teams.

---

* The author wishes to acknowledge Larry S. Barnfield as the source for this concept.

PHYSICALLY HANDICAPPED. Tape down the item to be transferred, and tape the newsprint over it. Use a bulldog clip around the crayons so that the child can more easily grasp them. A crayon that is thick and is flat on one side works best. The crayons can be flattened with a knife. With the texture hunt, it may help to work in teams, as some children will have more use of their hands than others. Remember that feet can always be substituted for hands. The crayon can be taped to a foot and the paper taped to the floor. With the texture game, tape the open side of the sack that *touches* the table so the child cannot look into the sack.

Evaluation

POTENTIAL OUTCOMES. The child has expanded his sense of touch by discovering one or more different textures and sorting them into rough or smooth piles. The child has learned the word for texture and can define it verbally or by pointing to different textures. The child has learned how to make a texture rubbing. He has completed one or more rubbings, demonstrating his knowledge of the process with 75 percent or more correct use of materials. During the texture game and the texture safari the child has followed directions and has given appropriate social responses 75 percent or more of the time.

CLOSURE. The class can match or write the words for the textured objects they have rubbed. This may become a class display, and a collage can be made from the collected rubbings. The texture game may be expanded by having the children bring in some of their own objects. A texture table can be set up in the room, with class contributions. The textures may be sorted according to a variety of categories.

WHAT'S IN A FACE?

Purpose/Rationale

This will be a series of suggested activities aimed at familiarizing the child with his face and its parts and learning the names for each part. At the completion of one or more of these activities, the child will have a better concept of his face and will have experienced success with a number of different media. The child will be able to use these media in imaginative ways.

Simple Faces

Motivation

Have several mirrors in the room, and have the children look at themselves in the mirrors. Ask them to point to their eyes, noses, ears, mouths, and hair. Ask for a volunteer to come forward and point to his facial parts as the rest of the class names them. (Most children love the chance to be teacher in front of the class.) Discuss what the facial parts do. Make several sounds while discussing ears. Have some different scents in discussing the nose. Have sweet and sour items for the children to taste. Another kind of motivation would be to have the children make different kinds of faces and express different emotions, such as happy, sad, angry, and funny. Have the class guess each other's facial expression.

Materials

Buttons

Cardboard in small pieces

Construction paper and other kinds of paper scraps

Old newspapers

Paint shirts or smocks

Paper plates, 1 or 2 per child

Pipe cleaners

Seeds in medium or large sizes

Synthetic foam packing pieces

White glue in squeeze bottles or small tins with ¼ inch (*c.* ½ cm) brushes

Yarn scraps, including yellow, brown, red, and black

Procedure

Have the children make a face. They might want to make one that expresses an emotion. Demonstrate how to put just a little glue on the area to be glued and then place the items down to make the facial parts. This activity should take about thirty minutes.

Adaptations

LEARNING DISABLED AND BEHAVIORALLY DISORDERED. Facial gesturing can be emphasized before beginning this activity. Discuss some things which make the child happy and sad. Some items might be candy or pictures of the zoo or a circus. The teacher will have other insights about these ideas since he should relate to each child in his class. Avoid having too many choices of materials, as this may be confusing for the child. The child can finish one part of the face with one material before going to the next part.

HEARING IMPAIRED. Suggest that the children construct their faces using a particular expression. Discuss the words for these expressions using many concrete examples. Tell the children that their work should be secret until they are finished. After the activity, each child in turn can share his creation.

RETARDED. Provide a choice of materials to use, and choose ones that can be easily picked up. A mirror will help the child in using his own face as a reference point. If a child omits something, go over the parts with him and point them out in the mirror or on himself. Key words are all the facial parts. Also each child can make a sentence about faces, i.e. "everybody point to their noses." A song may be sung about faces that includes the various parts.

VISUALLY IMPAIRED. Tape the plate down. It will be helpful to have different sizes of buttons, seeds, and synthetic foam pieces separated and set in a muffin tin that is taped or nailed to a work board. Have the child handle all of the items in the tin first, so he knows what is available. Pipe cleaners might be used instead of yarn, as they may be easier to manipulate.

PHYSICALLY HANDICAPPED. Do not use especially small items but rather items that can be easily picked up. Place these buttons, synthetic foam packing pieces, and cardboard pieces in distinct rows so that the child can easily grasp them. Instead of using glue in a bottle, put some in a weighted container and use a ½ inch stiff brush. The brushes should have short handles. Long-handled brushes may be shortened by cutting. The surface of the anchored plate can then be painted with white glue, and the child can drop the items into the surface. The child might want to use a cardboard funnel to assist in placement. If the child has very limited use of his hands, he can use his feet or a stick held in his hand or teeth to push the objects around to form the face.

Evaluation

POTENTIAL OUTCOMES. The child has named facial parts with 80 percent or better accuracy. He has made a simple face with the art materials and demonstrated appropriate use of glue. He has made his own decisions about which materials to use so that his face has at least one thing that is different from the others in the class.

CLOSURE. The class can review the facial parts by pointing to their own faces and to the correct part on their art work. The class may do some simple dramatics by holding up their faces and talking behind them. This activity is preliminary to the mask activity that follows.

Masks

Purpose/Rationale

Let a child make a mask and marvelous things start to happen. Put his mask on him and the *ham* within emerges. A mask is a license to play and to express all sorts of feelings and emotions which would not ordinarily emerge. A mask is an opportunity to reinforce what the child knows about a face and to be creative in putting that face together. Since different types of masks are best suited to different types of handicaps, these will be discussed under adaptations.

Motivation

Halloween is the natural place for mask making, but it should not be the *only* time in the year for the activity. A reading story can be the beginning for a mask and for some spontaneous drama. Capitalize on this occasion and develop a short play around the masks which each child makes. On a simpler level, each child can be given a chance to say or do something in front of the class as he wears his mask. Finally, have the children draw a story about themselves in their masks or make paper costumes to go along with the mask.

Materials

Aluminum pie tins, large size

Boxes, large enough to fit over the head

Brushes, ½ inch (*c.* 1 cm) wide

Buttons

Containers for glue, paint, and water

Crayons

Ice cream cartons, round, 5 gallon (*c.* 20 l)

Matt knife or sharp kitchen knife

Old newspapers

Paint shirts or smocks

Paper scraps in various sizes and kinds

Sacks, large enough to fit over the head

Scissors

Seeds, large and medium size

Stapler

Synthetic foam packing pieces (look like peanuts, popcorn, and *O*s)

Tempera paint

Watercolor markers

White glue

Yarn scraps, including yellow, red, black, and brown

Not all of these materials will be needed for each of the mask activities. Read through the adaptations, and then decide what is needed from this list.

Adaptations

LEARNING DISABLED AND BEHAVIORALLY DISORDERED. The decision on the type of materials for making masks depends on the interests, abilities, and attention span of the children. The paper plate faces easily become masks when eye holes are punched out, and the child can hold them up to his face. Paper sack masks are also appropriate. Always provide some choice of materials for the child, even if it is only a choice between two items. Remember that for some children, two choices will be as many as they can handle.

Place the sack over the child's head and mark where the eyes should be. Some children may become frightened when the sack is placed over their heads. Demonstrate what is going to happen with one of the class who would not get upset with a sack on his head. Have a classmate mark where the facial parts go on the mask. Then remove the sack and cut out the eyes and decorate with the materials provided. For small children, it may be necessary to cut out a place for the shoulders. This is done by cutting a half-oval in each of the small sides of the sack.

As important as making the mask is what the children do with their masks when completed. Have each child show and do something from behind his mask. Another possible starting point is to have a series of one-line situations like, "I'm a monster and am going to eat up everybody! Snarl! Snarl!" Or, "I'm superman and I'm going to protect you from the monster." Assign these judiciously to the members of the class.

HEARING IMPAIRED. Any material or type of mask can be made. It will be important to teach the concept of masks. Language can also be tied into the lesson. Some examples might be "cutting *out* the eyes" and "pasting *on* the hair." The choice of words depends on the level of the class. It is also crucial to demonstrate the type of mask the child will make (paper plate, sack, box, or pie tin). The box masks and the pie tin masks are discussed in the visually impaired and physically handicapped adaptations sections. Do not show completed projects that the child will be tempted to copy. Emphasize that each child is to do his *own* work. Have the child act or do something wearing his mask. This facilitates spontaneous language expressions.

RETARDED. Consider the level of difficulty in making the types of masks and the physical abilities of the children before deciding the types of masks they will make. The paper plate mask is the least difficult, followed by the sack, the box, and the pie plate (discussed in the physically handicapped section). The class may only be able to do one type of mask. This is fine. Again, be sure each child has a choice of materials (even if it is as simple a choice as using a marker or a crayon).

It may be best to use only drawing instruments on the masks the first time the child does the activity. This would take only about thirty minutes. Then repeat the activity, introducing other materials that can be used on the mask. If the children cannot cut paper to use, have them tear it. This activity will take forty-five minutes.

VISUALLY IMPAIRED. The best materials for masks are ice cream cartons (round, five-gallon size). They work best when they are empty, so have a party first! Help the child locate the spot for eyes and mouth. The child can brush glue (using a stiff ½ inch brush) on the items he is to attach. It is best to put the glue on the item and then press the item onto the carton.

Some of the same items which were used for the face plates work well. Add one or two other items to the pile. Small bottletops, pieces of string, wood shavings, or synthetic foam packing pieces are some suggestions. Give the child a reference point by tearing a hole in the carton or gluing on a piece of material so that the child knows where the front is. Other types of boxes may also be used. It should take about one hour to complete the mask.

PHYSICALLY HANDICAPPED. Again, the ice cream carton or another box that is a substantial stationary type (as opposed to one with a flimsy base such as a paper sack) is recommended. If the child wants to incorporate construction paper into his mask, use a tearing board and let him tear the pieces or strips himself. A tearing board is a flat board placed on top of the paper that leaves exposed the section that is to be torn. The child places one hand on the board and tears with the other hand. Let the child decide whether it is best to tear away from or toward himself.

Instead of gluing all parts, the child may choose to paint the mask. Avoid letting the child use too many different materials, as the result may look chaotic and the child may become confused himself. Depending on the abilities of the individual, this kind of mask should take between forty-five minutes and two hours to make.

Other materials that can be used for masks for the physically handicapped are aluminum pie tins and TV dinner trays.* The child will need help from the teacher or a classmate to mark where the eyes go and to cut them. This type of mask is held or tied on. Mask parts are stapled on using a large desk stapler. If the child has difficulty stapling, place a flat board on top of the stapler; this provides a larger area that is easier to press with one or both hands.

Aluminum strips can be torn from old pie tins by the children. These then may become hair, eyelashes, or other funny features. To tear the aluminum strips, first cut off the edge of the pie tin and then cut on the side with a series of two to three inch slits that are one to two inches apart. These slits are then torn from the pie tin. Paint cannot be used on these foil masks. Instead, color can be added by using *permanent* markers. Yarn and paper scraps may also be used. The child can tear the paper using a flat tearing board as described above. This kind of mask should take about an hour to make.

Evaluation

POTENTIAL OUTCOMES. The child has named facial parts with 100 percent accuracy. He has made a mask with the art materials provided. He has selected materials and used them demonstrating appropriate gluing and/or painting skills with at least 80 percent mastery. He has demonstrated his creativity by (1) not making a copy of anyone else's work, (2) having something uniquely added, and (3) uniquely using materials. (Unique is defined as a response that is different from all others in the class.) The child has put something on the mask that corresponds to some attribute he has himself (used the same hair color or same eye color, etc.). If he is making a mask of something else, such as a favored character,

---

* The author wishes to acknowledge Larry S. Barnfield as the source for this concept.

animal, or person, he makes it in such a way that it can be easily identified by others in the class or the teacher.

CLOSURE. The children can give a brief play wearing their masks. Have them put on their masks and say, do, or act at least one line for a brief time for the rest of the group. They can trade masks and create another short play. Costumes may be made to go with their masks. The masks may be used in other classroom activities. Masks of other persons or animals may also be made and used to dramatize social studies or current events.

PUTTING IT ALL TOGETHER: THE LIFE-SIZE PORTRAIT*

Purpose/Rationale

Although this activity may be done at any time in the series (as can all of the other activities), it is designed as a culminating experience in body awareness. Many children are not aware of how tall they are. This is especially true for physically handicapped children who are wheelchair bound and for the blind who need a point of reference about their height. Additionally, some children have difficulty in putting all the parts of the body together to form a comprehensive whole. This activity is geared to solving these problems. Additionally, since it requires teamwork, this activity facilitates cooperative skills. Decision-making skills are also involved in the choices that the child must make as he dresses his figure.

Motivation

For the younger children, start by simply asking them if they know how tall they are. Older children may be given a choice of doing themselves or dressing themselves in the form of a famous person (from entertainment, politics, and/or literature or history). Or, have a hatful of suggested names and let the child choose one. In each case, this should be a person of the same sex because it is important to have healthy sexual identification. If the child already has a good self-image and a healthy sexual identification, however, it will not be quite as important that the life-size figure be of the same sex.

Procedure

The child picks a partner (or one is assigned), and they take turns drawing around each other on separate sheets of paper. Mathematics may be tied in by having the child measure how tall he is and then by unrolling the paper according to this number, adding on an extra foot at the top and bottom. The child draws in his face and decides how he is to dress the figure. This is then cut out and put up in the room. It will take about one-half hour to measure and one-half hour to paint the figure. If cloth is used, it will take about one hour to complete the figure.

---

* The author wishes to acknowledge Larry S. Barnfield as the source for this concept.

Materials

Brown wrapping paper, in lengths about 3 foot (*c*. 1 m) longer than each child

Brushes, ½ inch (*c*. 1 cm) wide

Buttons

Cloth scraps that can easily be cut or torn

Containers for water and glue

Crayons

Masking tape

Measuring tape or yardstick (meterstick)

Old newspapers

Paint shirts or smocks

Paper scraps of various kinds and sizes

Pencils

Scissors

Yarn scraps, including yellow, red, brown, and black

Watercolor markers

White glue

Not all of these materials will be used on each life-size portrait, but the choice should be made from this basic list.

Adaptations

LEARNING DISABLED AND BEHAVIORALLY DISABLED. Think carefully about the materials choices given to the children. Some children who become easily frustrated will not have the patience to cut out the cloth to dress their figures. Other children will need a choice of only two types of materials, as they may well become overwhelmed by too many decisions. Different textured material and paper may be preferred choices for the learning disabled child.

HEARING IMPAIRED. This is an excellent opportunity not only to reinforce language of the body but also to introduce clothing words. As the child dresses his figure, give him the words for the clothing parts he is adding. The question form can also be reinforced by asking "Where is the shirt?" or "How many buttons are there?"

RETARDED. These children may not have the attention span for an involved dressing of their figures. Be sure they add the facial features, and give them a choice of coloring them in *or* making them with construction paper. (Give them very large sheets of paper to dress their figures.) This experience is an excellent chance to teach clothing words to the children. If they dress their figure with cloth, be sure it can be easily cut or torn. Have them brush on white glue as opposed to squirting it out.

VISUALLY IMPAIRED. Trace around the child with white glue that will leave a raised line. If the child has some sight, use a heavy black line that is easily seen. Provide a choice of materials. Have the child use paper, construction paper, cloth, and/or yarn. If he is using cloth, be sure that there are differing textures and that it is easy to cut or tear.

PHYSICALLY HANDICAPPED. If the child wishes to use cloth, be sure it can be torn or easily cut. Some children can use electric scissors. If the child prefers to use tempera paint instead of cloth, be sure it is thick (cream consistency) and that he uses a wide brush. The brush should be about one inch wide and stiff. It should have a short handle. Since this child probably cannot cut too accurately, it is suggested that his life-size picture not be cut out.

OTHER ADAPTATIONS. This activity may be done several times during the year so that the child can check his growth. Another alternative is to have the children choose a community helper and then make themselves as this person.

The life-size portrait may be done on strong cardboard and a free-standing picture made out of it. This may become a coat and hat rack for the child. Finally, the class can go out on the paved playground and use chalk to trace and finish their portraits. Tempera paint can also be used on the playground after the children are traced. Permission to use the playground should be obtained.

Evaluation

POTENTIAL OUTCOMES. In figuring how much paper to use, the child has measured with 90 percent accuracy or better. By tracing around another classmate, he has shown he can cooperate. The child has named all the visible body parts and included them on his life-size portrait with 90 percent or better accuracy of placement.

He has related at least three things about himself to his portrait by putting in, for example, the same hair color, eye color, or the same color of clothing. He has shown his independence and creativity by making his own choices of materials and by *not* copying others' work. He has gained an appreciation for others' work by spending time looking at a display of their completed work.

CLOSURE. Display the finished portraits either in the room or in the hall. The class should have some time to view the completed figures. Names of body parts and clothing may be reinforced by choosing one child to lead the class by pointing to various parts as they are named. The rest of the class can be the umpires in this game. Discuss the way materials have been used. Encourage *each* child by saying something *positive* about his work in front of the class.

REFERENCES

Fitts, W. H. et al. The self concept and self-actualization. *Dede Wallace Center Monograph III*. Nashville, Tenn.: Counselor Recordings and Tests, 1971.

Hamacheck, D. E. *Encounters with the self*. New York: Holt, Rinehart & Winston, 1971.

Wylie, R. *The self concept* (Vol. 1; Rev. ed.). Lincoln: University of Nebraska Press, 1974.

Chapter V

MAINSTREAMING ART

INTRODUCTION

RESEARCH CONFIRMS that integrated arts programming can help students with learning problems (Quinn & Hanks, 1977). A program called Reading Improvement Through the Arts and run in nine New York City high schools has documented that students who had mathematics and reading failure were able to dramatically raise their scores after experiencing an integrated art and mathematics program. After four months in this program, students' scores in reading and mathematics indicated growth equal to that typically expected in a whole year. In a related study (Quinn & Hanks, 1977), elementary children who participated in a core art program, which included six to eight times more art than usual, showed significant gains in their reading and mathematic scores on standardized tests.

In this chapter, attention is directed to the specific content of mathematics, science, and social studies and the ways that art can facilitate the child's learning in these areas (as well as in art). Because he is a specialist, the art teacher may not be as aware of curriculum content in other areas, and the classroom teacher may not be fully aware of the role art can play in the rest of the curriculum. An attempt is made to present a strong case for utilizing art in *other* learning and vice versa. Ways this has been accomplished with special children are discussed and demonstrated. As elsewhere, very few, if any, assumptions are made about the prior knowledge which the reader might bring to this chapter.

ART IN THE MAINSTREAM*

Frequently in the school year, teachers have that overwhelming feeling that there is not enough time to adequately cover any subject. In fact, part of the rationale behind having summer school for special children is to provide extra instructional time. Special children need a frontal attack on learning, resulting in an overlapping and consistent reinforcement of skills and concepts from week to week, day to day, and hour to hour. One solution to this dilemma is to use art (*in the best sense* of use) to clarify and reinforce concepts which impaired children have been studying in the rest of their program.

The examples that follow demonstrate that many different art activities

---

* Some of these ideas were initially developed by the author in the article "Mainstreaming Art as Well as Children" *Art Education,* 1975, 28(8), 26-27.

can serve to develop basic concepts and skills, not only in the expressive and perceptual and creative areas but also in other areas of learning such as mathematics, social studies, and science. Art has an integrity and a set of objectives and aims unique to its subject area. This integrity can be sustained and even embellished when art is integrated with the rest of the curriculum. Finally, in such a situation, children and adults view art in a different perspective. They see art in *the mainstream of life,* where it belongs.

Consider "mainstreaming art" from the perspective of the art teacher. The art educator often makes careful choices of media and topics which foster creative development in the child. For example, a class session may focus on painting and the art aim(s) may be to build expressive skills as well as skills in the use of a specific paint medium. The final crucial decision rests on what might be appropriate for the child and what motivates him.

Motivation might be the painting experience per se. If painting is not intrinsically captivating for the child, the teacher may also need to provide a choice of topics or suggestions to further stimulate the child. An immediate experience discussion, role playing, or a field trip can provide this motivation. Considering the additional time which may be needed to discuss topics and the time needed for instruction in the use of media, there may be little time left for the painting portion of the lesson. Therefore, it makes good sense to integrate the painting lesson with some subject that is already being studied by the child. Such a topic would be one that the child already understands and one which does not need elaborate explanations from the art teacher.

From the viewpoint of the classroom teacher, mainstreaming art by using such a painting activity may help his class clarify what they know about a subject they are studying. It may also indicate areas where there are misconceptions. Such an art activity will reinforce language that is being stressed in the classroom, math, or any other subject that is currently being studied.

This way, the children will not have to cope with too many tasks and too many concepts at the same time. For example, it may well be sufficient to instruct a class of retarded children in the appropriate use of tempera paint and then suggest they complete a painting of a country they are already studying in social studies. A group of deaf children who are studying "Winter" would be much more motivated to draw a picture about that particular season. A class of physically handicapped children might be highly interested in completing a mural about a recent field trip to the candy factory. All of these children are learning about art media and processes and are having their classroom activities underscored by engaging in these art activities.

Whenever possible in an art learning experience, the key is choosing a specific activity leading to artistic development that will also facilitate growth in other curricular areas. There are times when this is not totally possible. The point is to maximize those times when such an integration is *very feasible.*

Additionally, there are times during the rest of the school day when children can engage in art activity as a part of their math or language lesson. This does not mean that either of these subject areas gets slighted. It does mean that the child is engaging in *art readiness* activities. For example, the child might make a poster or bulletin board for the room, decorate his lesson folder, draw a picture of a science experiment, or create math cards by drawing his own sets on them (as opposed to just coloring in those drawn by the teacher).

Conversely in an art lesson, the child can be provided with opportunities to practice his language, reading, or math skills. He may build his readiness abilities in these areas as well. The child learns all the time, and this learning should not be fragmented so that when he gets to art he switches off his thinking processes in other areas or vice versa. Neither art nor math nor language is an isolated aspect of learning or of living. Fragmenting these subjects also fragments the child who is learning.

Art does have its own structure and content which is based on design elements and principles. Professionals in art do not recommend an undue instructional emphasis on these elements and principles, for they can become a block to artistic expression (Lansing, 1969; Art Therapy Training, n.d.). However, laymen should be aware that these elements and principles exist and that the art lessons described are built on line, color, shape, and texture. These design concepts are integral parts of each learning situation presented in this chapter. For example, in the section on geometry, the subjects are two- and three-dimensional shapes and colors. In the science section on windows, the focus is on color, while texture is emphasized in the nature study.

Design principles of harmony, unity, balance, proportion, and contrast have also been carefully considered in the way that each art activity is structured and in the materials selected for these activities. For example, a limited palette is a necessary component to insure harmony and unity in an art activity. Therefore, using synthetic packing pieces, pasta, rice, *and* paper scraps in a mosaic or texture picture offers too many different materials in one activity. The result: a picture with too much variety. A better choice would be to limit the materials to a variety of the *same* class of items. An example of this would be a mosaic or picture made with only two to four different sizes and shapes of the same kind of synthetic packing material.

A limited palette may mean using only different types of paper in a composition or a mural or offering only one or two colors of paint to cover a sculpture or a clay piece. It may imply limiting a wood sculpture to components of two or three basic geometric shapes and insuring contrast by providing a variety of different sizes of these shapes. Further limits might be set by specifying a *minimal* number of pieces that the child might use (for example, at least ten shapes, three of which must be triangles and three of which must be squares).

There is *not* any fixed formula. However, some limits and some freedom are needed in an activity to enable individual solutions in a diverse range of possibilities. A certain honesty and truth in materials selection and use is the guiding principle. In every instance, this kind of implicit design consideration has been given in specifying the materials and in planning the art learning situations presented.

If the aim of the art activities is primarily cathartic and self-expressive, then it may not be appropriate to focus unduly on the art content. However, by adhering to some of the limitations suggested, the outcome of the activity will be more aesthetically pleasing and thus more acceptable and more self-affirming to the child engaged in the activity.

Enough has been said. Each section that follows demonstrates ways in which art can be a learning partner to the rest of the curriculum. Also, suggestions are made about ways by which a number of art readiness activities can be incorporated into the classroom. Some examples are provided only as a catalyst to spark the reader's own thinking. The teacher and the parent know their own needs and the needs of their child or children. Therefore, the reader is encouraged to select, improvise, and amend what follows.

ART AND MATHEMATICS

Active learning is recommended in developing mathematics skills and concepts (Eicholz, O'Daffer, & Fleenor, 1973). Moreover, in learning mathematics, the child needs to see the relationship between the real world and mathematics (Trafton, 1975). Art provides an active involvement with materials and with materials that are a part of the child's world. Art can be an important link between mathematics skills, active learning, and the real world.

In learning about mathematics, problem-solving abilities are imperative. In problem solving from a mathematics perspective, the emphasis is on relating to the child's world, holding his interest, and actively manipulating materials. Moreover, the problems that are posed should be significant mathematically and should have several levels of possible solutions. Finally, the child should be aware when he has solved the problem (Nelson & Kirkpatrik, 1975). All of these qualities of problem solving are not unique to mathematics learning. They are essentials of art learning situations as well. The necessary addition of artistic significance to a problem provides the final ingredient to a valid problem-solving activity in art and mathematics.

Prenumber Activities

Classifying, sorting, comparing, and ordering are necessary prenumber activities (Gibb & Castanesa, 1975) and are skills important to developing logical thought processes (Nuffield, 1972). They are abilities that are called upon in the art activities already discussed in the texture section in Chapter IV. These prenumber activities are necessary in developing pattern concepts fundamental to higher math functioning (Nuffield, 1970). Art activities use pattern concepts. The printing series in Chapter IV focuses on rudimentary pattern development. Pattern concepts can easily be taught using simple everyday items such as buttons, metal nuts, cotter pins, and washers. The child can string these in a variety of sequences to make body adornment (jewelry). The more mature child may develop this activity further by creating intricate beads and patterns using clay.

In these pattern activities, it is important that the materials differ noticeably in color and/or size. A limited choice of materials can help prevent confusion for the child learning pattern concepts. Also having the child make jewelry from a limited palette (such as only buttons, or only metal nuts and washers, or only clay beads) builds in design unity. Weaving can also help in teaching number patterns and odd-even concepts (Nuffield, 1970).

Counting

Counting can enter an art activity in a variety of ways. Often by suggesting that the child have five or more things in his drawing, he may be encouraged to consider composition and filling the whole page. This can also provide appropriate limits for the child. Otherwise, the child may be frustrated by being asked, after the fact, to put more things in his picture. The child can count other items in his picture such as the colors, the geometric shapes, and the lines.

In a math lesson, a child can draw sets of things such as balls or trees or flowers. He can make rubbings of various coins. This would also help him identify money. These are not art activities per se, but they are examples of art readiness activities that reinforce art skills.

Finally, counting may be of great use in a gluing activity. Children can be told to hold the wood or paper and count to thirty or whatever number is appropriate. This may be easier for them and for the instructor than telling them to wait for the glue to dry.

Verbal Problem Solving

Numerous ways of introducing verbal problem solving are possible in art activities. For example, in a cut paper lesson the following questions may be posed: "I have thirty pieces of blue paper, and there are fifteen children in our class. How many pieces of paper does each child get?" Or, "I have twenty pieces of paper for our art lesson. How many pieces will be left if each child gets one piece of paper?" Or, "I have ten pieces of green paper, and everyone wants to use green in his art picture. What can we do to solve this problem?" Thus, the concepts of addition, subtraction, division, and fractions are utilized at a very concrete level. Most importantly, the problem situation becomes a part of the art lesson.

Having the child solve problems before he gets additional art materials is another way of using verbal problem solving in art. For example, the child adds two plus two, and the result is the number of wood pieces he gets for building his sculpture. Or, the same may be done with a subtraction problem. Finally, this approach can be used each time the child solves a math problem. He would get another piece of wood for each correct answer. These wood parts can then be used to make his construction. This same approach may be used with other art media, too. Such an approach should be used occasionally and only to reinforce skills rather than as a punitive activity.

Measurement and Proportion

Measurement is an important aspect of living. Art is no exception. Children will find it necessary to learn how to measure everything from making a frame for a puzzle to measuring their wrists for a bracelet. Measuring will also be necessary in mixing salt clay or wheat paste for papier-mâché. Moreover, the children will be greatly motivated to do such measuring and mixing if afterwards they can make an animal, some beads, or some other meaningful creation.

Learning to mix colors involves addition and proportion concepts. In introducing color mixing, the child can start by painting with only the three primary colors (red, yellow, and blue). Then, he may discover other colors. Or, the activity can be a problem situation such as "Today we have three colors for our painting. Can you make a fourth color by adding two of the colors together?" Finally, the children can be given the three primary colors and asked to make as many other colors as possible for their painting.

An older class can be encouraged to make the secondary colors by adding equal parts of two primary colors. If the class is fairly advanced, they can mix the tertiary colors by adding two parts of each primary color to one

67450

part of each secondary color (that is, two parts of red are added to yellow to make the tertiary color red-orange; two parts of blue are added to yellow to make the tertiary color blue-green).

PLEASE NOTE: Before reading further, examine carefully these visual examples of art and math activities. These illustrations are preparation for the discussion which follows.

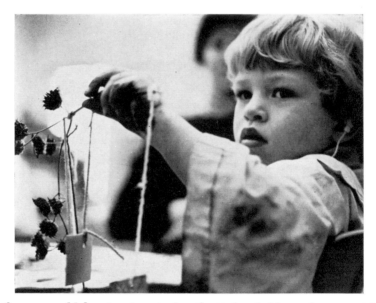

Figure 55. A three-year-old hearing impaired epileptic boy holds up the geometric shape mobile he has been making. Before beginning the activity, he played a matching game with shapes and then picked the ones he wanted to paint for his mobile.

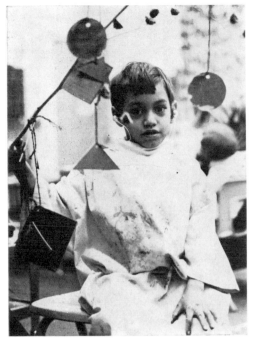

56

57

Figure 56. This four-year-old preprimary hearing impaired child has included circles and triangles in his shape mobile. The art lesson focused on shape identification and on color words. The child verbalized and signed the correct color word before being given that color of tempera paint for painting each shape.

Figure 57. Sometimes it helps to work in teams and pool the talents of physically handicapped children. This mobile was the cooperative effort of a cerebral palsied ten-year-old girl who had limited hand use and a nine-year-old orthopedically handicapped girl who had full use of her hands.

Figure 58. After discussing shapes and looking for shapes in the classroom environs and in photos or magazine pictures, this hearing impaired eight-year-old girl is composing her own picture using geometric shapes cut from construction paper.

Figure 59. This cardboard slotted sculpture is a team endeavor. Four hearing impaired children in a primary class are trying to find out how wide they can make their construction. The cardboard shapes were made by cutting discarded cardboard into a variety of geometric shapes and sizes. When the cardboard is slotted, slots have been cut in each edge of the shapes. The slots must be *slightly* wider than the thickness of the cardboard.

Figure 60. A teenage deaf student constructs her cardboard sculpture using a combination of free forms and geometric shapes. She has cut these shapes herself using a utility knife. The several slots in each cardboard shape enable the artist to try various combinations before finalizing the design.

Figure 61. Making choices and decisions is an important part of an art activity. Here, two hearing impaired children select the geometric wood shapes they will use for their sculpture. In this lesson, the specific number selected has been specified in terms of a range (between 5 and 10 different shapes, including at least 2 triangles). The activity may be more open ended, or the number of shapes selected may be the solution to a particular math problem. (Add two plus two, and that is the number of squares provided for the sculpture.)

63

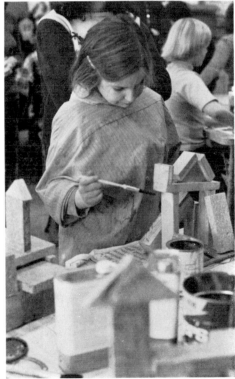

62

Figure 62. A physically handicapped nine-year-old glues her wood geometric shapes by brushing (painting) on white glue using a short handled ½ inch flat brush.

Figure 63. A nine-year-old deaf girl has decided to shellac her wood construction to "finish" it. A separate work table has been covered with old newspapers for this shellacking operation.

Figure 64. A multiply handicapped seven-year-old girl who has cerebral palsy and visual impairments holds her wood pieces as she waits for them to dry. Sometimes counting to thirty can help "speed" the time it takes to wait for glue to dry. (This reinforces counting skills as well.)

Figure 65. The finished wood sculpture has been painted with tempera paint.

66   67

Figure 66. Wood sculpture can become a very concrete creation. This particular sculpture has been titled "Robot." It is the creation of an eight-year-old boy who has perceptual learning problems and physical handicaps.

Figure 67. Children also can create abstract sculptural statements. Here is an untitled abstract construction by a hearing impaired nine-year-old boy.

Figure 68. After deciding the shapes to be made on her geoboard, a deaf eight-year-old girl pounds nails in her board. Pounding nails may be harder for the hearing impaired because they cannot hear when the nail has been firmly hit with the hammer. Note that a piece of cardboard has been placed under the wood to protect the table in case the child pounds the nails completely through the wood base.

Figure 69. Finally, the artist wraps yarn around the nails to create various shapes. The way the yarn is placed can be changed to create new shape combinations.

Figure 70. Different colors and thicknesses of yarn have been used to make the several triangles and parallelograms in this geoboard by a nine-year-old deaf boy. How many different shapes has he created?

Figure 71. A puzzle-making activity can integrate drawing and measurement skills. Some preplanning will be needed. After the topic of the puzzle is established, a black edge is drawn around the puzzle cardboard. (This black edge will make the puzzle easier to assemble.) *After* the black edge is complete, the rest of the drawing is made. In this picture, an eight-year-old hearing impaired girl is starting to draw a picture of her father at work. Parents' occupations were the topic for this puzzle-making activity; thus, social studies was also a part of the art activity.

Figure 72. After the puzzle picture is drawn and filled in, it is placed on top of a larger piece of cardboard. Then, one inch wide cardboard strips are measured and glued onto the larger cardboard to make the puzzle holder.

Figure 73. After the puzzle holder (frame) is made, the puzzle is divided into pieces and the pieces are numbered. These pieces are then cut out with a large pair of scissors as this nine-year-old deaf boy is doing with his puzzle.

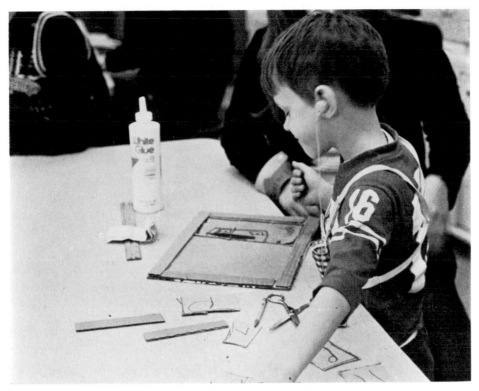

Figure 74. The proof of the puzzle is in the assembling! Here, a seven-year-old deaf child fits his puzzle into its holder.

Figure 75. This is a completed puzzle by a nine-year-old deaf boy showing his father at work driving his tractor in the field.

Geometry: The Wedding of Art and Math

Purpose/Rationale

The art learning sequence discussed at length in this section centers on geometry. Through these activities, the child's ability to recognize shapes and spatial relationships is developed. Children need to recognize the geometric shapes which are the building blocks of their environment. This is necessary for their perceptual development as well. This series also requires the child to see the patterns of these shapes around him. The ability to perceive and identify shapes and spatial relationships is important in developing mathematics concepts. These basic perceptual abilities are also necessary to artistic development.

These art activities are presented in a series and lead to more complex art learnings. The reader must decide at what point to enter this sequence with a child. It may be desirable to return to a simpler level for review or for reinforcement of the concepts.

SHAPE GAME

Materials

Brushes, ½ inch (*c.* 1 cm) wide

Cardboard cut in geometric shapes, 25 or more

Containers for paint and water

Hole puncher or scissors

Old newspapers

Paint shirts or smocks for each child

Paper towels

Sacks large enough to hold the geometric shapes

String or yard scraps

Tempera paint

Tree branches

Scrap cardboard can be used for the geometric shapes. It can be cut using a paper cutter, matt knife, or large scissors. Check before using the paper cutter because cardboard can dull the blade. Pizza parlors can supply cardboard circles.

Motivation

With the class or a small group in a circle, choose a child to be "it." First, he is given a shape and told its name. He is then asked to match this shape without looking and by searching in the bag. When the child has made a match, he keeps the shape. Tell the class that something will be made with the shapes later. Continue the game until all children have had a turn or until they know their shapes. Another game approach is to have each child and/or small group of children make the various shapes with their own bodies. Each child can be assigned a specific shape or can pick his own and have the rest of the class guess what it is.

Procedure

With the cardboard shapes that the children have earned in the Shape Game, they will make a mobile. (A mobile is a construction of a group of objects or shapes that hangs and moves or turns in the moving air.) Show the children an example. To avoid possible copying, the example should differ in some way from the mobiles that the children will make. A specific problem may be included in the activity such as "In each mobile you must have three (or more) of your favorite shapes and three or more circles. You must also have two or more of the other shapes already discussed." These are then painted with tempera paint. After the shapes are dry, holes are punched into them, and these are hung on the branches that are suspended in the classroom. Balance can be discussed as the mobile is assembled. To help achieve balance, distance between parts can be measured. It will take about one-half hour to complete the mobile.

Adaptations

LEARNING DISABLED. Extend the movement aspect of the motivation. Large shapes may be drawn on the floor with masking tape or made out of cloth. After doing the first part of the game described in the motivation section, have the children, either individually or in small groups, locate shapes as they are called out. The class and the teacher will probably think of other variations on these movement ideas. Weather permitting, the activity can be done on the playground and the shapes drawn with chalk.

BEHAVIORALLY DISORDERED. In addition to the above, the children can work in small groups as they make their mobiles. Select those children who will work best together.

HEARING IMPAIRED. Special emphasis might be placed on specific words. Key words in this activity might be *large* and *small, both, hang,* and color names. There probably will be some other words the teacher will want to stress.

RETARDED. Stress some specific words beginning with the shape names themselves. When the child can distinguish between two different shapes (or bigger and smaller sizes of the same shapes), he can proceed to the second part of the lesson. Have each child paint one or two shapes. All the children can then contribute to one group mobile.

VISUALLY IMPAIRED. Even though the totally blind child cannot distinguish colors, it is important that he paint his shapes. Color, even if experienced by name only, is still a part of this child's world. He has favorite colors also. Weight down the shapes with tape or a large stone before painting them. In stringing the mobile, incorporate small bells. Then the child can hear the mobile move.

Physically Handicapped. Secure the shapes with tape or a large stone so that they can be easily painted. Short-handled, stiff-bristled brushes are recommended. If the child cannot easily grasp the brush (even if it has been thickened with foam rubber), have him use a sponge instead. Paint that is thick like heavy cream will be the best to use.

Evaluation

Potential Outcomes. The child has played the Shape Game and identified the basic geometric shapes by touch and sight with 80 percent or more accuracy. The child has demonstrated his social skills and maturity by following rules and taking turns 90 percent or more of the time. The child has made a mobile using at least three of each kind of basic geometric shapes. He has painted these shapes with one or two of his favorite colors.

Closure. Have the class review the names for the geometric shapes. Each child can show and share his work with the class. Then, display the mobiles in the classroom.

SHAPE SEARCH

Materials

Cardboard examples of the geometric shapes: circles, squares, rectangles, triangles

Construction paper in assorted colors: 9 by 12 inches (*c.* 22 by 30 cm), and some scraps

Drawing paper about 9 by 12 inches (*c.* 22 by 30 cm) or larger

Magazine pictures that have geometric shapes in them

Old newspapers

Paper towels, some slightly damp to wipe hands

Pencils or watercolor markers

Ruler or straight edge

Scissors

White glue in small bottles or pot pie tins with ¼ inch or ½ inch (*c.* ½ cm or 1 cm) wide brushes

Motivation

Begin by playing a recognition game with the class. Hold up the shapes, and have the children identify them. Next, select one child and have him point out examples of geometric shapes in the classroom. Then, tell the class the story of Super Shape. Super Shape has discovered many, many geometric shapes, and he has hidden them in the classroom somewhere. Have the children find places where Super Shape has hidden his shapes. The same approach can be done by using magazine pictures and art reproductions. When they find geometric shapes in the pictures, the children can draw around them with pencil. This approach may be more motivating for older children. Finally, the class is asked to make their own picture of geometric shapes cut from construction paper.

Procedures

If the child does not readily comprehend how to make a shape picture, then partially demonstrate what is to be done by cutting out some shapes and pasting them down. After the demonstration, distribute the materials. Another approach would be to begin by building some objects from the shapes left over from the Shape Game. It is assumed that the children can cut out the various geometric shapes. If the child has difficulty cutting, he may need some practice. Or, provide some shapes already cut out. Finally, some starter sheets with several shapes already pasted down might provide the beginning point for the activity. This activity should take about one-half hour.

Adaptations

LEARNING DISABLED. Using highly contrasting colors of papers may help this child distinguish between shapes. Squares can be cut from one color and rectangles from another. If there is one shape that is giving particular trouble to the child, cut that shape from a textured paper such as sand-paper.

BEHAVIORALLY DISORDERED. Select several children to work together on a shape picture or mural. If the children are working individually, have them decide what shape(s) they want and begin with one or two of these. Having too many shapes from which to choose may be confusing.

HEARING IMPAIRED. It is important that the child really comprehend what he is to do. As the lesson is presented, have one or two of the children come forward and construct shapes on the felt board or draw them on the chalkboard. They may not understand a starter sheet with just a shape on it unless some pictures that have been completed are also shown. Through-out, emphasize that each child's work is to be different from the examples made in the class demonstration.

RETARDED. Extra practice in finding shapes and in seeing them in objects, such as houses, doors, windows, etc., may be needed; for those who do not have the cutting skills, it may be helpful to have shapes already cut for them. However, let the child choose the shapes he wants to use in his picture. This will help insure that the pictures are all different. Language can be emphasized; for example, "How many circles do you want?" Or, one limitation may be placed on the activity, such as "Use as many shapes in your picture as you want, but only use two triangles."

VISUALLY IMPAIRED. Have some shapes precut. It may help to have differ-ent textured papers for the square and the rectangle. After he has explored the shapes and can recognize them, let the child try his hand at cutting the shapes himself. To get the idea across, bring in examples of items that have these shapes incorporated in them: toy trucks, sailboats, or cups, for example. Be certain that the background paper (which could be a piece of cardboard) is secured to the work area. Glue should be in a container which is firmly attached to the table. The partially sighted will need shapes cut out of highly contrasting paper to stimulate what vision they may have.

PHYSICALLY HANDICAPPED. It probably will be necessary to use precut shapes. Ones that are cut from posterboard or cardboard will be more durable. It is suggested that students work on a cardboard background that can survive a lot of wear. The children can then brush on white glue with a short-handled stiff brush. Finally, shapes are placed on the glued cardboard background surface.

Evaluation

POTENTIAL OUTCOMES. The child has identified the geometric shapes by sight with 90 percent or more accuracy. He has analyzed and identified these same shapes in objects in the classroom and/or in art reproductions and magazine pictures with 80 percent or more accuracy. He has made one (or more) cut paper picture and has used only the basic geometric shapes. His picture has three or more of these shapes in varying sizes. He has been able to cut out these geometric shapes with 75 percent or more accuracy. He has demonstrated that he can use the correct amount of glue in his picture.

CLOSURE. The construction paper pictures can be displayed after each child shares what he has made with the class. Other pictures with geometric shapes highlighted can be brought in by the class members. A list of objects in the classroom that contain the various geometric shapes may become part of a continuing bulletin board display.

SLOTTED SHAPE SCULPTURE

Materials

Cardboard in assorted sizes of various geometric shapes, 10 to 15 shapes
    per child
Matt knife or paper cutter or scissors or single-edge razor blade

Scrap cardboard may be cut into the various geometric shapes with a matt knife, scissors, or paper cutter. Check before using the paper cutter because cardboard can dull the blade. A local pizza parlor can supply cardboard circles in various sizes. The geometric cardboard shapes are slotted with a cutting tool or paper cutter. The slots should be slightly wider than the thickness of the cardboard. When cutting slots, cut on top of other scrap cardboard. Test the slots to be sure they work. Depending on the size of the shapes, there should be two to six slots per shape.

Motivation

Give a review of the geometric shapes and then demonstrate how the pieces of cardboard fit together. Build some examples. Either concrete ideas or more free form abstract statements can be presented. The class will realize that problems of balance will have to be solved as they build their sculpture. Remove the class examples or take them apart and return the pieces to the cardboard shape pile before the children begin their own work.

Procedures

The class demonstration will immediately communicate the procedure involved. Some of the intermediate children can help in cutting the cardboard shapes and the slots. Encourage the class to experiment. If they do not like their first attempts, the children may pull their sculpture apart and start over. The activity should take about one-half hour.

Adaptations

LEARNING DISABLED. Some children may need help in visualizing sculpture ideas. If a child wants to make a specific item, he may need help in determining the shape components of that idea. For example, if the child plans to build an airplane, some pictures of airplanes will help. Have the child locate the various shapes that make up the plane, and even mark these on the picture. Once he has analyzed the shapes, he can easily proceed to constructing his sculpture.

BEHAVIORALLY DISORDERED. In addition to the above, after some exploration of the materials or after each child has built one sculpture on his own, the class may work in teams of two or three. Carefully choose the teams to insure good working relationships. It may reassure the children to know that if they do not like what they have made they may take it apart and start over.

HEARING IMPAIRED. In this kind of activity, having visuals of various everyday items around as well as pictures of sculpture by such artists as Alexander Calder and David Smith will help. Since the materials which the class is using are so varied and may be assembled in so many different ways, there will be little chance of copying. Have each child decide on a topic for his sculpture after some exploration of the materials. Encourage the children to do their own work. Stress that each person is different, so each person's work will be different also.

RETARDED. Begin with fewer shapes per child. When it is certain that the child understands what he is to do and has had a chance to experiment, he may use more shapes. Suggest some concrete things to make. However, the class does not have to be limited to concrete subjects; they may use totally abstract ideas. This depends on the individual child's response to the activity. Encourage each child to have a different subject for his sculpture.

VISUALLY IMPAIRED. Have several examples already taped together to show the children. They can explore these and then practice joining the slotted shapes. Each child can identify the shapes he is to use by sorting and selecting them from a large box in the classroom.

PHYSICALLY HANDICAPPED. In addition to lots of practice in joining, these children will probably need to work in teams. Have the children work from a larger cardboard base. This base with slots in it can be folded and attached to the worktable using *C* clamps or a vise. Enough of the edges should be exposed so that other parts can easily be attached.

Evaluation

POTENTIAL OUTCOMES. The child has identified a variety of geometric shapes by name with 90 percent or better accuracy. He has learned to construct with these shapes by interlocking the slots. He has made one (or more) construction by using ten or more different types and sizes of geometric shapes. He has made an artistic decision about whether he will keep his construction or take it apart and build another. He has been able to work with another student and do a group construction.

CLOSURE. After all the constructions are made, the children can show their work. Counting skills may be reinforced by having each child count the number of shapes in his sculpture. The rest of the class can check on his accuracy. The class may work in larger groups and see how wide or how tall their sculpture can become before it falls over. The constructions which the children particularly like can be glued together. Language arts may be tied in by writing words on each slotted shape. The child then tries to build various sentences. (The words and/or parts of speech can be shape coded. For example, verbs can be on circles only, etc.)

WOOD SHAPES

Purpose/Rationale

The child lives in a three-dimensional world. To avoid visual chaos, it is important that the geometric shapes in the environment be identified (Buktenica, 1968). This activity enables the child to explore the basic geometric shapes in wood and then to build with these. During the activity some related mathematics concepts can be discussed. For example, the children can be given all the same number of blocks and shapes and then asked whose building covers the most area. (None will.) Or, the children may experiment with making a building as tall as possible or as wide as possible.

Materials

Brushes, ½ inch (*c.* 1 cm) wide
Containers for water and paint or shellac and shellac solvent (alcohol)
Old newspapers
Paint shirts or smocks
Paper towels
Sandpaper, fine flint paper in approximate 6 by 6 inch sheets (*c.* 15 by
   15 cm), 1 sheet per pair of children
Tempera paint
White glue in small bottles or pot pie tins with ½ inch (*c.* 1 cm) brushes
Wood, in assorted shapes, 5 to 15 shapes per child
Wood base about 5 by 10 inches (*c.* 12 by 24 cm)

A local lumberyard usually has a scrapbox and gives away wood. The wood can be cut into shapes at the lumberyard or at the school wood shop. If a specific school does not have a wood shop, a nearby high school or the school district maintenance shop will have a power saw. Depending on how rough the wood is after cutting, sandpaper may be optional.

Motivation

In this activity, the materials may be motivating in themselves. Have several boxes of sorted wood shapes. Hold up the various shapes and have the children identify them. Suggest that they will be building with these shapes. Ask what can be made with these shapes. A specific number of shapes may be given to each child for his construction, or several problems with the shapes may be posed. For example, "What is two plus eight? That is the number of squares you will use in your construction." "What is three minus one? That is the number of triangles you will use."

Procedure

Have the children select the correct number of shapes that they will be using. Give each child the base for his construction. Demonstrate how to glue the pieces together. If too much glue is used, it will run down over the blocks. The children should paint the glue on with a stiff brush. They must wait for the glued pieces to dry, especially if they are dealing with a balance problem. The child can count to thirty while holding the pieces together before adding a second piece to the construction. No matter how fast or slow the count is, by the time the child gets to thirty the glue will be dry. After the construction is completed, let it dry overnight. Finish the work by painting with tempera paint or shellac. If shellac is used, water cannot be used for cleaning. A special alcohol solvent must be used to clean the brushes. Have a separate table covered with newspapers set aside for this final operation, and have the children use smocks or old shirts.

Adaptations

LEARNING DISABLED. Just explore and build with the shapes first. Then, when a desired structure is discovered, glue it together. Right/left concepts can be stressed by having the children add more shapes on the right side, etc. If the group is particularly active, suggest that each child get started with two or three shapes. When these are glued, the child can go to the wood box for more.

BEHAVIORALLY DISORDERED. In addition to all of the above considerations, some children may need to work in small groups. As a group activity, this lesson should come after the class has built with wood several times. They will then be familiar with all of the art processes and can concentrate on cooperative solutions. Suggest that in this problem no one talk. The group members must agree before a piece is glued, but no words should be spoken.

HEARING IMPAIRED. Care of materials is essential in any art lesson. It will help to demonstrate using *too much* glue and then *just enough*. This will also reinforce these language concepts. Carefully explain that shellac must be washed in a special solvent. The children should be able to smell the difference in the alcohol and water. An old brush with shellac on it may be used to show what happens when it is put into water.

RETARDED. Children enjoy building and having the chance to create different structures. They can begin with just a few wood pieces so they learn the process before getting involved in a large construction. Unless the group is older, it is suggested that the wood be painted instead of shellacked.

VISUALLY IMPAIRED. Have glue in a container that is very stable and does not easily tip. The children all should know where the woodbox is located. To avoid traffic jams, have them select their shapes individually or circulate the box around the class. To get the class going and to avoid the problem of having children wait too long, make several rounds with the box. This will allow each child to explore and to select the shapes that he wants on several occasions.

PHYSICALLY HANDICAPPED. Explain that the glue must dry before adding another shape to the sculpture. Emphasize this, or let the children discover this drying factor on their own. Part of the sculpture can be built and glued one day and finished the next. Work in teams to maximize abilities.

Evaluation

POTENTIAL OUTCOMES. The child has made a construction using five or more wood shapes. He has learned how to glue these shapes by using enough glue to hold them but not so much that the glue runs off the sides of the wood. The child has learned to wait for the glue to dry before adding upper parts to his work. The child has made his own decision as to how he will finish his construction. He has learned how to cover all surface areas with paint or shellac. If he has used shellac, he has learned how to clean it out of a brush.

CLOSURE. The children can share their work. Counting skills and shape recognition may be reinforced by counting the number of each kind of shape in each child's sculpture. A larger group construction can be planned, or several small constructions can be put together to make a larger one. Balance can be discussed.

GEOMETRY WITH NAILS AND STRING: A GEOBOARD FROM SCRAPS

Purpose/Rationale

The learning situations centering on geometric concepts which have been developed in the preceding art activities are extended here. If the students already have a good grasp of these concepts, some of the simpler art and geometry activities already discussed may be omitted. The geoboards are a more sophisticated art activity and will appeal to intermediate and older groups of students. It requires some preplanning and finer eye-hand coordination than the other art activities in this section. Once constructed, these geoboards can be used in a number of other additional lessons in math.

Motivation

A review of the geometric shapes discussed earlier may be helpful. Showing several examples of partially completed geoboards will convey the concept. Moreover, posing some specific problem for the class to solve will provide some boundaries and some open-endedness. For example, it may be suggested that the students include at least one triangle, one square, and one circle in their designs. Or, have some students figure out how many geometric shapes they can include in their boards.

Materials

Carpet scraps or thick cloth
Hammer, 1 for each child or share in pairs
Paper for sketching design (newsprint or computer paper)
Pencils

Roofing nails, 1½ inches (*c.* 3 cm) long, 10 to 20 per child
Scissors
Wood base about 5 by 10 inches (*c.* 12 by 25 cm) and ¾ or 1 inch thick
    (*c.* 1.5 or 2 cm)
Yarn scraps

The wood base can be a different shape or size. Usually the lumberyard scrap box is a good source of free wood. Roofing nails can be purchased (or begged) from the lumberyard or hardware store. Other nails may be used if they are about the same length and have large heads. The carpet scraps are used to muffle the sound of pounding the nails.

Procedure

Begin with a partial demonstration. Have the child draw the shapes that he wants to include on a piece of paper. This preplanning depends on the attention span of the child and on his ability to transfer ideas from a sketch to the wood. Some children will find it easier to plan (sketch) their shapes right on the base.

The children must hammer the nails in far enough so that they stay in and do not work loose as other nails are added to the board. The placement of the nails should be far enough apart so that it is easy to add and pound in other nails. About one inch of space between nails works well. Sometimes a child may pound in a nail too far, and it comes clear through the other side of the base. Such nails that are pounded completely through may scratch the table and be dangerous. To prevent scratching, scrap cardboard may be placed between the base and the table or surface on which the child is pounding. After the nails are in the base, yarn is tied to outline the various shapes. This should take from thirty to forty-five minutes to complete.

Adaptations

LEARNING DISABLED. For each different type of shape, the child should use a different color of yarn. This will help him with the discrimination of shapes. Some overlapping of shapes may also be attempted (see Figure 70). This activity will help the child to develop figure-ground perception.

BEHAVIORALLY DISORDERED. Be certain that the student knows how to use a hammer properly. To cut down on the noise factor, place an old towel or some large cloth scraps on the pounding surface (table or floor). Or, take the child outside (weather permitting) and have him work there. Hopefully, the expanded out-of-class environment will not be too unstructured for the child. The children will probably derive great satisfaction from the nailing portion of the activity. Another alternative might be to have the student construct a nail relief of one or more geometric shapes.

HEARING IMPAIRED. In addition to the adaptations already discussed, it will be helpful for this child to practice nailing. Have a certain number of times (a minimum) that the child pounds each nail. This is done because the child cannot rely on the sound to tell him when he hits the nails hard enough.

RETARDED. If this student has trouble with the eye-hand coordination necessary to hammer a nail, have him use pliers to hold the nail as he pounds. Such a procedure can also save several smashed fingers. Perhaps attempt only one shape initially. After the child has the concept, more complicated geoboards may be made.

VISUALLY IMPAIRED. It may be too difficult for the blind child to attempt to hammer nails. Therefore, the materials should be adapted for this activity. One possibility is to use ceiling tiles or synthetic foam as a base and large carpet tacks that can be pressed into the base. Initially, the child can just experiment making various geometric shapes with the tacks. Later he can try tying on yarn. If tacks are used, they must be pushed securely into the base; otherwise, they will come loose and may frustrate the child.

PHYSICALLY HANDICAPPED. It may help to substitute materials such as those suggested with the blind child if the student has difficulty pounding nails. Or, team those children who can use a hammer with those who cannot. Securely anchor the base to the work table by using C clamps. The activity will be less hazardous if pliers are used to hold the roofing nails. It may be easier to work on a larger base. There should be ample space between nails.

Evaluation

POTENTIAL OUTCOMES. The child has made a geoboard in which there is at least one geometric shape. He has been able to identify several geometric shapes by stringing yarn in different ways on his own geoboard. He has also observed and counted geometric shapes made by other classmates.

CLOSURE. The class can play a shape search game. Choose three or four of the most complicated geoboards and hold one of these up for just a few minutes. Have the class visually count the number of triangles present. Then, show the geoboard again, and, tracing with a pointer, count the number of triangles actually present.

A large class geoboard may be made and changed periodically to teach different shapes. Other geoboards may be made by using parts of drawings which the class has already done. In transforming a drawing to a geoboard, the class must analyze where the nails should be placed. This would be a good perceptual training activity.

Puzzles: Mathematics, Perception, and Art

Purpose/Rationale

This activity builds on the mathematics skills of measuring and count-ing and on the perceptual skills of discriminating shape and perceiving figure-ground and part-to-whole relationships which are necessary for other academic skills (Buktenica, 1968). As the child expresses himself, he learns some sensitivity to composition as he realizes that his space (his puzzle) must have interest and detail in each area. If it does not, then the puzzle will be very difficult to assemble. Not only the process but also the com-pleted artistic statement will have importance in this activity. As such, children who deal mostly in concrete concepts will be highly motivated in this learning situation.

Motivation

The activity can be presented by showing commercially produced puzzles and by explaining that the class will be making their own. Have several examples of puzzles made by other children. Emphasize that the class is not to copy these examples but rather to think of topics on their own. Sug-gest some topics such as a subject already under discussion in the classroom.

Materials

Cardboard, thin and about 9 by 12 inches (*c.* 22 by 30 cm), and thicker
  cardboard that is 11 by 14 inches (*c.* 27 by 35 cm), plus some additional
  thick cardboard strips 1 inch (*c.* 2 cm) wide and 14 inches (*c.* 35 cm)
  long or longer
Old newspapers
Paper towels, some dampened for cleanup
Rulers
Scissors that will cut cardboard, or a paper cutter
Watercolor markers
White glue in small bottles or pot pie tins with ½ inch (*c.* 1 cm) wide flat
  brushes

The kind of cardboard that is used on the back of school tablets works well as a source of thin cardboard. Discarded boxes are good sources for thicker cardboard. Check before using the paper cutter because cardboard can dull the blade.

Procedure

Have several puzzles in stages of partial completion, and use them to demonstrate the process. Determine the topic of the puzzle drawing be-forehand. First, a black line is drawn around the edge of the thin cardboard that will be the puzzle. This black edge will be very helpful later when the child is trying to assemble his puzzle. Next, have the children draw their puzzle pictures.

Before the children cut out their puzzle pieces, make a puzzle frame. This is optional, but it will provide a means of storing the puzzle and will greatly ease the assembly of the puzzle. Lay the uncut puzzle picture on top of a piece of scrap cardboard that is about two inches larger in dimensions than the drawing. Thus, if the puzzle picture were nine inches by twelve inches, then the scrap cardboard would be eleven inches by fourteen inches. Cardboard strips of varying lengths but of the same width can be provided for the frame edge. With these, the child can measure the appropriate length, cut them, and glue them onto the cardboard base. He will then have a cardboard frame (holder) for his puzzle.

Next, have the child cut his picture into pieces. Some sort of minimal number of pieces should be established. Ten to fifteen pieces would be a good number for this size of puzzle. The child divides the puzzle into parts and numbers them on the back. Cut the parts with scissors or a paper cutter. Finally, the child assembles his puzzle or tries his skill with his neighbor's puzzle. The puzzle will take one-half hour to draw. One-half hour will be needed to make the frame, and about one-half hour will be needed to cut the pieces.

Adaptations

LEARNING DISABLED AND BEHAVIORALLY DISORDERED. Limit the number of puzzle pieces to four or six initially. This will make the puzzle easier to assemble. The shapes of pieces should be limited to triangles or rectangles. Later, more complex puzzles can be made with many more pieces and shapes. Instead of drawing with markers, a variation might be making a puzzle from a crayon rubbing, paper collage, or a magazine photograph montage. (A montage is a picture created mainly from parts of magazine photographs.) This would appeal more to older children.

HEARING IMPAIRED. Encourage the group to make individual artistic statements. Scrutinize the activity for possible vocabulary building. Words such as *measure, limit, perimeter, assemble,* and *composition* could be stressed.

RETARDED. In addition to the above, the child may need help in cutting out his puzzle pieces. This can be done by using a paper cutter instead of scissors. Cut the puzzle into fewer pieces.

VISUALLY IMPAIRED. Instead of using markers for the drawing, use a "line" of white glue. The child can trail glue from a squeeze bottle. Emphasize that the space needs to be filled. Four or six pieces may be a good number for the first puzzle attempt. The child can use a box lid for a puzzle holder instead of making a holder of his own. The puzzle cardboard should be cut to fit inside the box lid before any drawing is done.

PHYSICALLY HANDICAPPED. If the group is not able to draw using their hands, feet, or mouth, their puzzle pictures can be printed. This can be done by using simple found objects that are easy to grasp. It might be desirable to laminate or cover the puzzle picture with a spray plastic coating before cutting it into the pieces. A box lid or just a large *L* made from thicker cardboard may be used here instead of a puzzle holder. This will facilitate the assembling of the puzzle after it has been cut. Large puzzle shapes are recommended, as they are easier to manipulate. Help probably will be needed with cutting these out.

Evaluation

POTENTIAL OUTCOMES. The child has learned what a puzzle is by making one. He has learned how to measure and make a frame for his puzzle drawing. His puzzle fits into this frame with 90 percent or more accuracy. All the space in the puzzle drawing has been filled with color or objects. He has divided his puzzle up into ten or more parts. These parts are some sort of straight-edged geometric shape that others can identify. He has learned to assemble his puzzle with 100 percent accuracy.

CLOSURE. Give each child a chance to show his work to the rest of the class. The children can trade their work, each child having another classmate assemble his puzzle. A larger, more complicated puzzle may be made by part or all of the class.

Puzzles can also be made from drawings or paintings that have already been done. Mount these on cardboard, and then cut the parts out. To focus on figure-ground relationships, have the child cut around one object in his drawing. The puzzle, minus the object, can be mounted on another piece of cardboard, with a recessed place left for the missing object. The same kind of puzzle may be made from art reproductions. Older students can sharpen their knowledge of artistic styles by trying to sort out two different types of art work represented by two art reproduction puzzles that have been mixed up.

ART AND SCIENCE

Art and science are not as unrelated as one might think. An examination of the contents of specially developed curricula materials in science and basic elementary science texts reveals many aims and attitudes that are shared with art and many opportunities where art either can be or already is integrated.* As with math, science curricula emphasize active learning

---

* *Elementary Science Study* curricula materials listed in reference section; Karplus & Lawson, 1974; Ennever & Harlen, 1971; Brandwien, Cooper, Blackwood, Horne & Fraser, 1972.

situations in which the child manipulates many objects. This emphasis is grounded in the research of Piaget on the ways that the child develops his cognitive abilities.†

The child's active involvement in science learning can be enhanced in many ways through art activities. For example, in a science lesson or unit on growing plants, the child explores growth through actually planting seeds and constructs the container that will hold the plant in clay or decorates existing containers, cans, or cups. Thus, a personal artistic statement is a part of the science activity. Or, in the process of studying wind concepts, the child gains deeper understandings of these concepts by constructing and flying pinwheels or kites. In making kites, the child designs the surface area using shapes and logos and colors that are artistic statements. These logos will help differentiate the kites when they are up in the air.

These are a few examples of ways of integrating the two fields. Several other ways are presented in the following discussion of more specific science aims and attitudes. These examples are presented to spark the reader to develop his own integrated art and science lessons.

Scientific Attitudes

Science educators stress four attitudes which are necessary to a child's scientific literacy. These are *curiosity* (which is described by science educators as the utilization of more than one sense to explore objects), *inventiveness* (which is the unusual and constructive use of scientific equipment), *critical thinking* (which is described as basing ideas, conclusions, and thoughts on evidence), and *persistence* (described as "sticktoitivity," i.e. persisting at an activity when others in the class have lost interest in the project) (*Attitudes in Science*, 1972).

These four attitudes are not the sole domain of the scientific world. They are necessary to artistic literacy as well. Every time a child picks up a brush or crayon and makes marks on a page, he is *inventing*. When the child is given a choice of materials and makes a decision to try the new material, the child is demonstrating artistic *curiosity*. When a child is given the opportunity to decide what he will do and to decide exactly when his particular art activity is finished, he is displaying *critical thinking*. Moreover, when a child sets his own problem in art and completes this set task, he is being *persistent*.

The art projects described in this sourcebook are designed to foster these "scientific attitudes." These scientific (and artistic) attitudes can be devel-

---

† Duckworth, 1964; Educational Development Center, 1973; Ennever & Harlen, 1971; Karplus & Lawson, 1974.

oped by providing a supportive environment that encourages the child to make decisions and to follow an art project to fruition and completion. Throughout the teaching/learning situation, careful questioning by the teacher will greatly facilitate attitude development.

A more specific example of the ways these scientific attitudes can be enhanced is illustrated by the life-size portrait discussed in Chapter IV. This activity can be introduced so that the child is curious about his height and how this height would appear on the paper. By providing a choice of materials, i.e. cloth, paint, or a combination of these, the child is able to invent ways to solve the problem of dressing his figure. The choice of materials and the specific ways that the child decides to place these on his life-size figure necessitates many critical decisions. Since the project requires an investment of time, persistence is encouraged on the part of the creator to complete the portrait.

Discovery/Inquiry/Exploration

Science curricula writers emphasize the importance of *exploration* in science learning. Exploration in elementary science is accomplished by providing the child with a variety of experiences with equipment, materials, and the actual, real world (Karplus & Lawson, 1974). In fact, the real world of the child and the objects that exist in it are his first science laboratory (Ennever & Harlen, 1971). The exploration of the child's own environs is preliminary to the development of abstracting abilities.

Moreover, science educators feel that as the child explores his world and the items in it, he begins to ask questions. If the child can ask questions, the belief is that he can begin to discover answers as well (Rogers & Voelker, 1972). In the field of art, the child deals directly with materials. These materials are familiar to him. One of the underlying philosophies of the art activities discussed in this sourcebook is that they must be created with familiar materials and media that are readily available in the regular classroom and the child's home.

The artistic process necessitates *inquiry* and *discovery*. This is readily apparent if a child is observed as he picks up a crayon or brush and explores the quality of lines or colors that emerge on his page. The learning situation is crucial in encouraging the student to explore and discover. Carefully posed problems or situations that require the child to ask questions are essential. The art activity leading to the discovery of the secondary colors discussed in the math section is an example of a discovery lesson. In such a situation, the child is invited to discover and explore.

There is a definite place for open-ended discovery and exploration in art. This is always necessary as the child learns about new materials and media. Art cannot be made without having a storehouse of knowledge about what is possible with media. Armed with this knowledge, the child is prepared to draw or paint or create in any media which he has mastered. Creation and expression do not occur in a vacuum. The artistic processes are enhanced with a deeper knowledge of media. The only way a child can attain such knowledge is through exploration per se. Exploration can be the major aim of an art lesson.

In many cases, however, exploration is but one phase in the total artistic process. Stopping at exploration and failing to encourage the child to go beyond can foster erroneous concepts about art activities and art learnings. Art is more than exploration of media. Art is also the expression of an idea, a feeling, and an experience. The expression depends on the abilities of the child and his knowledge of the materials which can be used to accomplish this expression.

Communication

Science curricula writers emphasize the importance of recording observations of phenomena which are observed in the environs. Science places a high value on such observation and on the communication of discoveries (Educational Development Center, 1969b; Karplus & Randle, 1970; Ennever & Harlen, 1971). Drawing, painting, and model-building activities are important art activities. They can also be important adjuncts to scientific observation and communication. Intermediate students who are learning about their environment, plant growth, or climate changes can record changes in these phenomena via drawings or a group mural.

Describing Properties

In science education, the child should be able to make comparisons of objects and describe the similarities and differences of objects. To do this, the child learns about the properties of objects (Herrera & Thier, 1975; Karplus & Lawson, 1974; Randle & Thier, 1970). Such observational abilities and the ability to discriminate likenesses and differences in objects are important to art as well.

Many art activities already presented focus on the child's involvement in doing just this. Good examples are the art learning section on texture rubbings presented in Chapter IV and geometric shapes already discussed in the math section of this chapter. In these art learning situations, the child is asked to make distinctions between objects. The child must match items by looking and feeling for similarities. He can also be asked to decide which items are hard, soft, heavy, light, etc. This same type of discrimination is needed in the art activities centering on shape and color distinction. Thus, art and science learning can be joint endeavors.

PLEASE NOTE: The next illustration section focuses on art and science activities. The reader is encouraged to examine the illustrations before reading further.

Figure 76. Making and flying kites can be an integrated art and science activity. First, a wrapping paper pattern is made, and the child decorates it. This kite was painted by a six-year-old hearing impaired boy.

Figure 77. The next step in the kite activity is to assemble it and go out on a windy day and fly the creation. In this picture, a two-year-old deaf boy with partial vision holds his kite as the teacher steadies the line. Often the best way of explaining something is to do it. What better means is there of communicating the concept of kite than to make and fly one? Wind concepts may also be tied into the activity.

78   79

Figure 78. Making stained-glass windows illustrates ways that media can be explored and discoveries made about light and color mixing. This picture shows the results of one such exploration by a group of intermediate physically handicapped children. The "windows" were made to actually fit over existing classroom windows so that part of the light would be blocked out and the rest softened.

Figure 79. A nine-year-old physically handicapped girl shaves crayon scraps with a hand pencil sharpener for the window filling. A vegetable grater or a dull flatware knife can also be used to shave crayons. She is experimenting with different sizes of crayons and colors of tissue paper.

Figure 80. An eleven-year-old with cerebral palsy irons the crayon and wax paper "sandwich" for the window. This is a good opportunity for a scientific discussion about what happens when heat is applied to a solid (to crayons).

Figure 81. A multiply handicapped eight-year-old shows the results of her *exploration* of overlapping tissue papers and melted crayons.

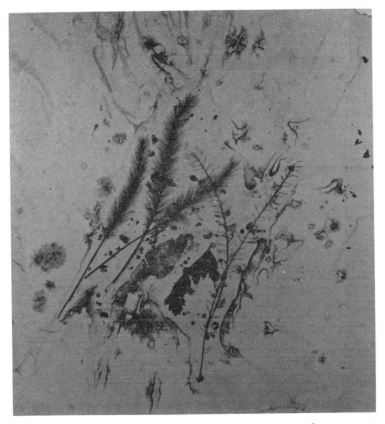

Figure 82. A variation on the window-making activity is to use other items instead of tissue paper and cellophane. This "window," made with the addition of natural forms (weeds), was done by a retarded teenager.

Figures 83 and 84. A physically handicapped group goes on a search for natural objects such as twigs, leaves, and pieces of bark. Each child makes her own decisions about what to collect. These will be taken back to the classroom and discussed in terms of both their scientific and their artistic properties.

Figure 85. Several deaf children also collect bags of treasures from outside.

Figure 86. After the natural items are sorted according to various categories, this deaf eight-year-old begins her collage.

87

88

Figure 87. This is a nature collage that has just been finished by a retarded nine-year-old girl. When the white glue is dry, it will not show. The artist has created a concrete picture of a tree.

Figure 88. A blind fourteen-year-old boy made this nature collage. He has repeated the bark and the moss to build design unity in addition to the unity provided by a collage of one category of objects, i.e. nature forms.

Figure 89. Combining movement and role playing often makes an experience more meaningful. Each of these impaired children first picked an animal and then discussed what the animal ate, where it lived, etc. Here, a class of primary deaf children "act" out their animal choices on the playground before drawing them during an integrated art and science activity.

Figure 90. After space is assigned to each child, a chalk drawing is started. Here, a zebra begins to emerge.

Figure 91. A backyard "habitat" is being made for a cat.

Figure 92. After all the drawings are completed, the class goes on a "viewing" walk around the playground "gallery."

Figure 93. After drawing on the playground, the class makes animal costumes. Here, a seven-year-old hearing impaired boy begins to paint tiger stripes on his costume.

Figure 94. Later, he draws his animal in its jungle environment. Note the overlapping in the drawing.

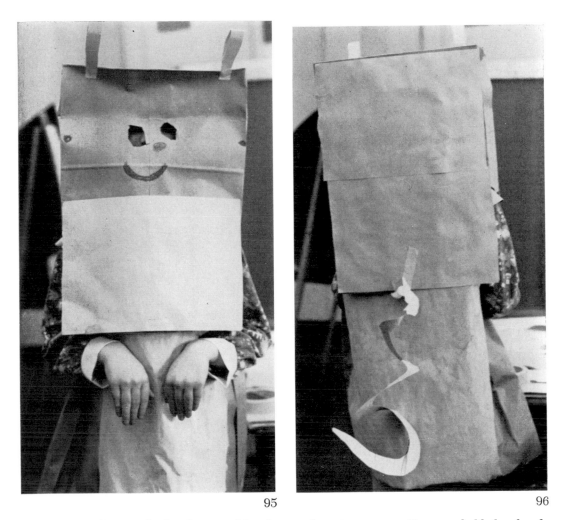

95   96

Figures 95 and 96. A deaf eight-year-old girl wears her pig costume. She even holds her hands empathically. Note the addition of the construction paper tail.

Figure 97. Scenery for a play can be as simple as a word on a card. In this "play" about animals, two aides become tree "props" for the raccoon.

Figure 98. The deaf children begin to act out their play by reading from cue sheets.

Figure 99. After the play, the children draw some part of their experience. Note the raccoon between the two trees. The child who was the raccoon "in the trees" drew this picture.

Figure 100. The direct experience of the play has even prompted this nine-year-old deaf boy to write the lines of the play in his picture.

Windows: Through a Glass Brightly

Purpose/Rationale

This activity focuses on a discovery/exploration approach to the art lesson. This is an inquiry lesson in art. It centers on several basic science concepts also. The child is asked to explore ways in which sunlight can be blocked. This discovery may lead to a discussion of the differences in meaning between the words *transparent* and *semitransparent* and an inquiry into the nature of different types of paper.

The child explores what occurs when heat is applied to crayons. Wax melts, and colors of crayons can be mixed. He also learns that color can be mixed by overlapping of colors of tissue paper and/or cellophane. Finally, measurement becomes important if an area is to be adequately covered.

Materials

Cellophane scraps in various colors	Ruler
Crayons, old broken ones, peeled	Scissors or vegetable grater or dull
Iron	knife
Masking tape	Tissue paper in various colors, sizes
Old newspapers	Wax paper
Paper clips	A window that needs covering

The cellophane can be omitted. Scraps of tissue paper can be used.

Motivation

A situation may actually exist in the classroom to prompt the solving of a specific problem. This actually happened in the classroom in which the windows pictured in this section were created. Too much light was pouring into the room, and there was a need to cut down on this. Blinds cut out too much light, so another solution was needed. Different types and thickness of papers were tried over the window. The activity as presented here was the solution.

A variation on this idea might be to make "sunglasses" instead of a window covering. Another means of exploration would be to have crayons and a warming tray available. The students can just explore what happens when heat is applied to the crayons. In fact, this can be a separate lesson in itself, and exploration and discovery may go on for several days or weeks.

If the class is an intermediate group and fairly bright, they can get into a discussion of the differences between the words *transparent* and *opaque*. They can also study Egyptian encaustic painting. (Egyptians used tempera suspended in a wax medium for their early painting on wood. This painting was called encaustic.) Finally, the class can discover what happens when primary colors of tissue or cellophane are overlapped; the same kind of exploration can occur by using pieces of scrap stained glass.

Procedure

Whether the lesson is to focus primarily on exploration or its aim is to actually make window coverings, the process is exactly the same. If a specific area is to be covered, it must be measured. *Two* pieces of wax paper, each having these measurements, are required. If the area is not too large, the wax paper can be folded over to make the two pieces needed. A sandwich of wax paper is necessary. The "filling" of this sandwich is the pieces of tissue paper and other papers or other items that are fairly flat. The sandwich is held together with crayon pieces or shavings that are melted. The crayon can be shaved by using a vegetable shredder or by taking scissors and scraping old crayons.

It is recommended that children work on a surface covered with old newspapers. When the sandwich is complete, it is covered with another paper layer of newspaper. The whole double-decker sandwich is then ironed with an iron set on a moderate setting. Some experimentation will be needed to determine the best setting for the iron and for how hard and long it will take to press the sandwich together. Before ironing, clip the sandwich together with paper clips to prevent slipping. This activity will take about one-half hour. If any of the children do some measuring, allow an additional fifteen minutes.

Adaptations

LEARNING DISABLED. Shorten the activity for those children who have a short attention span. Just demonstrate the process and let the children get involved in the activity without too much questioning and waiting. With this kind of process, there is no *right* or *wrong* way to accomplish the final design. The composition can be very abstract or realistic.

BEHAVIORALLY DISORDERED. In addition to the above, the child can crush the crayon pieces by putting them between newspapers and by using a hammer. After this, he can sprinkle these small pieces over the design he has created before the top waxed paper is added.

HEARING IMPAIRED. Vocabulary can be tied in with this activity. Examples of key words might be *press, iron, melt,* and *transparent.* Because the child will be actively using these words, the development of meanings for them will be facilitated.

RETARDED. Language can be tied into this lesson. Key words might be *cover, overlap, mix,* and the color names. Red, blue, and yellow tissue paper should be included in the materials for this lesson so that secondary colors can be "discovered." Some children will be impatient to see their finished project and may not iron long enough. To facilitate the long time needed for ironing, have the child count to a specific number. For example, each child can count to forty as he rotates the iron.

VISUALLY IMPAIRED. The blind child may not fully comprehend the value of making a window for the room. For this child, drawing with crayon on paper taped over a warming tray or set into an electric frying pan may be an alternative. With such an activity, the child can sense the heat and explore what happens as he draws and the crayon melts. The paper used should be slightly smaller than the tray or pan.

PHYSICALLY HANDICAPPED. It may be easier for these children to crush the crayon pieces. It is suggested that their designs be kept in the abstract realm to avoid frustrating students who do not have the motor control to create a realistic picture. Older children may enjoy looking and discussing the work of Abstract Expressionist painters such as Jackson Pollock, Franz Kline, and Willem deKooning in connection with this activity. (These painters, as the reader probably knows, created works that will look much like the outcomes of this activity.)

Evaluation

POTENTIAL OUTCOMES. The child has made one or more stained glass window. He has discovered that crayons melt when heat is applied to them. He has discovered that two primary colors overlapped produce a secondary color. Therefore, the child has discovered one new color. The child has explored what happens when light is partially blocked by semi-transparent paper. He has explored these light effects by taking time to look at all the stained glass window pictures. He has demonstrated his curiosity by wanting to try at least one additional combination of crayon pieces and cellophane colors in another stained glass picture.

CLOSURE. The class should spend time looking at the effects of each child's work displayed in the classroom windows. These window pictures can be studied at different times of the day and can evolve into a study of direct and indirect light. This light study may involve a study of stained glass. The students may also study paintings done by the Abstract Expressionist painters which will look very similar.

Nature Collage: A Walk in the Woods

Purpose/Rationale

Perhaps an obvious tie-in between science and art is an activity involving a field trip into nature and the construction of a collage with the items collected. The field trip offers numerous opportunities to study many objects and things (phenomena) in nature's own laboratory. Students can examine similarities and differences in natural objects such as leaves, grasses, and weeds and trees, twigs, and bark. Such an excursion also can provide the occasion to make comparisons between living and nonliving creatures. Students can also get a feeling for the concept of environment.

Decisions about how much detail and how many scientific concepts are to be incorporated in the activity depend on the level and interest of the class. It may be helpful to have several discussions prior to and during the excursion. Students will be asked to make collections of a variety of objects. Categories may be set up prior to the trip, or they may be discovered afterwards when the students are back in the classroom with their collections. Some observations may be recorded in drawings made during the trip.

Materials

Brushes, about ½ inch (*c.* 1 cm) wide
Cardboard about 6 by 10 inches (*c.* 15 by 25 cm) or larger
Nature items such as leaves, bark, weeds, etc.
Old newspapers
Paint shirts or smocks
Paper towels
Playground or woods for nature collecting
Sacks or plastic bags for nature collection
Water in container to clean brushes
White glue in small pot pie tins or other containers, 1 per child

Motivation

The field trip will provide much of the motivation. Having each child observing and searching for natural items (perhaps in some systematic way that has already been discussed) will insure active involvement in the activity. The children can be told that they will be doing several activities with their collections after the trip. Or, what is prepared after the field trip can be kept a mystery.

Procedure

After the trip, place the students' collections in one pile and discuss ways of sorting, classifying, and describing what they have found. This can be done individually or by working in pairs or teams. A series of collages can be made according to some of the categories suggested by the class. A collage usually refers to a picture made entirely from different kinds and textures of papers. Here it is defined more broadly to mean a picture made with a variety of items that are "found" and arranged as opposed to items drawn or completely created by the artist. Several examples of partially completed collages and a partial demonstration may help.

If the students have sustained interest, suggest that they plan their placements and experiment with these natural forms before actually gluing them down. This will enable a discussion of composition and ways that the space may be filled so that it is not wasted. The aim is to have items that are interesting to observe in each area of the page and a visual emphasis in one or two parts. This visual emphasis is created by using one or two larger nature items in the collage.

After design decisions are made, white glue is brushed on the cardboard surface and the natural objects are added. The collages should be left to dry overnight. Some students will discover that some items are too large to be included or are too heavy or bulky to be glued down. In this case, a discussion might emerge about weight and gravity and strength of glue. This is just one example of how discovery and experimentation may emerge from an activity. The nature walk will take about forty-five minutes. The discussion afterwards may take up to another hour, depending on the interest and level of the class. The collage will take another one-half hour to make.

Adaptations

LEARNING DISABLED. Perhaps a more structured approach will be called for. If the class cannot go on a field trip or it is not feasible to do this, then bring natural objects and collectibles into the classroom. The composition discussion may be especially helpful if left and right and top and bottom are emphasized. The student may prefer constructing a more realistic picture using the natural objects. The relief quality of the collage will help the child separate the figure from the background.

BEHAVIORALLY DISORDERED. The field trip may be stimulating to the more withdrawn child as he is given responsibility to make a personal collection. Set some rules and limits on what and how items are to be collected. In this way, respect for the environment is also taught. With a larger piece of cardboard, the students can work in small groups and make a mural or group picture. The children should be aware that patience is needed in gluing and that items must be left for several hours before they will adhere to the background. Tell students that some objects will not glue as easily as others. This may prevent some frustration.

HEARING IMPAIRED. In addition to the above, stress meanings of words such as *similar, different,* and *same.* Demonstrate some of the problems encountered in gluing heavy objects to the cardboard. This may lead to a discussion of what happens and why. It may stimulate scientific thinking and some spontaneous language as well. Different leaf names and tree names can also be discussed.

RETARDED. Simple distinctions and words should be emphasized. It may be helpful initially to get the child to make distinctions among leaves, grass, and bark. Matching leaves that are similar or the same may also be an important discrimination activity. The collage may be as simple or as complex as the teacher wants to structure it.

VISUALLY IMPAIRED. Some more planning for the field trip may be needed. Perhaps begin by bringing in some natural objects first and by letting the child explore these *before* the field trip. Place the collected objects in a large box with low sides or in a tray. The child then may explore what is there and make his choices in this way. Larger cardboard background pieces are recommended. Secure these to the work area with clamps or tape.

Make the child aware that it takes some time for glued items to dry. It may help to have the child work from left to right in his collage so that he will not unglue or knock off items already glued. Or, work in stages on the project and let each section dry before going on to the next.

PHYSICALLY HANDICAPPED. Secure the cardboard with tape or clamps, and have the children brush on a good coating of glue. Items that are added to the cardboard can then be placed on the prepared surface. If the child desires to shift positions of these items, he can use a short stick to move them into the desired position. It may help to complete one section at a time and leave it to dry as described in the visually impaired adaptations.

Evaluation

POTENTIAL OUTCOMES. The child has made a collection of five or more nature objects. He has learned to sort these according to various categories (such as shapes, colors, textures, sizes, and forms). He has learned some of the names for these natural objects. He has made a collage with nature objects. He has used enough (but not too much) glue to hold all the items. He has learned to wait until the glue dries. The child has demonstrated his understanding of composition by filling the surface of the collage with a variety of shapes and sizes of items and by not leaving large empty areas.

CLOSURE. Each child should have a chance to share his work with the class. The different nature objects can be pointed out and discussed in terms of their names and how they are similar and different. The various ways each child has solved the problem of filling the available space may also be discussed. The emphasis should be on the positive aspects of each child's work. Display the collages on a shelf, or line them up along the chalk tray. For added color interest, construction paper can be glued to the cardboard before the children begin their collages.

Animal Study

Purpose/Rationale

Investigating animals is a part of many elementary science curricula. In this series, the children communicate what they know about a particular animal in terms of how the animal looks, how it moves, what sounds it makes, where it lives, what it eats, who its foes are and with whom it lives peaceably, etc. The same type of art learning series may be developed for a number of other science topics. This, therefore, is but one example of what can be accomplished through art.

The focus of the study is on actual animals in the real world. The teacher can extend this study to imagined animals if it seems appropriate and desirable for the class to delve into the fantasy world. Science concepts of food habitats, food chains, and environments would be a part of the learning.

ANIMALS ON THE PLAYGROUND

Materials

Chalk of various colors
Playground with blacktop or concrete
Permission to draw on the playground
Relatively warm, sunny day

Motivation

Prior to going outside, the class discusses and reviews animals they have been studying. Ask each child to select an animal. If he has trouble doing this, the child can pick one from a list of names on the chalkboard. Another alternative is to have a box of animal names from which each child may choose. After this selection is made, each child demonstrates how his animal walks, what sounds it makes, and discusses where the animal lives. Tell the class that they will go outside and dramatize their animal. Once outside, give each child a space on the playground to draw.

Procedure

When outside, start the children in a circle, and, one by one or in pairs, tell them to become their animals. Then, in a line, lead them to their drawing areas. In some playgounds, there are natural areas marked off already by the lines of a volleyball or basketball court. If these lines do not exist, mark off areas for each child. After each child has his area, have him draw the animal in his habitat. At the end of the lesson, line up the class and go on an animal-looking expedition. The activity should take about fifteen minutes for the discussion and forty minutes on the playground.

Adaptations

LEARNING DISABLED. Set specific limits in terms of how involved each student can become in acting as his animal. For example, the lion cannot really eat up everyone. Left and right dominance can be emphasized in part of the acting. For example, the raccoon can dig and eat with his right (or left) hand (paw). If the class cannot go outside or there is not a good blacktop on which to draw, have the class draw with colored chalk on the chalkboard.

BEHAVIORALLY DISORDERED. In addition to the above adaptations for the learning disabled, establish more structure. Provide a carefully selected list of animals from which the child can choose. Include animals with cooperative characteristics and which are known to cohabitate well. A large group mural can also be made on the chalkboard or on the playground.

HEARING IMPAIRED. Some pictures of various animals may spark the discussion. Because the children will be actively involved in creative dramatics and will be doing their drawing outside and away from these pictures, there will be less opportunity to copy.

RETARDED. If possible, do not have the same animal chosen by more than one child. Then, the children will not be tempted to copy each other's work. If going out on the playground presents too many management problems, have the class draw on the chalkboard or on large paper. This type of acting and drawing activity will reinforce what the children already know about animals. Another approach may be to do this activity *as* the class is learning about animals.

VISUALLY IMPAIRED. Each child will not need to pick a different animal because there will be less tendency to copy. A zoo visit or exploration with actual animals, such as gerbils in the classroom, will help transmit the concepts. Constructing clay animals in a prior art lesson will help establish animal concepts and prepare the children for this large outdoor drawing activity.

These children also need the experience of working and drawing on a large scale. The playground can be used for this with the following changes. Anchor large brown wrapping paper sheets using weights and/or tape. The children can then draw on this with large crayons. The rough texture of the blacktop will leave a texture on the paper. The child can feel and know where he has already drawn.

PHYSICALLY HANDICAPPED. Tempera may be easier to manipulate than the chalk. Thicken the paint brush handle as needed for grasping, or use a sponge instead. In making this decision, let each student experiment with the materials. The child can then decide which he prefers to use. If the child cannot be taken out of his wheelchair, have a piece of chalk (or a brush) attached to a stick so that he can reach the drawing surface.

Evaluation

POTENTIAL OUTCOMES. The child has discussed animals and demonstrated his knowledge of one of them by dramatizing that animal (making appropriate gestures, actions, and sounds) with 75 percent or more accuracy. He has drawn his chosen animal and has included appropriate background details.

CLOSURE. Some time may be spent looking at each child's playground drawing. Some specific facts about each animal can be reinforced as this is done. Mention the next activity (making animal costumes) to build anticipation and expectancy in the group.

ANIMAL COSTUMES

Materials

Brown wrapping paper, 36 inches (*c.* 1 m) wide, in lengths about as long as each child is tall

Brushes, ¼ inch (*c.* ½ cm) wide, plus some smaller

Construction paper in assorted colors and some scraps

Containers for water and paint	Stapler
Masking tape	Tape measure or yardstick (meterstick)
Old newspapers	
Paint shirts or smocks	Tempera paint in appropriate colors
Paper towels	
Pencils	White glue in small bottles or pot pie tins with ½ inch (*c.* 1 cm) brushes
Sacks large enough to fit over the child's head	
Scissors	

The brown wrapping paper will be folded in half for each animal costume. Children will choose either paint or paper for use in finishing their costumes.

Purpose/Rationale

This is an extension of the animal drawing activity. Now that each child has more knowledge of his animal, he becomes that animal via making a costume.

Motivation

Animals are again discussed. Even some animal pictures again may be helpful to the students. This time, however, the students are going to construct costumes. Show some examples of completed or partially completed costumes. Partially demonstrate how the costume is made. The students will then *use* these costumes in some special way. (This is explained in the next lesson.)

Procedure

One child is asked to lie down so that a pattern can be traced on the brown wrapping paper. To provide for the back and front, the paper is *doubled* before any tracing is done. About two inches of extra room is needed on the sides so that the two parts can be taped or stapled together. A sack mask is also made (see discussion of masks in Chapter IV) to complete the outfit. Measurement can be brought into the activity in a number of ways. The child can use a ruler to measure how much paper is needed and where the eyes go on the mask. Thus, math is also a part of the lesson.

The costume is painted and cut out and worn. If the child desires, he can also use construction paper to complete the project. It will take about one-half hour to make the mask and an hour to complete the costumes.

Adaptations

LEARNING DISABLED. This provides a good opportunity to reinforce directions, i.e. left and right, up and down, and back and front. The use of textures cut from either newspapers or construction paper and added to the costume may be more motivating for the child.

BEHAVIORALLY DISORDERED. Gauge the interest span of the class. If making a costume is too involved, then have the students concentrate only on the mask. It may be appropriate to make an imaginary beast. Remember, though, that some children prefer the security of making an actual animal. Additionally, limiting the activity to actual animals may help the child remain in the real world.

HEARING IMPAIRED. The vocabulary that is most crucial to this project should be carefully thought out. Key words might be *front, back, paws, claws, whiskers, ears, fur, measure,* and *patient.* Again, many different pictures of the animals that the children are making may help. Since the materials used are so different, it will be impossible to copy. Therefore, picture references are recommended, since these will help the child to clarify his concepts.

RETARDED. As with the behaviorally disordered student, this child may not have the patience and extended interest to follow through on the costume portion of the activity. Perhaps only a mask should be made (see mask discussion in Chapter IV).

VISUALLY IMPAIRED. Textured materials are recommended for use in covering the wrapping paper. Such materials include cloth scraps or construction paper. The child may want to experiment with ways of creating textures that are appropriate to his animal idea. Such ways may include tearing or curling paper textures or using already textured types of papers.

PHYSICALLY HANDICAPPED. Use ice cream cartons for the masks (see discussion of masks in Chapter IV). Those children confined to their wheelchairs may want to cover the whole chair with the wrapping paper so it becomes part of the costume. This will require some team effort and preplanning. The body part of the costume can be covered with paint. Tempera paint is recommended, as it covers easily and takes less time to dry. The costume can be painted first, or the children may wrap each other and then paint each other's costume. These decisions must be made jointly with the children.

Evaluation

POTENTIAL OUTCOMES. The child has made an animal paper costume and mask. The costume includes characteristics (colors and/or textures) of a specific animal that make it recognizable by the teacher and classmates. The child has measured accurately enough so that the costume fits. The child has demonstrated the appropriate use of art materials and his complete mastery of the art skills involved.

CLOSURE. The children can put on their costumes and briefly dramatize their animals. Each child then may guess the animal being dramatized. The costumes are then put aside until the next art activity when they will have a special use.

ANIMAL DRAWINGS

Purpose/Rationale

This final part of the series ties in writing and dramatics with science and art. The class is asked to make up a story which they will act out wearing their costumes. If the class has trouble coming up with a story line, provide a situation or take an idea from a story which the class already knows. The class must incorporate all the animals into a short play. This activity will graphically illustrate how powerful direct experience can be in motivating children to draw.

Materials

Animal costumed children
Cue sheets with lines written on them
Drawing paper about 9 by 12 inches (*c.* 22 by 30 cm)
A story
Watercolor markers

Any kind of paper such as newsprint or computer printout paper or manilla drawing paper can be used for the drawing part of this activity.

Motivation

The fact that all students will be in a short play will be motivating in itself. It may help to provide (capture) an audience for this play, i.e. parents or another class.

Procedure

When the story is written, the parts are assigned and practiced. Props can also be made if they are needed. Then the class presents the story for their audience. After the story, the class and the audience, if there is one, draw some part of the story. An example of one such story that was developed in this way follows:

Rabbit: (has props of candy and Easter eggs). He goes visiting each animal in his own habitat. As he visits, he says, "Hello, Raccoon! Will you come with me on my rounds as I bring goodies to all the animals?"

Raccoon: "Yes, I will. Do you have something for me?"

Rabbit: "Yes. Here are some candies for you." They go together to the next animal, and the scene is repeated until all children are following behind the rabbit.

Each animal is encouraged to act his part and to make the appropriate sounds, etc. After the play, the class draws a part of their dramatics experience. At the end, a party is held where they all enjoy their candy. It should take about fifteen minutes for the play and one-half hour for the drawing.

Adaptations

LEARNING DISABLED. Adapt the script to focus on the strength of each child and to reinforce concepts with which they might be having trouble. To emphasize right versus left concepts, the rabbit could hop on his right foot. If it is not a threatening situation for him, the nonverbal child can have a larger part in the play. Children may be encouraged to read their lines.

BEHAVIORALLY DISORDERED. Include some cooperation concepts in the play. For example, the lion could become a friendly one, or the group could make a large mural working together to illustrate the play.

HEARING IMPAIRED. Having cue cards may provide more security for these children as they perform the play. New vocabulary can be included in the lines as a means of reinforcement. Several plays can be written and performed.

RETARDED. Specific lines may help these children as they perform their play. (It is assumed that the children understand what a play is.) They may begin writing their play just by answering questions about their animals, writing down these answers, and then becoming the lines. For example, "What animal are you? What do you eat? Where do you live?" The play then can be centered around a pretend walk in the forest or woods and the discovery of the animals that live there. Noises can be taped and used as a part of the play. Those who are less verbal or shy can just move when the noises are heard.

VISUALLY IMPAIRED. These children will need some help figuring out where they can move in the stage area. Give them a choice of either drawing a part of the play (using a drawing screen) or working in clay. Their animal can be constructed along with a cage of cardboard and props for the habitat. This then would become a group project.

PHYSICALLY HANDICAPPED. Those students with limited language can just move and make animal noises on cue. Naturally, lines and parts should be carefully assigned so that all are included. The parts may be divided up so that those children with more language and mobility will have roles that match these abilities. With careful assignment of the tasks, a group mural

Figure 101. Impaired children need many opportunities to play. Having an opportunity to dress up and role play helps to clarify concepts about various roles. It is also fun. A deaf nine-year-old looks at himself dressed as a construction worker.

Figure 102. Then he begins to draw himself in this role. Note that he has also included the frame of the mirror in his drawing.

Figure 103. An eight-year-old deaf girl dressed as an elegant lady and still regaled in her finery draws herself.

Figure 104. An eight-year-old deaf boy shares the partially completed drawing of himself as a soldier. Notice that he even is adding his glasses and the stripes of his shirt to his drawing.

Figure 105. Constructing a house can lead to making a number of design decisions and can also spark a discussion of the family. A primary deaf girl who is eight years old works on constructing her house from cardboard.

Figure 106. This is a completed house by a nine-year-old deaf boy. Note that he has added details such as cellophane windows, a doghouse, and "smoke" coming from the chimney.

Figure 107. This house was designed by a learning disabled nine-year-old. He has added curtains on the windows.

Figure 108. A very exciting way of learning about transportation is to make some vehicles. A group of handicapped children are painting the bus which they have constructed from a furniture box. Note that the floor of the box has been taped up so that children will be able to ride and move in the bus when it is finished.

Figure 109. Two deaf children who are eight years old begin to draw a plan (map) for their neighborhood model. This active learning will clarify the many concepts about maps, towns, neighborhoods, and models which they are studying in social studies.

Figure 110. Another child adds a parking lot and cars to the model. The cars have been cut from thin scrap cardboard, and other rectangular pieces of cardboard have been slotted and added to make each car "stand up."

Figure 111. The completed model is left in the classroom so the children can discuss traffic patterns, city planning, and other neighborhood concepts.

Figure 112. To better understand the concept of a piñata, students can make one. Here in this picture, a team of handicapped children paint their papier-mâché piñata. The boys are so engaged in the activity that they have climbed right on top of the table to work.

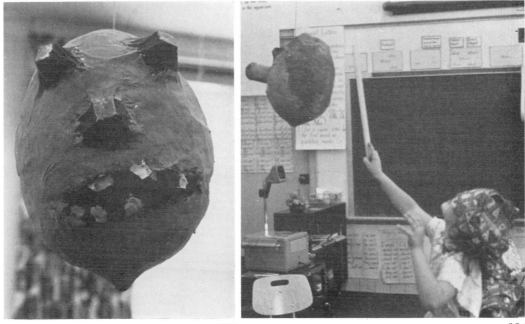

113   114

Figure 113. A finished piñata hangs in the classroom awaiting the inevitable.

Figure 114. A handicapped eight-year-old attempts to locate the piñata by touching it with a stick before she breaks it to get to the "goodies."

Figure 115. Murals may have many, many different themes. Holidays are a good topic. A mural can also be a way of building cooperation and cohesiveness in a group because each and every child can contribute in some way. Here, a Thanksgiving mural is discussed with a handicapped class of eight-, nine- and ten-year-olds. Already having the background paper up creates interest in the project.

Figure 116. A nine-year-old deaf child makes a Pilgrim from cloth scraps for the mural. It is easier to make separate items to put onto the mural. The whole group can then discuss the best placement and composition of these items on the mural, and separate items can be rearranged if necessary.

Figure 117. This eight-year-old deaf boy has decided to use crayons for his Pilgrim. He is cutting his figure out so that it can be easily arranged on the background paper.

Dressing Up: It's More Than Just Play*

Purpose/Rationale

Many persons, whatever their ages, enjoy dressing up or putting on a costume and pretending to be another person. Usually, most children have many opportunities to do this because they can initiate such activities. Impaired children may not so readily have opportunities, partly because they cannot play as easily on their own. When children are dressing up, they are doing much more than trying on clothes or hats or other props. They are trying on various roles and exploring them.

Thus, a child playing the role of a parent is testing to see how it feels to be a mother or a father. In other situations, the child may do the same with various occupations, exploring the work of a firefighter, a doctor, a nurse, a teacher, or a member of the police force.

The child needs ample opportunity to do some role playing in addition to just wearing the various clothes and using the various props. In this way, roles can be clarified and social studies concepts can be formulated. This activity may be repeated with more of an emphasis on the world of fantasy rather than on real persons and occupations. After this activity of dressing, role playing, and discussing, it is important for the children to further clarify these experiences in some art expression.

Materials

Clothing, props, and various hats
Crayons or watercolor markers
Drawing paper or newsprint 12 by 18 inches (*c.* 45 by 60 cm)
Mirrors, including a full-length one

Often an SOS to a community-oriented radio station will result in contributions for this type of activity.

Motivation

In most instances, the clothing and props, such as hats, will be all the motivation needed. In other instances, discuss what some of the roles are. This can be done by asking what kinds of things mothers, fathers, and children do at home. If the lesson is to center on vocations, then questions about what police or construction workers do, etc., will help, as will having the children actually role play. Spontaneous dramatic situations may also emerge.

Procedure

With the class still in their costumes and hats, have them examine how they look in the mirrors. The children will then draw themselves. They

---

* The author wishes to acknowledge Larry S. Barnfield as the source for this concept.

can use the mirror as a reference or draw themselves as they were in playing their various roles. Some questions may help in this situation. Dressing up should take about one-half hour to do. If desired, more time can be spent dramatizing the various roles. Allow another one-half hour for the class to draw something about their experience.

Adaptations

LEARNING DISABLED. It may be motivating for these children to make their drawings by using a variety of papers or cloth scraps. Several choices should be provided. In using cloth scraps, check to be certain that they are not too difficult to cut or tear.

BEHAVIORALLY DISORDERED. It may be preferable to encourage the child to take on the role of an imaginary character or mythological person. This might facilitate the expression of scary feelings or emotions which ordinarily would not be expressed. For example, the child might choose a large cape and pretend to be Dracula. Allowing the class to do this requires some organization and *sensitivity* on the part of the teacher. Clear limits in terms of what is to be acted and for how long will provide needed structure for both the child and the teacher.

This type of adaptation should be attempted only when the teacher knows his children very well. It will be helpful to try the activity *first* as part of a unit on a less controversial topic such as community helpers. Consider how to handle potential traffic problems and possible conflicts as the child chooses his props. Perhaps letting each child go one at a time to a pile of props and make a choice will prevent traffic jams.

HEARING IMPAIRED. Key questions and clarification of the roles which the child will be playing are most important. The activity lends itself to the development of new vocabulary. Words related to the various occupations and what is done on the job may be emphasized, and experience stories can be written after the activity.

RETARDED. In addition to the adaptations discussed above, it may help to keep the roles and characters in the real world. These roles (and the props available) should be of people to whom the child can relate and who are within his reference frame. Later, the activity can be expanded to include roles and persons that are more remote.

This activity would be a good adjunct to a field trip. For example, in studying occupations, the class can visit a dentist's office. Later, they can role play with props and then draw themselves. To prevent classroom management problems, have only a few children at a time actually dress up and role play. The rest of the class becomes the audience. As he draws, it will be important to have each child remain in the props and clothes used.

VISUALLY IMPAIRED. It may help to have this child use different textured papers for his portrait. It may be more appropriate to have the child use a three-dimensional material such as clay and make several figures depicting the dressing-up experience.

PHYSICALLY HANDICAPPED. As with the visually impaired children, the physically handicapped children may have had less of an opportunity to do this kind of activity. Their handicaps may often prevent them from dressing up, so it is important that they have these experiences. For those children who are too involved, it may help to have them use starter sheets with heads and hats that represent the various occupations or whatever the theme of the activity is. The child may then complete the picture using either thickened paint or markers.

Evaluation

POTENTIAL OUTCOMES. The child has discussed various roles of parents or community helpers. He has picked one occupation and dressed up using props for that role. The child has done some dramatization as that particular role (pretended to do whatever job the person does). He has made one or more drawings of himself as the person in the chosen role.

CLOSURE. The drawing can be displayed and the occupations represented discussed. The activity can be repeated with the children changing their choices. A large mural may be made in which the children in their chosen roles are the topic. The children can also make life-size portraits in their chosen roles.

Come to My House and Visit!

Purpose/Rationale

Constructing cardboard houses can be tied into a variety of art and social science concepts. From an art standpoint, solving the construction problems and making design choices in interior furnishing and in exterior colors are all valid art activities. Making a house can tie into a discussion of types of shelter in our society and who designs and builds them. The activity may also be an extension of a discussion of families.

Materials

Boxes, shoe and other small ones
Brushes, ½ inch (*c.* 1 cm) wide and some ¼ inch (*c.* ½ cm) wide
Cardboard scraps
Containers for water and paint
Magazine pictures of house exteriors and interiors
Masking tape

Old newspapers
Paint shirts or smocks
Tempera paint
Wallpaper books or rolls
White glue in small bottles or small pot pie tins with ½ inch (*c.* 1 cm) wide brushes
Wood scraps

The local paint store will gladly donate outdated wallpaper rolls and books.

Motivation

Because this activity will be a part of a unit on a social studies topic such as the family or shelter, the students will already have a grasp of the key concepts of housing, shelter, family, etc., and will already be motivated. Magazine pictures may help the initial discussion of various types of houses. Each child will build a house from the materials available. It will be advisable to have the child think about the type of house to be built before beginning.

Procedure

Partially demonstrate some ways of attaching the cardboard parts. Cardboard can be scored and bent to form two, three, or four walls. The fewer pieces attached, the easier the constructing will be. This requires some pre-planning. Sides can also be taped together. It is best to tape the inside of the walls. Paint does not cover tape smoothly, so hiding the tape is a good solution. Hiding the tape inside the house also results in a better-crafted building. It may help to attach the walls to a cardboard base. Windows and doors can be cut out with a knife (if an adult is around to help). Or, openings may be drawn in.

If the house has a roof that lifts off, finish the inside with wallpaper and details of furniture made from wood scraps. The project can become as complicated as the interest and abilities of the class allow. The activity will take an hour to ninety minutes to complete, depending on how involved the interior designing becomes.

Adaptations

LEARNING DISABLED. It may help to use several boxes instead of building with flat pieces of cardboard. This will be less time consuming. After the project is finished, use the houses for other activities. Children can go and visit one another in their houses, write stories about the houses, or arrange a neighborhood by using the houses and making a map.

BEHAVIORALLY DISORDERED. Again, the box approach may be preferred, especially if the class has a short attention span. This can be turned into a group project, with each child making one room for a house. If such is the case, then one or maybe two sides should be cut off so that the different rooms can be attached.

HEARING IMPAIRED. With these children, visual props such as magazine pictures may help clarify concepts of houses. After they are shown, put the pictures out of sight so that the children will not be tempted to copy. Consider some of the key vocabulary words that can be incorporated into the activity. Some possible words are *fold, cut, tape, wallpaper, window, curtain, home, house, architect, construction, rooms,* and *family.* Emphasize that each child must plan a house that is unique and personalized, possibly using his own home as a model.

RETARDED. As with the hearing impaired child, this child may relate best to making a replica of the place where he now lives. Perhaps constructing a house from pieces of cardboard may be too frustrating for these children. In this case, begin with a large box. One side can be cut away to enable access to the inside. Then, the child can divide up the interior space and can proceed to decorate the interior and exterior.

VISUALLY IMPAIRED. Use a box instead of constructing all the walls of the house. Wood pieces can become furniture. Several boxes can be used so that each box becomes a particular room. The boxes should be large. The child can make a series of these, and he can actually represent his room at home or at the school. In this way, the children get a more complete grasp of the spatial relationships within each room and its furnishings.

PHYSICALLY HANDICAPPED. The box should become the basic building unit. Larger boxes with a side removed are recommended. The children can work in pairs, with one child who has fuller use of his hands working with a more involved child. In this team arrangement, the less able child can still make design decisions.

Evaluation

POTENTIAL OUTCOMES. The child has discussed houses and constructed his own model from cardboard. He has learned how to make the parts by scoring or taping them to form a well-crafted building in which the masking tape is hidden from view. He has made his own choices about how to finish the outside and the inside. Each room has the fundamentally appropriate furnishings (kitchen appliances in the kitchen, beds in the bedroom, etc.). He has learned something about size and proportion by determining how small or large the furniture must be to fit into the rooms.

CLOSURE. Give each child an opportunity to take the class on a tour of his house. Furnishing can be discussed. The class can design a neighborhood by using the houses that they have made. Stores, businesses, and schools may be added, and city planning on a simple level may be incorporated. Try various kinds of street and house arrangements.

A Box Is a Box, Is a Bus?

Purpose/Rationale

In learning about transportation and modes of transport, one way of reinforcing concepts is to construct vehicles. In doing so, many important details of the vehicle can be examined. This particular art/social studies learning activity focuses on the construction of a bus from a large furniture box. Upon completion, the class can actually play in the bus and take turns being the passengers and the driver. Issues of group transport are then discussed as well as traffic problems and safety issues. Many other types of vehicles (or other items) can be constructed from large boxes. This depends on the particular social studies topic under discussion. Because this is conceived as a group project, issues of working together must be discussed.

Materials

Boxes, large appliance or furniture kind
Brushes, ½ inch (*c.* 1 cm) and 1 inch (*c.* 2 cm) wide
Containers for water and paint
Matt knife, kitchen knife, or utility knife
Old newspapers
Paint shirts or smocks
Paper towels
Tempera paint

Appliance or furniture stores will save their large boxes for the class.

Motivation

Since the class has been studying transportation, they should already be familiar with the topic. The idea of actually making a large bus will no doubt be sufficient motivation. If the class does not usually come to school by bus, a field trip on a bus will enhance the motivation.

Procedure

Divide the class into groups of five or six, and designate a leader. Each group should decide who is to do what task. (Hopefully, there will not be too many chiefs and too few Indians.) Consult with each group and see that equal division of labor has been made and that the plans are good ones. It will help to go out and examine a school bus periodically as the project progresses so that the children have an actual frame of reference. When the parts of the bus such as windows and doors are designated, they can be cut out with a knife. The cutting should be done by an adult. The bus is constructed so that it has no floor. The children can then move the bus along by walking inside it.

Next, the bus is painted. The tempera should be thick enough to cover the box with one coat. Details such as making bus tickets, or a bus route in the school hall, complete with a traffic control or police officer, may also be planned. If the classroom is too small to accommodate the buses, they can be left in the hall or elsewhere. Check with the administration to be sure that the hall can be used as a parking lot. This activity will take probably two hours to complete.

Adaptations

LEARNING DISABLED. Class activities with the transportation vehicles could emphasize directions. A child, acting as a driver, can be given a map to follow. Also, place traffic directions such as No Left Turn, Right Turn Only, etc., along the route. Have the children acting as passengers check to see that the driver is obeying the law.

BEHAVIORALLY DISORDERED. The teacher may have to assign work tasks for each group member. If the class is small enough, all can work on the same box. If there is a large class, then perhaps have several groups.

HEARING IMPAIRED. The children should have ample opportunity to use the buses they make in numerous other activities. The idea of a bus trip or going through rush hour in the bus should stimulate much spontaneous language.

RETARDED. A trip on a bus and several trips outside to examine the school's buses will be invaluable in conceptualizing the problem. It may be best to have only one group working at a time. The teacher may have to be the leader, advisor, and facilitator in the group. Later, another group can make a different transportation vehicle. Having the whole traffic fleet constructed at the same time in the same room may cause too many traffic jams.

VISUALLY IMPAIRED. This activity would be of particular significance for the blind child, especially when one considers that a totally blind person will never have a chance to actually drive anywhere. The same basic driving activity described under the learning disabled adaptations can be utilized. The highway will have to be carefully laid out, and someone will have to give verbal directions. When the bus is being painted, the children will have to be well covered, since paint may not always end up on the vehicle. Mark off sections to be painted with straight pins and string; have the group work in pairs moving in the same direction. As soon as one section is finished, mark the next section to be painted. Establish a set place for the paint container, and anchor or weight it to prevent tipping.

PHYSICALLY HANDICAPPED. The tempera paint should be thick enough to cover the cardboard with one coat. Thicker paint will not drip or run as easily and therefore will not become frustrating. The door to the bus should be large enough so that all wheelchairs can enter without getting stuck. Be sure the brush handles are shortened so no one gets poked. Sponges can be used instead of brushes.

Evaluation

POTENTIAL OUTCOMES. The child has learned about one form of transportation by making a bus. He has cooperated in his group by working with the others on his assigned task. He has used tempera paint and brushes appropriately, thus demonstrating his mastery of painting skills. He has helped clean up without prompting from the teacher.

CLOSURE. Take the group on an imaginary trip. Tickets and maps can be made, and the group can take turns being the driver. Passengers can be picked up along the way, or stories can be written about the trip. Traffic rules might be discussed and signs made. Have the children take turns being the traffic cop. If the trip is made outside on the playground, a route can be drawn in with chalk. Have the children draw pictures of their trip afterwards.

Neighborhood Model

Purpose/Rationale

This activity provides a concrete idea of a neighborhood and the basis for discussing the relationships between the people and the structures in that neighborhood. In doing this activity, the child can study directions and traffic patterns and can make a map from the completed model. When the model is completed, the child considers some ways of improving the neighborhood. The class might even get into environmental issues in urban planning and design. They can experiment with possibilities of changes by removing buildings and adding others. The class can go beyond this activity and create a whole city if they wish.

Finally, the child learns how to use cardboard and small boxes to create buildings and details such as cars. He also learns about proportion. This activity may be a part of a series of art activities, beginning with making houses (homes) and large box vehicles and finally ending with the creation of the school neighborhood.

Materials

Boxes, small ones such as shoe, cereal, film, and toothpaste
Brown wrapping paper to cover the base
Brushes, ½ inch (*c.* 1 cm) and ¼ inch (*c.* ½ cm) wide
Cardboard from large box flattened for a base
Containers for water and paint
Masking tape
Matt knife or kitchen knife or utility knife
Old newspapers
Paint shirts or smocks
Paper towels
Pencils
Tempera paint
White glue in small bottles or small open containers with ¼ inch (*c.* ½ cm) wide brushes

Bicycle boxes or other large boxes with wide uncreased areas make the best bases when flattened out. Local stores will save these on request.

Motivation

A walk around the school neighborhood after a discussion of neighborhoods will help the class get started. Next, suggest that the class build a model of the neighborhood. Have the base ready. Make the base from several large pieces of scrap cardboard taped together and covered with the wrapping paper. A chalkboard list of items in the neighborhood that need to be included will help. The class may need to visit the neighborhood several times to clarify details.

Procedure

After the class has discussed the task, divide them into groups to work on specific sections of the model. Some direction about where buildings should go will help. Either pieces of cardboard or small boxes may be used for the buildings. Pieces should be taped together on the inside with masking tape. To make sides of the buildings, cardboard pieces are scored and folded. Discuss proportion. This can be done by relating to buildings in the real neighborhood. For example, if one building is six stories high and another is three stories high, then the first is twice as high as the second. This two to one relationship can be transferred to the cardboard model by simply measuring with a ruler or by locating a box that is twice as high as another.

After the buildings are made and placed on the base, cars and other details can be made from cardboard scraps and added. The model is then painted. It will take one-half hour to plan the model and ninety minutes to construct and paint.

Adaptations

LEARNING DISABLED. The children can make special note of the signs in the neighborhood. These signs can be an important part of the model and may help reinforce reading abilities.

BEHAVIORALLY DISORDERED. Carefully choose the groups so that the members work well together. It may be best not to have everyone working at the same time on the project because there may be some traffic jams. If the class cannot work in small groups, assign a specific task to each child and have the child work independently on the model parts. Assemble these into one large class project.

HEARING IMPAIRED. Location and direction words may be stressed after the class has constructed its models. They can write experience stories about their projects, thus tying in language and writing with the activity.

RETARDED. Begin with some examples of commercially made toy models to convey the concept of model. It may be best to use assorted boxes instead of trying to construct buildings from parts of cardboard.

VISUALLY IMPAIRED. Use different sizes of boxes. Several field trips will be needed for this group. It may help to make a model of the classroom first so that the group has a concept of a model. Initially, arrange the neighborhood on the base using the boxes. This will give the child a grasp of the model and neighborhood concepts. After the boxes are painted, tape them to the base.

PHYSICALLY HANDICAPPED. Assorted boxes or wood scraps that are already in the shapes of buildings might be best to use. Cutting and taping cardboard pieces may be too frustrating for these children.

Evaluation

POTENTIAL OUTCOMES. The child has used skills he learned in the earlier house-constructing activity to make a neighborhood model. He has learned the definition of model by making one. He has been able to cooperate in a group and has shared materials and tasks.

CLOSURE. Discuss the neighborhood, including things that happen during different times of the day. Mapping, traffic patterns, and other social studies concepts can be studied. Situations like rush hour traffic could be role played, or better ways of arranging the neighborhood (city planning) can be discussed and the model changed. Have the class write stories about the group endeavor and/or ways of improving the neighborhood.

Holidays: A License for Murals

Purpose/Rationale

A class mural is an important ongoing activity that is always valid. Inspiration for a mural comes from a season, a story, or just the teacher's pragmatic need to change a bulletin board. A natural source for a mural is a holiday. A mural personalizes and clarifies the event that is portrayed. No matter how limited his ability, each member of a class can contribute to a mural.

Materials

Construction paper in assorted colors, about 9 by 12 inches (*c.* 22 by 30 cm) and some scraps

Cloth scraps that can be easily cut or torn	Straight pins
	Watercolor markers
Masking tape	White glue in small bottles or in
Old newspapers	small pot pie tins with ½ inch
Other paper scraps	(*c.* 1 cm) wide brushes
Paper towels	Wall or large area covered in light
Stapler	blue, pink, or grey paper

Motivation

It may help to put up the background paper several days before the activity is even discussed. This should make the class curious and spark interest in the project. Pictures from reading books, library books, or a visual file will help spark the discussion about what is to go on the mural. In this case, the topic is Thanksgiving.

Procedure

Put the class names and a list of things to be included in the mural on the chalkboard. The class may choose the things they want to make, or topics can be assigned. Some of the items can be written on separate pieces of paper, and each child can pick one out of a hat. The class may work in small groups. The parts of the mural should be made separately and then placed on the background. In this way, items can be rearranged if need be. If one group finishes earlier than others, they may pick another item from the hat, or ask them to look at the partially completed mural and make what is missing (provided no other group is making these missing parts).

Discuss the importance of making good use of the space. A discussion of proportion can be made simply by using three sizes of the same item. When these are placed on the background, ask the class which size looks best on the background and in relation to other items already on the mural.

If possible, include people in the mural. Depending on the abilities of the children, each can make a person to go on the mural. The mural will take about three forty-five minute periods to complete.

Adaptations

LEARNING DISABLED. Have children pick the written mural words out of a hat. This will be a good means of motivating them to read. Cloth scraps and textured papers may also be used to make the mural parts. This activity will help the child distinguish figure from background.

BEHAVIORALLY DISORDERED. It may be best to assign specific things for these children to make. Divide up the mural space so that there will be no misunderstanding about what goes where.

HEARING IMPAIRED. If a child needs clarification about how a Pilgrim looks, let him look at pictures or visuals. Encourage him to make his own version and not copy. Some key vocabulary words associated with the Thanksgiving mural would be *Pilgrim, Indian, corn, turkey, dinner, pie, table, thanks,* and *woods.*

RETARDED. In addition to the above suggestions for the hearing impaired, the abilities of the group need to be considered. Let the more able children make the more difficult project items—for example, the people. Tasks should be individually tailored to fit the skills represented in the class.

VISUALLY IMPAIRED. Set the background paper low enough to enable the children to explore the whole area to be covered. Masking tape should be used instead of pins to attach the parts to the background. Designate specific work areas.

PHYSICALLY HANDICAPPED. The children should be given specific assignments. In this way, those children who can draw will make the Pilgrims. A child who is especially limited in his fine motor skills can still tear paper for parts such as the tree leaves.

Evaluation

POTENTIAL OUTCOMES. The child has worked as a part of a group creating a mural. He has made one or more objects relating to the theme. These are recognizable to the teacher and/or his classmates. He has demonstrated 90 percent mastery of the media he used. He has discussed composition and noted one or more missing items and empty spaces on the mural.

CLOSURE. Some time should be spent looking at and discussing the whole mural and the items on it. Positive comments about the ways each child used materials will reinforce good work habits. Other classes or teachers or staff can be invited to see the finished masterpiece, and the class can spend some time looking at murals done by well-known artists. Some suggestions are works done by Ben Shahn and Diego Rivera.

Art South of the Border: Piñatas

Purpose/Rationale

This activity demonstrates ways of tying in art with a study of another culture, this time that of Mexico. It also provides an example of a papier-mâché activity. Papier-mâché, as art educators know, is a very inexpensive media that can be used to make a wide variety of things. By actually making a real piñata, the children are able to fully comprehend what one is and how the children in Mexico feel when they break the piñata and get the goodies inside.

Materials

Balloons, large	Paint shirts or smocks
Brushes, ½ inch (*c.* 1 cm) wide	Paper towels
Candy, individually wrapped	Tempera paint
Coffee cans with lids	Scissors
Containers for water and paint	Wheat paste or white glue and
Masking tape	water mixture
Old newspapers	

The hardware store can supply wheat paste. Mix it according to directions and add a few drops of disinfectant. This mixture can be kept for several days in covered coffee cans. The class can work directly from the cans. A substitute papier-mâché mixture can be made with equal parts white glue and water. This glue mixture is more expensive but does not shrink nor mold as does wheat paste. Paper towels may be used instead of newspaper. Because they do not have a printed surface, paper towels are easier to paint. Usually only one coat of paint is needed to cover the towels. It will probably take two coats of paint to cover newspapers.

Motivation

The activity itself should be sufficiently motivating. Knowing that a piñata is to be made with lots of candy inside will certainly spark any class. Pictures of piñatas may be helpful.

Procedure

After the class is motivated, demonstrate the procedure. First, a balloon is blown up. A large class can use more than one balloon and work in groups. The balloon is set in a shallow butter tub. Strips of newspapers about 2 inches wide are dipped in the wheat paste mixture.

If the newspapers get too saturated with the papier-mâché mixture, it will be difficult to cover the balloon. Point this out by showing the class strips with too little, too much, and just enough of the mixture. If there is too much on a strip, it can be slid off by pulling the strip between two fingers. If the balloon seems to be getting too wet, then add dry strips. The newspaper strips should be overlapped and crisscrossed. Sometimes using the analogy of bandaging the balloon will work. The balloon should be allowed to dry after the first wrapping.

When it is dry, turn up the balloon and pop it. Fill it with candy and cover the hole with newspaper strips and papier-mâché mixture. At this point, add facial features or other details to the balloon. This is done by adding a part of an egg carton or wads of newspaper for the eyes, ears, nose, etc. Tape these on and cover with papier-mâché. After the third coat is dried on the face, the piñata is painted with tempera paint. Variations on this procedure can be done by adding appendages to the balloon "head" to make a person or an animal. After the piñata is finished, it is hung and broken. This activity will take about two hours of class time. It will be best to work in several blocks of time so that the papier-mâché can dry between coats.

Adaptations

LEARNING DISABLED AND BEHAVIORALLY DISORDERED. To insure good working groups, all groups should be chosen by the teacher. If a child is really averse to getting his hands in the papier-mâché mixture, then do not push him. Have this child do other parts of the project such as tearing or cutting the newspapers. Set some ground rules before beginning so that the paste ends up in the right place.

HEARING IMPAIRED. The children may need help in inflating the balloon(s). After the piñata party, stories can be written about the experience. The breaking of the piñata may be a topic for a drawing activity.

RETARDED. A step-by-step procedure should be specified in demonstrating the papier-mâché process. Also, specific class rules about cleanup and who is to do what will be needed. If the child cannot follow the procedures, then he may have to watch the others and not participate. Emphasize that the mixture is to go only on the newspapers. Wheat paste will be the preferred mixture as it is nontoxic. In painting, a limited number of colors will be appreciated by the children who sometimes get overwhelmed by too many choices.

VISUALLY IMPAIRED. Discuss the papier-mâché process, and have several partially completed projects in various stages so that the child can examine each. Stress that getting one's hands in the paste is very much a part of the activity. Place a bell on the completed piñata to help those playing locate it.

PHYSICALLY HANDICAPPED. Assistance and teamwork will be needed to get the balloons blown up. Even the most severely handicapped child can participate by tearing the newspaper strips and sponging on paint. The balloon should be weighted down while being papier-mâchéd. Rocks can be put in the butter tub and the balloon taped to it with masking tape. Tempera paint should be as thick as cream so it will cover and not run too much. Then the children will be better able to control the paint. Fewer colors will also prevent the possible chaos resulting when children try to use many colors and they all run together.

Evaluation

POTENTIAL OUTCOMES. The child has learned how to papier-mâché. He has demonstrated a 90 percent or better mastery of the papier-mâché process. He has worked in a group and helped to make a piñata. He has learned more about Mexican culture in doing this and can explain how piñatas are made and how they are used. He has demonstrated he can cooperate in a group and share materials.

CLOSURE. The piñata should be hung up in the room for a day or so. Then, a party can be planned around breaking the piñata. A plan should be designed so that each child has a turn at trying to break the piñata. Some rules should be set up so that when the piñata does break, no one is hurt getting to the candy. Perhaps the candy can be equally divided afterwards so that each child will get his share.

REFERENCES

Art therapy training, information brochure. Houston: American Art Therapy Association, n.d.

Attitudes in science. *SCIS/material objects evaluation supplement,* The Regents of the University of California, 1972.

Berlyne, D. E. Recent developments in Piaget's work. In H. L. Wayne, Jr. (Ed.), *Current research in elementary school social studies.* New York: Macmillan, 1969.

Brandwein, P. F., Cooper, E. K., Blackwood, P. E., Horne, E. B., & Fraser, T. P. *Concepts in science: Red, green, blue.* New York: Harcourt, Brace, Jovanovich, 1972.

Buktenica, N. A. *Visual learning.* San Raphael, Calif.: Dimensions, 1968.

Dienez, Z. P. *Mathematics through the senses, games, dance and art.* Windser, Berks, Great Britain: N.F.E.R. Publishing Co., n.d.

Duckworth, E. Piaget rediscovered. *The Journal of Research in Science Teaching,* 1964, 2(3), 172-175.

Educational Development Center. *Elementary science study; chart and teacher's guide.* New York: McGraw-Hill, 1973.

Educational Development Center. *Elementary science study; light and shadows.* New York: McGraw-Hill, 1963.

Educational Development Center. *Elementary science study; match and measure.* New York: McGraw-Hill, 1969.

Educational Development Center. *Elementary science study; musical instrument recipe book.* New York: McGraw-Hill, 1968, 1971.

Educational Development Center. *Elementary science study; pattern blocks.* New York: McGraw-Hill, 1968, 1970.

Educational Development Center. *Elementary science study; printing.* New York: McGraw-Hill, 1969.

Educational Development Center. *Elementary science study; sand.* New York: McGraw-Hill, 1969, 1970.

Educational Development Center. *Elementary science study; the structures unit.* New York: McGraw-Hill, 1968, 1970.

Educational Development Center. *Elementary science study; teacher's guide for mapping.* New York: McGraw-Hill, 1968, 1971.

Educational Development Center. *Elementary science study; teacher's guide for tracks.* New York: McGraw-Hill, 1968.

Educational Development Center. *Elementary science study; the whistles and strings unit.* New York: McGraw-Hill, 1968, 1971.

Eicholz, R. E., Martin, E., Brumfiel, C. F., & Shanks, M. E. *Elementary school mathematics.* Menlo Park, Calif.: Addison-Wesley, 1971.

Eicholz, R. E., O'Daffer, P., Fleenor, C. R., & Burke, T. *Investigating school mathematics,* teacher's edition (Book 2). Menlo Park, Calif.: Addison-Wesley, 1973.

Ennever, L., & Harlen, W. *With objectives in mind. Science 5/13.* Bristol, England, Nuffield Foundation and The Scottish Education Department, Schools Council Publication, 1971.

Gibb, G., & Castanesa, A. Experiences for young children. In J. Payne, H. Hashman, & D. Wells (Eds.), *Mathematics learning in early childhood.* Reston, Va.: National Council of Teachers of Mathematics, Thirty-Seventh Yearbook, 1975.

Herrera, S., & Thier, H. D. *Beginnings; science curriculum improvement study, teacher's guide.* New York: Rand McNally, 1975.

Karplus, R., & Lawson, C. A. *Science curriculum improvement study, teacher's handbook.* Berkeley: The University of California, 1974.

Karplus, R., & Randle, J. C. *Interaction and systems.* Berkeley: Regents of the University of California; New York: Rand McNally, 1970.

Lansing, K. M. *Art, artists and art education.* New York: McGraw-Hill, 1969.

Lavatelli, C. S., Moore, W. J., & Kaltsouns, T. *Elementary school curriculum.* New York: Holt, Rinehart and Winston, 1972.

Mitchel, L. S. *Young geographers.* New York: Agathon Press, 1934.

Nelson, D., & Kirkpatrik, J. Problem solving. In N. Payne, H. Hashman, & D. Wells (Eds.), *Mathematics learning in early childhood,* Thirty-Seventh Yearbook. Reston, Va.: National Council of Teachers of Mathematics, 1975.

Nuffield Mathematics Project. *Environmental geometry.* New York: John Wiley, 1969.

Nuffield Mathematics Project. *Logic.* New York: John Wiley, 1972.

Nuffield Mathematics Project. *Mathematics: The first three years.* New York: John Wiley, 1970.

Quinn, T., & Hanks, C., (Eds.). *Coming to our senses; the significance of the arts for American education: A panel report.* J. D. Rockefeller, Jr., Chairman; The arts, education and Americans panel. New York: McGraw-Hill, 1977.

Rogers, R. E., & Voelker, A. M. Programs for improving science instruction in the elementary school; Part I, ess. In R. G. Good (Ed.) *Science children: Readings in elementary science education.* Dubuque: William C. Brown, 1972.

Randle, J., & Thier, H. *Material objects: Science curriculum improvement study teacher's guide.* Berkeley: Regents of the University of California; New York: Rand McNally, 1970.

Romney, W. *Inquiry techniques for teaching science.* New York: Prentice-Hall, 1968.

Sigel, I. E. A teaching strategy derived from some Piagetian concepts. In W. L. Herman, Jr. (Ed.), *Current research in elementary school social studies.* New York: Macmillan, 1969.

Spodek, B. Developing social studies concepts in the kindergarten. In W. L. Herman, Jr. (Ed.), *Current research in elementary school social studies.* New York: Macmillan, 1969.

Spodek, B. The role of materials in teaching social studies to young children. Unpublished manuscript, University of Illinois, 1968.

Trafton, P. The curriculum. In J. Payne, H. Hashman, & D. Wells (Eds.), *Mathematics learning in early childhood,* Thirty-Seventh Yearbook. Reston, Va.: National Council of Teachers of Mathematics, 1975.

Figure 122. Puppets enable the child to role play and act through many kinds of emotions and situations. They are a safe way of creating, expressing and verbalizing. They also are *great fun* to make! The teacher introduces the puppet making activity via a spoon puppet turkey. This is a good way of immediately involving and motivating a child.

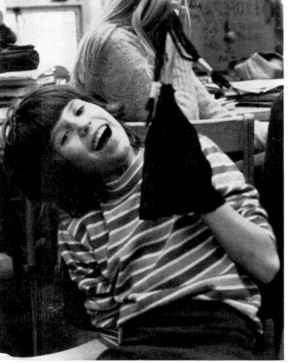

Figure 123. A ten-year-old cerebral palsied child shows her finished Indian spoon puppet. She has used a marker and drawn in the facial features. Yarn has been glued on for hair, and the puppet's dress has been tied on.

Figure 124. (Left) A teenage girl who is severely handicapped with cerebral palsy and cannot talk made this sack puppet. Just controlling the marker and some of the marks made was a major artistic triumph!

Figure 125. (Right) Cloth scraps were used for the "dressing" of this sack puppet done by a seven-year-old physically handicapped child. A mouse is one of her favorite animals.

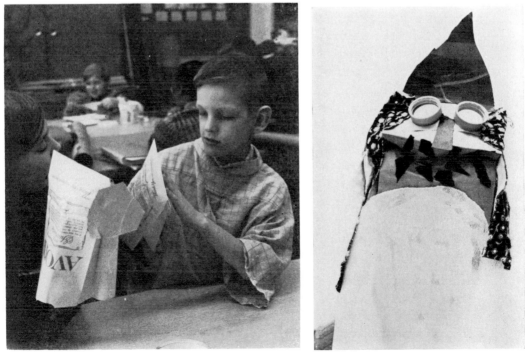

Figure 126. (Left) Playing with the puppets after they are made is an important part of the activity. Here, a seven-year-old hyperactive aphasic child plays with a classmate. During the half-hour art lesson he made four puppets using markers and construction paper scraps.

Figure 127. (Right) This witch puppet was made by an eight-year-old behaviorally disordered boy. He used discarded bottle tops for the eyes.

Figure 128. A seven-year-old deaf child shows the rabbit puppet she has made with a sack.

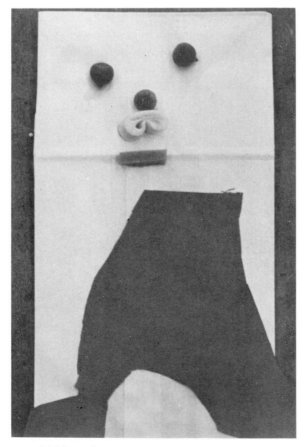

Figure 129. The nine-year-old blind child who made this sack puppet even cut out the trousers. He used seeds for the eyes and nose, a synthetic foam packing piece for the moustache, and a piece of foam rubber for the mouth.

Figure 130. A visually impaired six-year-old glues construction paper hair to her sack puppet.

Figure 131. A group of primary deaf children have an impromptu show after creating their sock puppets. Their eyes and facial expressions indicate that the children are really excited and very much involved in the activity.

PUPPETRY

Purpose/Rationale

Bring a puppet into the classroom, and learning is suddenly fun. Give a puppet to a child, and the play begins. Let a child make his own, and creative juices overflow in an outpouring of fantasy, fiction, and reality. Have a puppet show, and the child can try on many roles, become many types of persons, and think (and act) through some difficult situations. A shy child may become a bellowing giant. A belligerent child may become a friendly helper. Behind a puppet, the child expresses, communicates, and socializes. He laughs, cries, fights, sings, and rejoices. Puppets are a safe means of constructive, creative expression and verbalization. This happens no matter how simple or complex the puppet might be. Often, in fact, the simpler the puppet, the more direct and fresh the verbal communication and "play."

Stationary Puppets

Among the various types of stationary puppets there are finger puppets, drawn puppets, and spoon puppets. In each case, there is no moving part to the puppet itself. A finger puppet may be as simple as a face drawn on one finger with a pen or a marker. By simply making a cone of paper that fits on the finger and decorating the cone with markers or scraps of paper that are pasted on, more complicated finger puppets are created.

One variation on the finger puppet is to make an *O* with the index finger and the thumb. Eyes are drawn on the index finger and a mouth marked on the thumb. Hair can be added by putting some yarn between the index and middle finger. This *O* puppet is capable of movement by bending the thumb.

Puppets can be made by cutting out a figure the child has drawn and putting it on a short stick, tongue depressor, or toilet paper roll. If more durable figures are desired, puppets can be drawn on oak tag board or old file folders. The child may need help in cutting the cardboard.

Spoon puppets can be easily made from large plastic or wooden spoons. Faces can be marked with permanent markers and hair glued on with white glue. Scrap fabric can become the clothes by tying it on the spoon just below the head. The finger and *O* puppets will take about twenty minutes to make. The stick and spoon puppets will take about one-half hour to construct. Be sure to allow additional time for puppet shows.

Materials

Brush ½ inch (*c.* 1 cm) wide	Cloth scraps
Cardboard rolls from paper towels or toilet paper	Construction paper scraps
	Containers for water and paint

Hands and fingers

Masking tape

Old file folders

Old newspapers

Paint shirts and smocks

Scissors

Stapler

Tempera paint

Watercolor markers, some with wide tips

White glue in small bottles or pot pie tins with ½ inch (*c.* 1 cm) brushes

Wooden spoons

Yarn scraps

The list covers items needed for all kinds of stationary puppets. Items for specific kinds of puppets will be chosen from this list.

Motivation

Use one or two puppets to introduce the lesson. Explain that these puppets need some friends. Or, puppets can be made for a story the class is reading.

Puppets That Move

Among the simpler puppets that move are sack and sock puppets. In both cases, a simple grasping movement is necessary to work the puppets. Such action in a puppet is often more exciting and stimulating both to the creator and to an audience than is a stationary puppet.

These puppets can be very simple artistic statements. If the child does not have the attention span or fine motor skills to sew or to cut and paste on features, he can draw on the desired features and details.

Sack puppets will take between fifteen minutes and one-half hour to make (depending on the materials used). The sock puppets will take a little longer to make. Plan for enough time to have a puppet show.

Materials

Buttons

Cloth scraps

Needle and thread

Old newspapers

Paper scraps of various kinds

Paper towels

Pipe cleaners

Sacks, slightly larger than the child's hand

Scissors

Seeds

Socks, old, some with light colors

Synthetic foam packing pieces that can be marked on.

Watercolor markers, and some permanent ones for drawing on socks

White glue in small bottles or small pot pie tins with ½ inch (*c.* 1 cm) brushes

Yarn scraps

Usually grocery stores will willingly donate sacks. Selectively choose from this list after reading the adaptations and discussion that follow.

techniques but who still have a great desire and need for a constructive, creative outlet. The camera solves the technical problems of illustration and leaves the most important issues of design, communication, and type of message in the domain of the person behind the lens.

Cameras are now within the economic means of many, and even class-rooms may be able to acquire simple cameras. Cameras can be used collectively to illustrate class stories and events. Communication skills can be increased via photography. The whole area of nonverbal communication can be a topic of study. Questions such as the following might be asked: How do we express ourselves without words? What does one picture communicate? What kind of story can be told in just four pictures? Ten? Soon it will become fairly easy to tell when one or more photographs in a sequence successfully communicate an idea. This kind of nonverbal series can also be done using a storyboard mockup or series of stick-figure sketches or magazine photos.

Camera Adaptation[*]

This camera adaptation was developed to enable physically handicapped students to take pictures. It accommodates a simple camera. The dimensions of the holder can be shifted to almost any simple instant-loading camera. It is so conceived that a child with functional use of only one hand can become a photographer (Fig. 132).

Materials

Aluminum or copper conduit; ⅝ inch (*c*. 1.56 cm) telescoping tubing, 10 inches (*c*. 25 cm) long; ½ inch (*c*. 1 cm) telescoping tubing, 6 inches (*c*. 15 cm) long

Copper T fitting, ⅝ inch (*c*. 1.56 cm)

Keychain and plastic belt, 1 inch (*c*. 2 cm) wide and 1 foot (*c*. 1 m) longer than child's waist

Loop and pin with blunt point

Acrylic sheeting (Plexiglas®) 5 inches by 5 inches by ⅛ inch thick (*c*. 12 cm by 12 cm by 3 mm)

Sheet metal, 24 gauge (*c*. 1.93 mm), 8 by 4¾ inches (*c*. 20 by 12 cm) for camera box

Sheet metal, 18 gauge (*c*. 1.44 mm), 2 pieces; 1 by 14 inches (*c*. 2 by 35 cm) for shoulder straps

With different makes of cameras, the dimensions of the 24 gauge sheet metal box will change, since the camera fits into the metal box. A plumber's supply store can provide the materials.

---

[*] The camera adaptation was conceived by the author and constructed by Gary McKinley. Two modifications in the support structure were added by Bruce Horne.

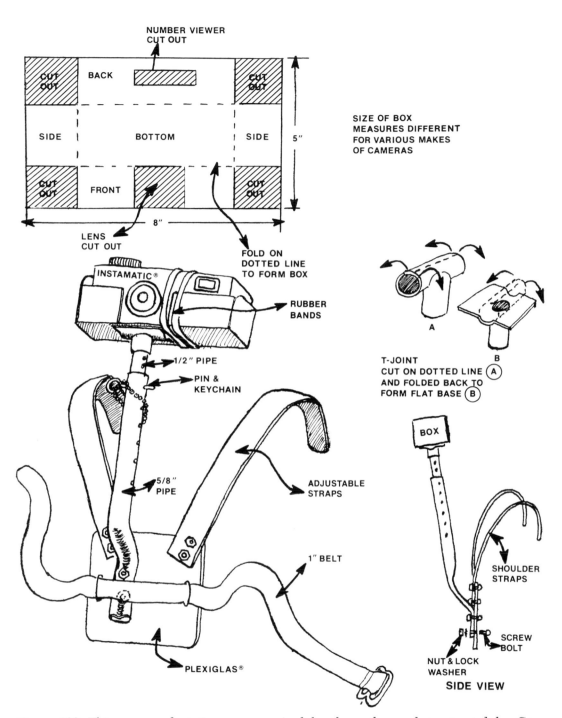

Figure 132. This camera adaptation was conceived by the author and constructed by Gary McKinley. This rendering was made by Bruce Horne and is reproduced by permission from Goodwin, P., Spurgeon, J., Wills, J., and Woodson, B. (Eds.), *Adaptive Media and Functional Devices for the Physically Handicapped*, Normal, Ill.: Students and faculty in Education of the Physically Handicapped, Illinois State University. Project No. 600-05, Illinois State University Mid-Central Association Center for Research and Development in Education of the Handicapped, 1975.

Procedure

1. Cut 24 gauge sheet metal as per drawing (dimensions may vary to fit the camera being used). File and smooth edges.
2. Bend and fold, then braze corners to form a box to fit camera.
3. Split top of copper T fitting lengthwise, fold back, and braze to underside of box (see drawing).
4. Insert ½ inch pipe into ⅝ inch pipe. Drill ⅛ inch holes through both at 1 inch intervals. (Size of hole may vary to fit pin).
5. Crimp and bend bottom of ½ inch pipe (see drawing).
6. Flatten 3½ inches of ⅝ inch pipe with a hammer.
7. Make a 45 degree bend (A) 2 inches from flattened end.
8. Bend again slightly (B) 1½ inches from previous bend to form a reverse curve (approximately 75 degrees).
9. Drill two ³⁄₁₆ inch holes in flattened end of pipe at ¾ inch and 1¾ inch.
10. Round and sand corners and edges of acrylic sheeting.
11. Drill first hole in exact center of acrylic sheeting 1¾ inch from top. Second hole should be drilled after ⅝ inch pipe has been screwed into plastic. Use bottom hole of pipe as template for second hole.
12. Drill second and third set of holes 1 inch on either side of center holes.
13. In lower part of acrylic sheeting, make two 1 inch slots ½ inch from each side. (Drill series of holes and smooth out with coping saw.)
14. Round and sand top corner edges of shoulder straps.
15. Clamp one end of both shoulder straps to plastic at a 15 degree angle. Drill two ¾ inch holes ¾ inch apart through both metal and plastic. Fasten with ¾ inch nut and bolt assembly with lock washers.
16. Bend tops of shoulder straps to fit over child's shoulders.
17. Fasten keychain through loop end pin. Slip keychain over bent pipe section.
18. Slide ½ inch pipe section into ⅝ inch section and adjust to eye height of student. Insert pin through holes.
19. Hold camera in box with one or two heavy-duty rubber bands.

Variations

Bent pipe may be placed either on the right or left set of holes in the stomach pad for right or left eye/handed students. Several holes may be made to fit on the tubing if it is planned to use more than one camera. An automatic camera that does not have to be turned is desirable, although any camera may be used. This device may also be adapted to fit on a wheelchair (see drawing).*

---

* Reproduced by permission from Goodwin, P., J. Spurgeon, J. Wills & B. Woodson (Eds.), *Adaptive Media and Functional Devices for the Physically Handicapped.* Normal, Ill.: Students and Faculty in Education of the Physically Handicapped, Illinois State University. Project No. 600-05, Illinois State University Mid-Central Association Center for Research and Development in Education of the Handicapped, 1975.

Figures 133 and 134. A tremendous experience awaits any child who makes his own slides by drawing on acetate. Seeing these drawings enlarged on the screen is also a great thrill. These two slides were drawn by two cerebral palsied teenagers. They used permanent markers and drew on larger pieces of acetate. Then, they decided which part of these larger drawings they wanted for their slides. An aide helped to mount the slides. The bold line qualities in these slides is reminiscent of work by Abstract Expressionist painters such as Franz Kline.

133

134

Figure 135. The child can also draw directly on a premounted clear acetate slide. Here, a hearing impaired seven-year-old boy drew a car.

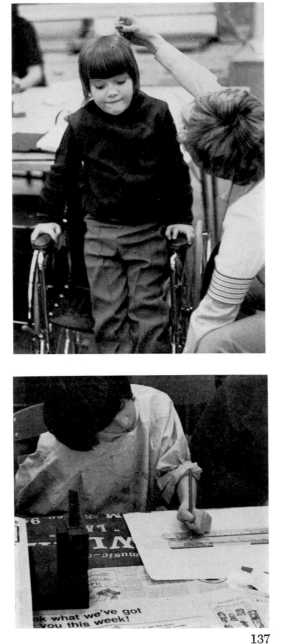

Figure 136. Drawing on film has some of the same excitement as slidemaking. Children, no matter how involved, can make some kind of mark on the acetate. An important part of the activity comes when the lights dim and the "world premiere" is shown. Here, a primary physically handicapped child stands up so that a length of film that is her height can be measured. Making a film that is as tall as the child creates added interest and relates the activity more to the individual. The "old" film has been recycled by soaking in bleach, which lifts the emulsion.

137   138

Figure 137. A drawing guide made with two rulers taped to a white piece of paper helps this intermediate physically handicapped child draw on her length of film. Narrow, felt-tipped *permanent* markers are best for this kind of drawing.

Figure 138. A five-year-old visually impaired, multiply handicapped child works on her film. Since white paper may produce a harsh glare, another color is used.

Photography Without a Camera

The activities that follow are all related to photography and are presented in a sequence progressing to more involved and complex activities. This does not imply that they are to be always or only used in this order. Such decisions must be made with care, and the types of student and the particular learning situations must be considered.

SLIDE MAKING

Purpose/Rationale

It is fun to draw. It is exciting to see those drawings displayed. Imagine the astonishment which a child has when he sees his drawing enlarged over fifty times and projected on a screen. It is a tremendous experience in affirmation. The child probably will not stop with only one slide. If the experience begins with a challenge to discover what happens when certain items are projected (such as overlapping tissue papers, paper clips, or rubber bands), few children can resist. These children will be studying about art and doing important scientific discovery as well.

Materials

Acetate or used film	Permanent markers (alcohol base
Aluminum pie tins	or waterproof)
Brushes, old ones, or sticks wrapped	Rubber cement
with small pieces of cloth	Rulers
Cellophane scraps	Scissors
Cellophane tape	Screen or white surface for pro-
Hole puncher	jecting
Iron	Slide mounts
Old newspapers	Slide projectors
Paint shirts or smocks	Strong soap solution or strong
Paper clips	bleach
Paper towels	Tissue paper scraps

Acetate can be recycled film or used overhead transparencies. These can be provided by the school media center or a local camera supplier. Slide mounts can be cut from thin cardboard, made from used file folders, or purchased at a camera store.

Motivation

With younger children, keep the activity a surprise. Have the class draw on premounted slides, and then slip these homemade slides into a group of commercially made slides and project them. After the surprise showing, more slides can be made by the children.

For older students, the activity can be tied into ecology and the recycling of used film (see procedure section). The activity may also be centered around producing a light show. Several images can be projected using several slide projectors; taped music or sound effects can also be created for the show.

Procedure

If used film is to be recycled, clean it in a strong soap solution or (preferably) bleach. Leave the acetate soaking for awhile, or let the students clean it by using old brushes or rags wrapped around a twig. Direct contact with the strong bleach solution should be avoided. (A friendly talk with the janitor may produce some institutional-strength bleach.) Students should be aware of what happens when bleach spills on clothes. In fact, that may be a part of the lesson. The acetate should be thoroughly rinsed and dried.

There are basically two ways to approach the activity. The students may begin by drawing directly on larger sheets of the acetate. These can be used as is with an overhead projector. Different kinds of permanent markers and colored pencils may be used. Let the child experiment and determine what drawing material he prefers.

Then, the student can work on the smaller scale of a 2 by 2 inch slide. Acetate that is premounted in the slide mounts can be used. Or, the student can draw on a larger piece of acetate. Then, by moving the slide window around his drawing, he selects the area he prefers for mounting.

The size of the acetate piece must be *slightly* larger than the slide window (so it will not fall through). The best size is 1½ by 1¾ inches. This size will sit inside the slide mount but will not touch the glue border. Next, iron the slide that is sandwiched between two pieces of newspaper. The iron should be on a hot setting. Rotate the iron for about thirty seconds. Finally, project the slides which the class has made.

If a group desires, divide them into teams. They can create their own series of slides or illustrate a story from a selected list which has emerged in class discussion.

Finally, experimental slides can be made by sandwiching bits of different papers, punched holes, and trails of rubber cement between a folded piece of acetate that is 2¾ by 1½ inches.

It should take about fifteen minutes to do the drawing. Another fifteen minutes will be needed if the class is also mounting the slides. Some time will be needed for viewing the completed work.

Adaptations

LEARNING DISABLED. This activity will assist in developing figure-ground perceptual skills. Once projected, the images can be discussed and figures can be clearly seen. If the slide area is too small for some students, they can use larger pieces of acetate and project these by using the overhead projector. Those students with short attention spans will probably draw several slides in one short work period. Slide topics may be placed in a box, and each child can go and choose one.

BEHAVIORALLY DISORDERED. When students understand the process, have them make some slides individually. Then, divide the class into groups and have them work together on a project. A list of suggested stories or ideas may help the groups get started. Consider ways that sound effects can be incorporated into the activity.

HEARING IMPAIRED. Each child can try writing or telling a story by incorporating groups of slides which the class has already made. As with other art activities, key vocabulary words should be stressed. Some words might be *slide, projector, series, illustrate, acetate,* and *bleach*. Explain what happens when bleach gets on clothes. A demonstration will probably be most effective.

RETARDED. Present a step-by-step demonstration of how slides are made. Many examples will help. Stress the concept that the image projected is indeed the same image that is drawn on the acetate. It may help to work on the larger acetate and use the overhead projector. Those students who have the fine motor skills can then draw in the smaller slide area. If they cannot draw specific images, encourage them to explore lines and colors. The mounting and ironing process may be too hard for those students with less developed motor skills. Have these children draw on acetate that is already mounted in the slide mount.

VISUALLY IMPAIRED. Contrasting colors of markers should be used. Have the student draw abstractly. Do not give undue emphasis to drawing representationally unless the child really desires to do this. Place the acetate on a light background so the lines drawn can easily be seen. It is doubtful if the totally blind child will benefit from this activity. If a light show is planned, he can help with sound effects.

PHYSICIALLY HANDICAPPED. Whether the student works on a large piece of acetate or a premounted acetate slide, it should be taped on the top of a white surface. The markers may have to be thickened by using a piece of foam rubber attached with a rubber band for easier grasping.

A more "abstract expressionistic" approach to the drawing can be encouraged. Show examples of this kind of painting by Abstract Expressionist painters such as Franz Kline, Willem deKooning, and Jackson Pollock. Then project slides done by the students. In this way, the students can more fully appreciate the truly dynamic expressive qualities of lines in these paintings and compare them with their own slide drawings.

Evaluation

POTENTIAL OUTCOMES. The child has made or drawn at least one slide. He can explain or demonstrate the whole process involved with 80 percent or more accuracy. He has learned to simplify an idea into one slide or a series of up to five. He has studied the work of at least one Abstract Expressionist painter and can compare the lines in these famous art works with lines made in slides by the class. He has spent time looking at each student's work on the screen and expressed a verbal reaction to it (named colors, described lines, compared thicknesses of lines, or expressed a preference for colors and lines).

CLOSURE. The slide show can be enlarged and sounds created and incorporated. The class can make up a story to go with the slides as they are projected on the screen. This becomes a real test of creative thinking. Another group can be invited to view the show. The class can illustrate a well-known story or one they created themselves by using handmade slides.

MOTION BOOKS

Purpose/Rationale

Can the child draw identifiable images? Can he plan ahead? Can he analyze? All these abilities are reinforced in making motion books.

Does the child like magical things? Most children do. If being the creator of a motion picture or a picture or image that moves sounds exciting, then motion books will be fun to make. Motion books will also lead into the more complicated process of film making.

The activity requires planning and thought. A student must really think about motion, analyze it, and break this motion into its simplest parts. He must be more observant of the world around him. He also has to think more carefully about the placement of images on a page and the proportion of these images.

Materials

Index cards, 3 by 5 inches (*c.* 7 by 12 cm), 10 to 20 per student
Pencils
Stapler
Watercolor markers or crayons

Drawing paper cut to the 3 by 5 inch (*c.* 7 by 12 cm) size may be substituted for the index cards. Carbon paper can be used to assist in drawing multiple copies of the same image.

Motivation

Begin with a series of questions. State that the class is going to make a picture move. That may seem magical. Some examples of finished motion books will probably be the most immediate means of motivation. After showing these, ask the group to describe how some things move. For example: What does the sun look like when it is going down? How do we know that it is setting? How do we know when a glass is being filled with water?

The class can do some movement activities themselves. They can jump, walk, or bend over in slow motion or in ten or fifteen movement steps. These steps then will be the individual parts or images for the motion book. The group can make a list of other things that show movement. The examples must be simple. Suggestions for the list might be a ball bouncing, leaves falling to the ground, someone jumping, the sun rising, a snake moving across the ground, or a name or word being written.

Older students will probably appreciate a discussion of animation. A motion picture is a series of still pictures that is shown in quick succession. The first motion pictures were a series of progress drawings that were put on a cylinder and rotated.

Procedure

The key to this activity is the choice of a simple topic to be animated. The student must have the persistence to repeat the image ten to fifteen times with only slight changes. Carbon paper can be used to make multiple images. The cards should be numbered when the sequence is finished. Sometimes it helps to set the cards out to check on their sequence before they are stapled.

Keep the drawing of the image on the half of the page that will be *away* from the stapled side. The changes in position or size of the image depicted should not be too great. The emphasis is on gradual, not abrupt change. After the drawing is complete, order the cards and staple on the edge opposite the images. The motion book is then flipped either forward or backwards in the hand. The activity should take about an hour to complete. If interest and time permit, more than one book might be made.

Adaptations

LEARNING DISABLED. This activity will facilitate the child's visual sequencing abilities. It will also assist him in analyzing and visualizing movement and motion. Have the children do some movement exercises before beginning. Actually dramatizing the simple images will help the child analyze the movement sequence that he will include in his motion book. After the initial motion books are made, more complicated ideas can be tried.

BEHAVIORALLY DISORDERED. Repeating an image can be a welcome task. Or, it can become very frustrating for this child. Be alert to both of these possibilities. Provide a list of simple ideas and suggestions. This may reduce any anxiety the child might have in choosing a subject. Include enough items on the list to enable each student to work on a different idea. The students may work in pairs on this activity.

HEARING IMPAIRED. This would be a good opportunity to develop some action or movement vocabulary. Some examples follow: A ball *bounces,* the sun *rises,* a glass is *filled,* and a flower *grows.* Several completed books should help explain the idea. Emphasize that each child must have a different subject for his book. These can be listed on the chalkboard. Some ideas can be placed in a hat, and the child may choose from these.

RETARDED. This activity is more appropriate for older, brighter students. As with the hearing impaired students, vocabulary building throughout the activity will be an important objective. Less complex images and ideas will be easier to draw. Something as simple as a found object print may be used instead of having the student draw the same image repeatedly. However, the student might enjoy drawing the same image several times with slight variations.

VISUALLY IMPAIRED. Highly contrasting colors should be used. Fluorescent crayons are a possible solution. Students can use larger size images and cards. The totally blind child may not fully grasp the motion book concept, and it is not recommended for him.

PHYSICALLY HANDICAPPED. It may help to work on heavier, larger size paper. Oak tag board or file folder cardboard would be preferable to drawing paper. If the student has difficulty drawing, torn paper or magazine pictures can be used instead. The magazine pictures may even be reproduced by means of a photocopier. Then, one image such as a drawn line or a piece of construction paper can be added. An alternative to photocopying the picture might be to collect several copies of the same issue of a magazine for use. Another means of repeating the same image is to have the student print an image with a found object. The position of this printed image is changed slightly in each subsequent "frame" of the motion book.

Evaluation

POTENTIAL OUTCOMES. The child has grasped the concept of moving pictures and made a motion book. The book shows his ability to analyze the separate motions or movements of an item with 75 percent or more accuracy. After completing the initial book, the child will be able to produce at least one other idea for a second book. His interest has been maintained during his repetition of the several drawings necessary. His first drawing is as carefully executed as the last, thus demonstrating continued interest.

CLOSURE. The class can trade their completed books and take time to view all of them. They can write a story to go with the book or can make a whole series of motion books based on a single theme that might be the start of a motion picture, i.e. a longer motion book.

FILMMAKING

Purpose/Rationale

It is a fantastic experience to see one's drawing enlarged and projected on the screen. It is even more exciting to create an image that actually moves. Combine these two experiences by drawing on actual film and projecting it to see what happens. Excitement, chills, exclamations of "Wow! Gee, did I do that?" or dead silence—all of this may happen and more. This kind of an exhilarating, heady experience is one each person needs, especially very special children.

Some planning may be needed in determining desired lengths of film. The initial experiments will not need a lot of preplanning. Later efforts will need more thought and even some mathematical ability to determine the desired lengths of film in relationship to the time that the images are seen. Do not let such calculations bog down the important expressive efforts.

Materials

Aluminum pie tins	Popcorn for premiere
Cellophane tape	Rags
Film projector	Rulers
Masking tape	Scissors
Old newspapers	Sixteen millimeter film
Paint shirts or smocks	Sticks wrapped with rags, or old brushes
Paper towels	
Permanent markers, or alcohol base ones	Strong soap or strong bleach
	Takeup reel

The film can be scrounged from the athletic department in the school district. Ask for old game film.

Motivation

Have several pieces of film for the children to see. This film can be projected first, and then the students can examine it closely. Thus, they can see the separate images in the separate frames that make up the film. This might be related to the motion book concept. Explain that the class will recycle film, and each child is going to make his own film. It may be additionally motivating for each child to draw on a length of film that is as long as he is tall.

Perhaps it is best for younger children to just explore line quality and color and not try to draw on *each* separate frame. Older children may want to actually draw images in each frame. Challenge older children to try to communicate a feeling with images only. If this is too abstract, have them try some simple concepts like those drawn in the motion books. Also, the group can try to illustrate a common saying, song line, poem, or proverb such as "Bingo," "Happiness (a smiling face) is (=) an ice cream cone (a circle drawn on top of a large 'V')," or "Sadness (a frowning face) is (=) a rainy day (a cloud with 'rain' drawn from its base)." Plan a world premiere after the project is completed, and invite other classes or parents to attend.

Procedure

Recycle the film by soaking it in a strong bleach solution. The process can be speeded up by wrapping a piece of rag around a twig and rubbing the emulsion off. A flat, wide old pan or can that can be discarded is best to use for the bleach solution. Rinse bleached film in water and dry it. Avoid bending the film. (A film *leader* does not need to be cleaned. Scratch into the leader by using a straight pin or paper clip.) A large amount of film can be cleaned first, or it can be measured off for each child's height. Then, each child can help clean his own section of the film.

Set up a special work area for the younger filmmaker. To do this, tape two rulers down on a white piece of paper. The rulers should be just far enough apart so that the film can be pulled through as each section is completed (see Fig. 137). Perhaps the images should be mostly abstract lines and color patterns. In this way, the child will not be forced to stay in the small confines of each frame.

An older group with fairly well-developed fine motor skills can draw images on each frame. If this is to be done, outline several frame sizes in black on white paper. Instead of pulling the film through a ruler arrangement, pin the film to the cardboard (placed under the paper) using the sprocket holes. One frame is as wide as two sprocket holes.

The same image must be repeated in ten or more frames before changing it in any way. Twenty-four frames will make seven inches of film, and two feet of film will make three seconds of viewing if the film is projected at normal sound speed. At this speed, thirty-six feet of film will result in one minute of viewing. When the projector is running on slow motion, it takes twenty-seven feet of film to produce one minute of viewing.

It is generally too complicated to incorporate actual words onto the film. However, if this is desired, work with the film sprockets on the left. When finished, flip the film over so that the sprockets are on the right and thread the film counterclockwise on the reel from the bottom. If there are no words to be written on the film, mark the beginning of each piece of film the child is using with a piece of masking tape. The starting point of each part will have the sprockets on the right-hand side. Splice together each child's section of film by using cellophane tape. The film should not overlap too much, and the tape should not cover any sprocket holes. Be sure to allow about five feet of film leader to thread into the projector.

It will take about one-half hour to clean the film. If only abstract lines are drawn, it will take about one-half hour. If individual frames are drawn in, more than an hour might be needed.

LEARNING DISABLED. If the student is going to draw images on a frame-by-frame basis, experiment and explore with a shorter piece of film first. It may help to have the student plan ideas on a story board first.

BEHAVIORALLY DISORDERED. Have these students do an abstract film. Trying to draw in the small area of each frame may be too frustrating. Have the students create sound effects and a possible story line to accompany the film.

HEARING IMPAIRED. Most will have the drawing skills to add images in each frame. Experiment with a short piece of film first. If students need help with some topics, an idea taken from their motion books or some story they have been reading in social studies can be used. If they are to illustrate such a story, it may help to work in teams.

RETARDED. Have these students explore colors and lines on their lengths of film. Working in the small frame areas may be too difficult or frustrating unless the students are older and have developed motor skills and conceptual abilities.

VISUALLY IMPAIRED. Provide one or two highly contrasting colors for them to use in their overall abstract drawing. Encourage the development of sound effects or original music to accompany the film. The totally blind child probably will not be able to relate to the actual filmmaking. He can help with the sound effects, however.

PHYSICALLY HANDICAPPED. The guides provided by the two rulers will enable even the most involved child to mark on the film. The marker may have to be thickened with foam rubber so that it can be easily grasped. Making a film piece as long as the child is tall will be particularly motivating, especially to those who are confined to wheelchairs.

Evaluation

POTENTIAL OUTCOMES. The child has demonstrated his knowledge of the filmmaking process by drawing his own segment of film. He has measured his height and made a section of film that length. If he is drawing on individual frames, he has accurately figured the correct length of the film and repeated his images ten times before changing them.

CLOSURE. A world premiere might be held and all film spliced together shown. Sound effects and/or a story narrative can be added. After this pre-

liminary experience, a larger group film project might be planned and executed. If there is video equipment available, the filmmakers can learn to
use it and videotape some planned sequences that they dramatize themselves.

Figure 139. Two primary physically handicapped children explore the medium of printing. Large, easily grasped objects are being used. The girl, who is seven years old, is evaluating the designs she made with a potato.

Figure 140. This cerebral palsied eight-year-old boy is experimenting with the kinds of patterns that can be made with a piece of scrap wood. To his left is a "stamp pad" made by folding two or three paper towels in the center of an aluminum pie pan and then pouring tempera paint on top.

Figure 141. A six-year-old deaf boy glues different thicknesses of yarn to a large tin can that has both ends cut out.

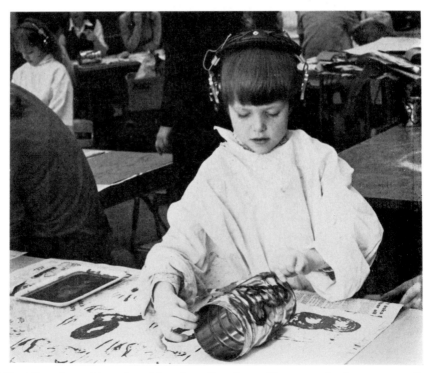

Figure 142. After the white glue dries (usually about 40 minutes), the can is rolled in tempera paint and wrapping paper is printed by rolling the can across the page.

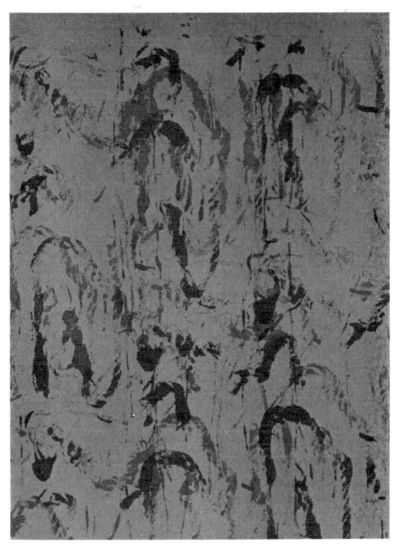

Figure 143. More than one color has been used on this printed wrapping paper. The paint is rinsed off the tin can before it is rolled in another color.

Figure 144. A string print can also be made by painting a flat piece of cardboard with white glue. This cerebral palsied child has found her own best working position.

Figure 145. If the child has limited use of her hands, pieces of yarn can be dropped on the glued surface. By placing a piece of waxed paper on top of the cardboard and rubbing, the yarn can be pressed down to insure the glue will hold it. After the glue dries in about an hour, the printing plate can be inked with water base printer's ink by using a brayer. Prints can then be made on construction paper.

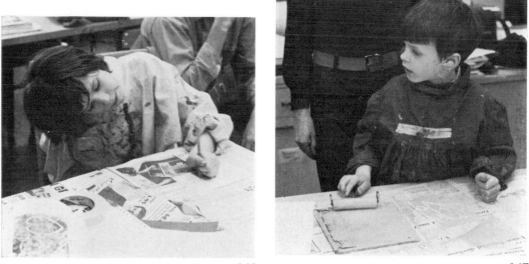

Figure 146. Another simple kind of printing is done by drawing with a dull pencil into a piece of styrofoam or a beadboard meat tray as is being done by this eleven-year-old physically handicapped girl.

Figure 147. Next, water base printer's ink is put on an easily washed surface such as a piece of metal, cardboard, or wood. A brayer is used to spread the ink and to ink the meat tray printing surface.

Figure 148. Finally, paper is placed on top of the printing surface and it is rubbed with a clean part of the hand or a clean brayer. Two finished valentine prints by this eight-year-old deaf boy can be seen on the left.

Figure 149. This is a print by a six-year-old physically handicapped boy. He has drawn a tree and a house.

PRINTMAKING
Purpose/Rationale

Making one drawing is fun and exciting. Printing two or five or ten of the same drawn image is really exciting. Making cards or stationery with messages in them is even more fun. Giving these cards can say and mean a lot of things. When a child gives a printed card he has made, something may be written inside, but mainly it says, "Hey, look at what I did. I can do something that is good and fun. I can give it away to someone I like without having to say aloud 'I like you.' " All of this is part of the experience of printmaking. All through the process, a lot of art learning is happening also.

The sections that follow discuss monoprinting and three kinds of relief printing. These are but a *few* of many kinds of printmaking. They are, however, some of the most direct and least complicated of the printing processes. Most special children can master at least one of these processes. Once the child has mastered these, some of the more complicated processes, such as linoleum, woodcut, or silk screen printing, might be tried.

As elsewhere, a sequence of printmaking ideas, materials, and processes is discussed. An attempt is made to progress from the less difficult to the more complex. Some simple printmaking has already been discussed in Chapter IV in conjunction with the discussion of the development of body-concepts. The following activities might be extensions of those foot- and handprinting activities.

Motivation

In most cases, a simple demonstration of the printing processes will provide much of the motivation. Many examples of finished prints *briefly* shown will also provide motivation. Tie in the printing activity with some holiday. Christmas, Easter, Hanukkah, Mother's Day, or Father's Day are obvious times to make prints, since cards can be made from these prints.

Prints can also be used to create wrapping papers, wallpapers, and stationery. Prints can illustrate poems and stories and can decorate fronts of homemade books or folders. Finally, prints can enhance tee shirts and hand towels, table mats, handkerchiefs and scarves. (If printing is to be done on fabric, textile inks should be used.)

Monoprinting
Materials

Construction paper in various sizes and colors
Containers for water and paint
Cookie sheet or easily cleaned counter or desk top
Old newspapers

Paint shirts or smocks
Paper towels
Sponges and water for cleaning

Tempera paint, thickened like cream, or *water base* printing ink
Watercolor markers

Procedure

Mark off the surface area with masking tape so that the child knows the limits of his printing surface. If a baking pan is used, the raised sides will provide such limits. Let the child choose one or two colors with which to work. Put a small amount of paint or ink on the printing surface. Scratch into this surface with a stick, finger, or paint brush handle. Place a sheet of construction paper on top of the design, and rub with clean hands.

Generally, only one print results from this process. After each print, new paint or ink usually needs to be added. Sometimes a second print can be made from the same design. Often a sprinkle of water on the design will help keep the paint and/or ink from drying out too quickly. The monoprints are left to dry and then made into cards or displayed as pictures. This type of printing will take about one-half hour to do.

Stamp Printing With Found Objects

Materials

Aluminum pie tins
Found objects such as bones, spools, pencil erasers, wood pieces, jar lids, bottle tops, etc. (5 per child)
Construction paper in assorted colors, 9 by 12 inches (*c.* 22 cm by 30 cm)

Newsprint, 9 by 12 inches (*c.* 22 cm by 30 cm) or larger
Paint shirts or smocks
Paper towels
Old newspapers
Tempera paint

Make a stamp pad by setting a pad of paper towels into aluminum pie tins and pouring tempera paint on them.

Procedure

The collection of the found objects is an important part of this activity. Encourage the children to do this themselves and to bring in all sorts of items. Have the class sort and classify various items in terms of types of categories. Some categories might be textures, shapes, different kinds of wood or bones, etc. In this way, science concepts can be integrated with the activity. The group may think of some other way of sorting the items.

Begin by just experimenting. Have the class make a variety of different prints by using the tops, edges, and sides of the found objects. Then perhaps try some other prints of found objects.

Solve some specific problems: use only two colors and one found object from the same category in a print, or use only one color and three found objects from the same category in a print. Also, probably no more than two colors should be used in the same print. In this way, structure is established for the total activity, and aesthetic harmony is also incorporated in the prints produced. Encourage the group in subsequent lessons to try creating various repetitive patterns in their prints. Experimenting with the basic found object printing should take about one-half hour. Another thirty minutes or more will be needed if other printing problems are given.

STRING PRINTING

Materials

Aluminum pie tins, large
Brayers, 4 inch (*c.* 10 cm)
Brushes, ½ inch (*c.* 1 cm) for glue
Cardboard, about 5 by 7 inches (*c.* 7 by 17 cm)
Construction paper in various colors, larger than cardboard
Containers for water and glue
Cookie sheet, baking pan, or piece of wood or cardboard for inking surface

Old newspapers
Paint shirts or smocks
Paper towels
String and yarn scraps
Tempera paint
Tin cans
Water base printer's ink
White glue in small pot pie tins

Omit the tin cans and tempera paint if the cardboard and string prints are to be made.

Procedure

In this process, a printing *plate* (relief surface) is made by brushing white glue onto cardboard or different sizes of tin cans. String and/or yarn is placed on the glued surface. The cans and cardboard are left to dry overnight. The cardboard plate is perhaps best for making cards, while the tin can plate is best for overall designs such as those needed in making wrapping paper.

The cardboard plate is inked with *water base* printer's ink. Squeeze out the ink onto the baking pan, cookie sheet, or wood and spread it with the brayer. Then ink the cardboard with the brayer. Pick up the cardboard and turn it over on top of the construction paper. This is then pressed and rubbed. Or, place the construction paper on *top* of the inked cardboard and rub. Some experimentation will quickly indicate which way is best for each child's particular print. If simple words are desired, put them on the cardboard *backwards.* If the children do not understand the backwards writing, write words in after the print is made.

In tin can printing, tempera paint is put in wide pie tins and the tin cans with yarn glued on them are rolled in the paint. Experiment to determine the optimal thickness of the paint. Next, roll the tin can on the construction paper, making a continuous pattern. Thick yarn makes the best prints because the yarn is more absorbent and holds more paint. It will take two separate half-hour periods to complete either of these printing activities.

BEADBOARD MEAT TRAY PRINTS

Materials

Brayers, 4 inches (*c*. 10 cm) wide
Beadboard meat trays, 1 per child, plus a few extras
Cookie sheet, baking pan, cardboard, or wood for inking surface
Old newspapers
Paint shirts or smocks

Paper towels
Pencils
Scissors
Soap and water
Water base printer's ink, 2 or 3 colors in 1 inch by 4 inch (37 cc) tubes

Printer's ink comes in large 1½ inch by 6 inch (155 cc) tubes. Buying in larger quantities may be cheaper, but the ink may dry out before it is all used. Beadboard meat trays look like styrofoam.

Procedure

Collect beadboard meat trays from the local grocery or in a recycling drive at school. The trays should have all edges trimmed off before starting. The surface of the meat tray should be smooth, with no indentations or brand names. Any indentation will show up in the final print. The design of the print is drawn with a pencil on the surface of the meat tray, which becomes the printing plate. Whatever is marked with the pencil will show up as a white outline in the print. The pencil should not be too sharp, and the child should not press down too hard on the plate with it.

Next, the ink is squeezed onto the baking pan, piece of wood, or cookie sheet. Spread this ink out with a brayer, and then ink the printing plate with it. A good covering of ink is recommended. Next, lay the print paper on top of the plate and rub thoroughly with the back of the hands or a clean brayer.

Another way of transferring the plate is to turn the inked plate over and put it on top of the paper that is to be printed. Lining up the plate with the paper is easier than placing the paper on top of the plate. Trim the print paper after it is printed. In this way, if the print is slightly askew, it can be trimmed up. It looks better if a border of about one inch is left all around the print, so do not trim it too closely.

If words are desired in the print, they will have to be drawn *backwards*.

This is often too frustrating for students. However, if there is a great desire to do this, the following method is recommended. The words that are to be printed are drawn out on another paper. This paper should be fairly thin. A sheet of computer printout paper works very well. Draw the words with a very black pencil. Turn this paper over and place it *on top* of the meat tray. The message, which can be seen through the thin paper, is now backwards. Incise the words with a pencil onto the tray.

Adaptations

LEARNING DISABLED. There should be few problems in using any of the printing activities described. Decide whether the child can incorporate words into his prints. Because words must be made backwards, it may be confusing. In some cases, including words in the print may help the child who has reversal problems. Set limits in terms of number of colors that can be used in any one print. The monoprint is recommended for those who have a very short attention span.

BEHAVIORALLY DISORDERED. In addition to the above adaptations, try a group printing project. Have the children in small teams make wrapping paper using the tin can and string process. With some organization, this can become an income-producing project, and the class can sell their wrapping paper. If wrapping paper is made, white butcher paper is recommended.

HEARING IMPAIRED. All of the printing processes can be accomplished with this group. Consider the problems involved in incorporating words before letting the children try this. Some will be able to reverse their writing without too much difficulty. Examples of meat trays or cardboard prints with incorrectly written words will help explain why the words must be backwards.

RETARDED. If the sequence of printing activities is followed, there will be few problems. Many students will quickly grasp the monoprinting process. In fact, this can be introduced as a part of a fingerpainting lesson. Fingerpaint directly on a cleanable surface such as a formica countertop. Then place a sheet of fingerpaint paper or newsprint over the design and lift a print from the surface. The more able, older students will also be able to do the found object printing and the meat tray printing. In the found object printing, emphasize that the objects are not to be used like paint brushes. They are to be *gently pressed, lifted,* and then *dipped* into the paint. Then, the steps in the process are repeated.

VISUALLY IMPAIRED. The baking pan or cookie sheet (with edges) is recommended over the wood or cardboard inking surface because it has edges which set boundaries for the student. *C* clamps can be used to hold the inking pan or tray to the table. It is further recommended that a second cookie sheet be set out and clamped to the table. In this second pan, the cardboard or meat tray plate can be set (weighted, clamped, or taped down), and the child can then roll on ink by himself. Words written in the print will have little relevance for the blind child. Braille may be added later.

PHYSICALLY HANDICAPPED. In addition to the above, the cardboard or meat tray plate should be taped down to the working surface. If tin can printing plates are being made, *C* clamps can be used to hold them down by running a length of wood through the can and clamping this with the clamps to the table. The yarn can be tied directly to the can, eliminating the gluing step. Teamwork may be needed in inking the printing surface and transferring the print to the paper. Again, the cookie sheet or pan with an edge is recommended for use as an inking surface. It can be clamped down, and its edges will provide a guide for the brayer. The handle of the brayer may have to be thickened so that it can be held by the child. In the found object printing, the objects should be large enough to be easily picked up by the students.

Evaluation

POTENTIAL OUTCOMES. The child has shown that he understands at least one of the printing processes by making one or more prints. He has been able to follow directions with 80 percent or more accuracy. He understands that more than one print can be made from the same cardboard or meat tray plate, and he has done this. He has learned how to fold or trim the paper after making the print so that the print can be made into a card. He has written a greeting inside for a parent or a friend that is appropriate to a specific holiday or occasion.

CLOSURE. Time should be spent looking at each child's print. The concept of sharing can be reinforced by having the children give (exchange) prints. A lesson in language arts can be incorporated, and prints can be used to illustrate stories written by the class or groups of children. This can become a limited edition of a book. Cards and books made by the class might be sold.

Figure 150. There is no right or wrong way to fold and dye paper. Each time the folded paper is dipped into the dye, a new discovery is made. An aide helps this seven-year-old deaf child unfold his first experiment with folding and dyeing paper.

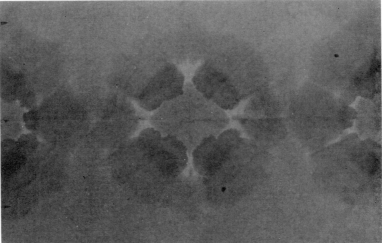

151

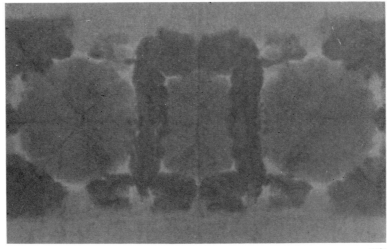

152

Figures 151 and 152. Examples of completed fold-and-dye designs by the same seven-year-old deaf boy.

Figure 153. A deaf six-year-old puts his tied cloth in the first dye bath. The cloth must be tight-ly tied with string or rubber bands.

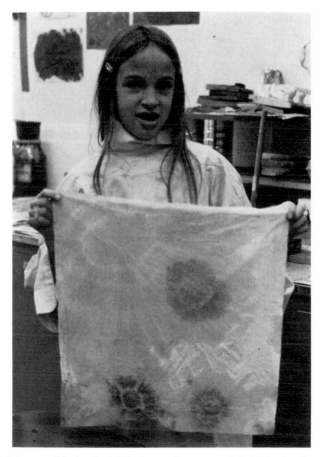

Figure 154. An eight-year-old deaf child shows her completed tie-dyed material. The white lines in the cloth are where the material was tied.

DYEING ACTIVITIES

Purpose/Rationale

Everyone needs to experience success. Success breeds success. Very special children need a larger measure of success, for they have had less successful experiences. Fold-and-dye and tie-dyeing activities provide a large measure of the needed success. There is also a magical element of surprise in these activities, for no two are precisely alike.

If providing successful experiences is not sufficient rationale, other learning can be integrated into the dyeing activities. Mathematics learning in terms of counting and learning geometric shapes can be taught through these dyeing activities.

Scientific experimentation and accurate recording of that experimentation can also be encouraged by both activities. As he experiments with various color combinations and the length of time the cloth or paper is immersed in the dye, ask the child to remember how long and in what sequence various dyes were used. Ask him also to keep a record or to remember how the cloth was tied or the paper folded if the effect is to be repeated. It is not always necessary or desirable to attempt to repeat various effects. However, some of the outcomes are quite spectacular. Often, others in the class are desirous of discovering how some special effect was obtained. This is the nature of scientific as well as artistic inquiry.

Motivation

The demonstration of the various processes is a very effective means of motivation. Have several examples of the various stages to communicate what is involved and how the processes work. Additionally, some completed dyed pieces will help the class understand the process and will provide added motivation. These completed pieces can be in the form of simple wall decorations, book covers, or placemats.

Stress throughout the presentation that there are no right or wrong outcomes and that each piece of dyed work will be different. The element of surprise and wonderment is always present in this activity.

Fold and Dye

Materials

Clip clothespins, 1 per child
Food coloring, 2 or 3 different colors
Newspapered surface for drying, or strung clothesline
Paper towels
Paint shirts or smocks
TV dinner trays or other small, shallow containers for colors

The larger sizes of food colors are much cheaper. The clothespins are optional, but using them prevents food colors from getting on the hands. Kitchen cleanser will clean any food coloring that might spill on tables or desks.

Procedure

Experiment to determine the desired strength of the colors. A dye container, approximately four inches in diameter, should have about one inch of water in it. Children usually prefer stronger colors, so a strong dye bath will be needed. Add ten to fifteen drops of the color to the water. The yellow will probably need to be stronger. Demonstrate some of the various ways of folding the paper towels. Squares of smaller and smaller sizes, triangles, or a fan-fold are examples of some of the basic shapes. These can be combined for other effects.

Each corner of the folded towel is dipped into a different dye. If some color mixing is desired, use only the three primary food colors. Occasionally, the dye bath will have to be replenished. Anticipate this. After the final dipping, unfold the towel and spread or hang it up to dry. Once dry, it can be mounted, attached to the front of a folder, or used for wrapping paper or a placemat.

The number of folds can be specified as well as the shapes for some of the papers which the children dye. Thus, mathematics concepts may be reinforced. This activity will take about thirty minutes to complete.

Tie and Dye

Materials

Containers for water and dye	Paint shirts or smocks
Dye liquid in 8 ounce (*c.* 230 g)	Pebbles
bottles, 1 bottle of each of the	Pipe cleaners
primary colors	Rubber bands, 3 or 4 per child
Elastic thread	String
Fabric for dyeing	Thread and needles

Cotton dyes best. Test the fabric before using it because some of the newer synthetics and synthetic mixes do not take dye.

Procedure

Mix the dye as per instructions and set in large pans. Also have several pans with clean water. Encourage some experimentation in tying the fabric. Found objects can be tied into the cloth. The cloth must be very *tightly* tied. For tight knots, have the child twist the rubber bands (or string) five times or more. Check on their tying. Some parts can be stitched instead of tied. Begin with a small sampler so that the total dyeing process is easily grasped. Some limits can be placed on the things tied; for example, each tied piece must have three or more tied areas.

When the fabric is ready to be dyed, place it in the lighter colors first. Before each dyeing, rinse the cloth in clear water. Experiment to determine how long the dye must be left in each color bath. The longer a piece is in the bath, the darker it will be. Encourage further experimentation by tying up different areas *after* dyeing in one color. After a final rinse, the fabric is untied. Usually the knots will have to be cut. Then, the fabric is hung to dry.

Care should be taken in dyeing and in working with dye because it is permanent. The children should have their clothing covered by smocks. Rubber gloves may also help. Even with commercial dyes, colors often do not set. Therefore, the material should be boiled in the final bath for thirty minutes to set the dye. The dyes can be stored in glass jars and reused. The fabric may be ironed and hemmed for placemats, scarves, or other functional items.

Adaptations

LEARNING DISABLED. Trying to repeat (replicate) different design effects will facilitate visual memory. Begin with a limited color palette. As the group understands the process, expand the color choices. Tie dyeing can be frustrating; therefore, the fold-and-dye process is recommended. It is a less complex process and will hold the interest of even those with a very short attention span.

BEHAVIORALLY DISORDERED. In addition to the above, tie dyeing may increase attention spans, since the longer the cloth is in the dye bath, the darker and more stunning the colors. Have another activity for the less patient child so he can draw or paint or perhaps do some fold and dyeing while waiting for the fabric dye to set. Since tie dyeing is more involved, it is recommended for intermediate and older primary children.

HEARING IMPAIRED. In addition to the above, be sure that the child understands the process. Have one or two children explain their understanding of the process before beginning. Set up traffic rules around the dye stations to prevent jams. This will be a good opportunity for language development. Some possible words to reinforce might be *tie, tight, accordion fold, food coloring,* and *dye.*

RETARDED. The fold and dye will probably be the preferred activity. It does not require the fine coordination needed to tightly tie knots. However, older students can do both processes. Some dyeing can be done in pairs or teams of students.

VISUALLY IMPAIRED. The visually impaired will have few problems with the fold-and-dye activity. The brilliant colors that result will be greatly appreciated. It is doubtful whether the blind child will be motivated or interested in this process. Be certain that the dye bath is securely attached to the work area. Help may be needed in unfolding the dyed paper.

PHYSICALLY HANDICAPPED. Team up the children so that aesthetic decisions can be made by all even though the actual folding or the dipping is not. Use a bulldog clip or a clip clothespin to hold the folded paper towel so it can be dipped easily into the dye.

Teamwork is also recommended in the tie-dyeing activity. Use string instead of rubber bands. The ends of the string need to be long enough to permit a "tug of war" as two children tie up their cloth. Help will be needed to cut the knots. A large group project can be done with pairs of children tying various parts of a large piece of cloth, a tee shirt, or a whole sheet. The children can decide what colors to use, and the art work may then be used as a backdrop, a tablecloth, or any number of other things for the classroom.

Evaluation

POTENTIAL OUTCOMES. The child has shown his understanding of the fold-and-dye and/or the tie-dyeing process by creating his own dyed art work. He has followed directions with 90 percent or more accuracy. He has made at least one dyed project in which all folding and color decisions were his own. He has produced one dyed project that is different from all others in the class. He has remembered the specific steps and colors used in one dyed art project and has accurately repeated them.

CLOSURE. Have the class share their work during the activity. Set some time aside for each child to show his work and to explain how the effects were achieved. If material has been dyed, a fashion show can be organized. A whole wall could be covered with fold-and-dye papers. The dyed paper towels may be laminated and used as folder covers, bookcovers, or placemats.

155   156

Figure 155. The paper loom has been taped to the work table so that this cerebral palsied child can concentrate on learning to weave while not being frustrated by a loom that moves around. The dark dots cue the child to begin these rows by covering the dots with the strip.

Figure 156. This is a training loom developed at the Arizona Training Program at Tucson to teach mentally handicapped adults to weave. The warp strings are color coded. The black-and-white photograph does not show this, but the ribbons are also of two different colors.

Figure 157. Nature weaving does not require great accuracy. Because it is a freer open-ended process, mistakes will not detract from the project. Here, an aide helps a cerebral palsied eight-year-old add a weed to his nature weaving.

Figure 158. A trainable mentally handicapped teenager makes a Giordes knot for his Persian hand tie. Each end of the black yarn goes around a warp string. Then, the ends are pulled up through the middle. The knot is finished by pulling the ends toward the body.

Figure 159. After knotting three rows, he weaves three rows. The yarn has been tied to a large wooden needle to make it easier to weave.

Figure 160. This blind teenager is just beginning a row of weaving on his Persian hand tie. The boards of his loom overlap so that it is easier to get his hands underneath. The warp nails in the loom have been staggered so it is easier to put the warp string onto the frame. Only part of the loom is being used for this project.

Figure 161. This completed Persian hand tie was done by a trainable mentally handicapped teenager at the Arizona Training Program at Tucson. Notice that the rows of weaving do not show in the completed wall hanging.

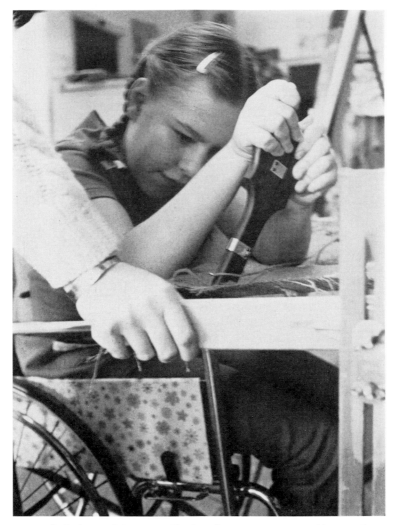

Figure 162. A retarded (trainable mentally handicapped) physically handicapped teenager hooks her rug with a Susan Burr rug hooking machine. She is working at a large table-height floor loom.

163

164   165

Figures 163, 164, and 165. Weaving can become a vocation for adults (impaired or nonimpaired). These are several examples of the work being done at the Arizona Training Program at Tucson. None of the young adults in this sheltered workshop has an IQ of over 50!

FIBER EXPERIENCES

Purpose/Rationale

Intermediate and older primary students need to begin to understand that artists and artistic statements often require a longer commitment and involvement than that which is encountered in one or two periods of art. Such artistic involvement is demonstrated in this section on fiber experiences. These activities not only provide a grounding in composition and visual organization, they also build important skills which may later culminate in a vocation.

As with the other activities discussed in this chapter, important concepts are learned and/or reinforced through these fiber experiences. Laterality, sequencing, visual memory, and counting skills are all necessary in other areas of the child's personal and academic life and are required to master any of these art activities. Just as crucial is the learning of an artistic process and the self-actualization that emerges as the result of a job that is well done. One major outcome of these fiber experiences is the affirmation of the child as a person and as a unique, creative, and productive individual.

A sequence of activities moving from paper weaving to nature and yarn weaving culminates in Persian hand tying. Many students may not reach the final phase until they reach adulthood. Nevertheless, the basic foundation can be laid.

Weaving

Motivation

If the group is unfamiliar with weaving, show some examples of very loosely woven fabric. A magnifying glass may help the children as they examine the cloth. They can even unravel part of the cloth to discover how it is made. Some examples of very large paper weavings can also help. Show some simple woven baskets, and then demonstrate the weaving process.

Materials

Construction paper strips 2 inches (*c.* 5 cm) wide and 12 inches (*c.* 30 cm) long in 2 contrasting colors, 6 per child
Masking tape
Paper loom about 8 by 12 inches (*c.* 20 by 30 cm), 1 per child
Stapler or white glue

Thinner strips and larger looms may be used when the child learns the basic tabby weave.

Procedure

Make the paper loom by taking a piece of 8 by 12 inch construction paper and cutting strips in it that are 2 inches by 7 inches. The last inch of the paper loom should not be cut. This is taped to the work surface. In this way, the warp (strips cut and still attached to the paper loom) can be easily lifted to make the over/under weaving of the weft strips (those that are cut separately and are actually woven into the warp).

If the group has difficulty catching onto the over/under process and the alternation of the weft strips, demonstrate the whole process on a large scale. Using four ropes (as warp), have eight students hold these to make a huge loom. Then, with a rope (as weft) of a *second* color (black, for example), weave it onto the loom. Next, take a third color of weft rope (red, for example) and weave it through. Finally, take another black rope and weave it onto the loom. This rope loom may be hung in the room by tying both ends onto dowel rods. This way, the children can test their weaving skills before being given the paper to weave.

Once they have mastered the basic weaving process, they can move to a simple wooden box or cardboard loom and use yarn instead of paper. The correct basic (tabby) weaving pattern must be mastered before any innovations or other patterns are introduced. This kind of weaving will take about one-half hour to finish. Thinner paper strips will take longer to weave.

Some Design Considerations: Persian Hand Tie and Rug Hooking

Almost any type of design can be incorporated into hand tying and rug hooking. Design is very important, and there are several ways to plan what is to be accomplished. Either a symmetrical or free form design can be done. If the student is having difficulty in deciding on a design, transform something from his art folio into the design for the rug. Other design sources might be a part of a fold-and-dyed or tie-dyed project, or a small part of a drawing or texture rubbing. A photograph of a landscape or a cityscape from a magazine such as *National Geographic* or *Arizona Highways* may also become the basis for the design.

Whatever design source is used, the original idea must be changed somewhat. Eliminate small details because they are often lost in the transposition. Two or three main shapes are perhaps better than six or nine small shapes. Make sketches of the ideas, including several in color using crayons or torn paper. The torn paper more accurately reflects the kind of edge which will be obtained by the finished project. Therefore, the student will not be disappointed when he realizes that neither hooking nor hand tying will produce a clean, straight edge.

To prevent visual chaos, limit the colors to two or three and possibly a lighter or darker shade of one of these colors. Use colors in related families: for example, the cool or the warm groups of colors. These naturally go together; thus, a greater harmony is automatically insured. After two or three color sketches are made, let the child choose one of these. If one of these sketches seems to be too chaotic or has too many details, eliminate it before the child makes his final design choice.

Sometimes a student may want to do a monogram or some other less original pattern. There is nothing wrong with this design approach because in executing it the child learns the whole process. It will, however, be important to encourage the child to *go beyond* these less original ideas and use a design idea that is much more his own. Thus, it makes good design sense to transform a piece of art already created into a textile design. Probably a child's tempera painting, drawing, or print will be good for this purpose.

PERSIAN HAND TIE

This relatively uncomplicated process is the same basic one used in making Persian rugs. Only the scale and size of the threads has been enlarged. By a combination of weaving and knotting, a sophisticated rug and/or hanging is the result. Once the basic idea is learned, the only limitation to the process is the time available to spend on the project.

Motivation

The presentation of partially completed as well as totally finished examples is the best means of motivation. By realizing that their efforts will result in a rug, a pillow, or a wall hanging, the class may be even more motivated.

Materials

Dowel rods

Fabric for pillow backing

Good design idea

Masking tape

Nails, 1 inch (*c.* 2 cm) wire nails, 17 gauge (*c.* 1.37 mm)

Rug backing

White glue and nails for frame

Wood frame, ½ to ¼ inch (*c.* 1 cm to ½ cm) thick and 2 to 4 inches wide (*c.* 5 cm to 10 cm) strips

Yarn, assorted scraps plus 5 or more skeins of 4 ounce (*c.* 110 g) or heavier yarn

The frame size will vary. Wood can be obtained from the lumberyard scrap box and cut to desired lengths. The amounts and colors of yarn depend on the design. Pillow backing material is needed if a pillow is to be made. Dowel rods can be used to make a wall hanging, and rug backing is necessary if a rug is being made. (Rug backing usually must be mail ordered from a commercial art supplier.) The number of nails needed depends on the size of the loom (see procedures section).

Procedure

It is recommended that nothing smaller than a 12 by 12 inch frame be used. This can be made from scrap wood. The wood strips should be slightly larger than the desired size. The frame strips should overlap instead of being made flush. This enables the student to get under the warp threads to tie knots. Glue and nail the wood strips together with larger nails. The smaller nails are hammered into the frame on the top and bottom. No smaller nails are needed on the sides of the frame. Arrange the nails so that there are two rows of staggered nails on the top crosspiece. The nails should be ½ inch apart from each other. The nails are hammered only partially into the frame (see illustrations at beginning of this section).

Next, string the loom with warp string. A double knot is tied onto the first nail, and a two inch *tail* is left. This tail will be tied onto the next warp thread when the student has finished stringing on the warp. The warp string is wrapped around the bottom two nails and then across the loom and around the next two top nails. Continue the process until the whole frame is strung. At the end, the string is tied off again, leaving a tail which can be tied into the neighboring warp string. The warp string should be fairly tightly strung around all the nails.

A full-scale color mock-up of the rug design may be made and taped under the frame. This guide can then be followed in changing yarn colors.

A length of yarn long enough to weave three rows is tied on the frame, and three rows of straight over/under/over (tabby) weaving is done. This should be fairly loose. The length is tied off at the end of the third row with a simple knot.

Next, tie two or three lengths of yarn that are four or six inches long onto the warp. Do this in groups of two or three lengths of yarn per knot. Since it will be very tedious to continually cut four inch or six inch lengths of yarn, make a *butterfly* for this purpose. A butterfly is a length of cardboard that is about five inches long and two or three inches wide. Yarn is wrapped around and around this butterfly, and then it is cut along the top edge. The result is a number of short pieces of yarn of uniform length.

The knot used is called a Giordes knot. To tie the knot, the yarn lengths are wrapped around the first two warp strings and the ends of the yarn are pulled up through the center of the warp strings. The knot is pulled toward the weaving that has already been done (see Fig. 158). If the students have trouble grasping this simple knotting process, it may help to do a "walk-through." Have two students be the warp strings, and have two others hold a short length of rope. Have the rope holders walk through the process of tying the knot. Repeat until the knot is learned.

idea has been developed by changing it in some way (eliminating details, changing the color scheme, or both). He has demonstrated persistence in completing the project without constant prompting.

CLOSURE. The completed weavings should be displayed. The Persian hand-tied projects should be finished by adding dowel rods or branches if they are to be wall hangings. If the projects are to be pillows, then a pillow and cover can be made and the hand tie stitched to it. Completed Persian hand ties can be sold at local art fairs.

RUG HOOKING

Another way for students to make their own rugs or wall hangings is by means of rug hooking. This process is simplified by the use of a manually operated hooking machine. There are several on the market, and they are usually available at local craft stores or through large mail order art material suppliers. One that is relatively inexpensive is the Susan Burr® rug hooker. As with all artistic endeavors, the key to this process is the design which will be made into the rug. One of the child's own paintings or drawings is one of the best design sources. Magazine photographs of landscapes or cityscapes may also be used. Detail should be eliminated, and all the space must be filled so the hooked project will be more than an outline drawing in yarn.

Materials

C clamps

Burlap, good quality, 2 inches (c. 5 cm) larger in diameter than loom

Carpet tacks, #10 size, ⅝ inch (16 mm)

Good design

Nails, #4 common, 8 per frame

Hammer

Susan Burr rug hooker or other rug hooking needle

Rug backing, liquid, for sealing and skidproofing the rug

White glue for frame corners

Wood for box frame, ¼ to ½ inch (c. 1 cm to ½ cm) thick, between 3 inches and 5 inches (c. 7 cm and 12 cm) wide, and about 12 inches (c. 30 cm) long

Yarn

The size of the frame may vary. Wood can be obtained from the lumberyard scrap box and cut to desired dimensions. The amount of yarn and colors would vary, depending on the size of the frame and type of design. The rug hooking machine or needle can usually be purchased from a local hobby shop or mail ordered from a commercial art supplier. Rug backing will probably have to be mail ordered from a commercial art supplier.

Motivation

For younger children, introduce the activity by talking about a magic machine that eats yarn. This machine walks across burlap and leaves yarn footprints. At this point, show the machine, thread it, and demonstrate. If this presentation is too abstract or sophisticated, show the group some examples of hooked rugs or samplers. Have an unfinished sampler so that each child can try the machine.

Procedure

Stretch burlap over a wood *box* frame that is the desired size. The burlap should be tightly stretched and tacked or stapled around the sides of the frame. Allow enough burlap border to easily stretch it on the frame. Sketch the design onto the burlap with a pencil. By following the directions, thread the hooker with yarn. No knots are put in the yarn. The yarn is just completely hooked into the burlap. More yarn is then threaded as needed. Mistakes can be easily taken out by pulling. Most yarns work quite well. Have the child practice on a sampler or on the class demonstration frame first. Thus, he will really understand how to use the hooking machine.

Always hook at a slight angle instead of holding the machine exactly perpendicular to the burlap. To do so, point the hooker slightly in the desired direction. There is a rhythm that comes with a little practice, and it will be obvious when this is achieved. Finally, it will be easiest and most aesthetic if the hooking is done in rows in either a right/left or up/down pattern instead of a more random style. To change directions, turn the machine and point it in the new direction.

It may help to weight down the frame with bricks on the corner or with C clamps so that a good tension can be achieved. The hooking machine does not remain in one place but must walk along. If the child does not move the machine along, then a hole may be punched in the burlap. This can be easily mended, but try to avoid such holes. When complete, seal the back with rug sealer, remove from the frame, and hem the edges. The time necessary to finish this project depends on the size of the loom and the child's working speed. It would take at least ten hours to complete a rug that was 12 by 12 inches.

Adaptations

LEARNING DISABLED AND BEHAVIORALLY DISORDERED. This activity may help the child's figure-ground perception. However, since the process is somewhat involved and time consuming, begin the project as a group activity. Then, several children may work, taking turns at various times during the class day. Those children with greatest interest can go on to make one of their own rugs. In this case, the size of the frame should not be too large. It takes less time to work on a smaller frame, and none of the children will get discouraged. Limit the colors used to two or three to build in harmony.

HEARING IMPAIRED. As with the hand tie, it is essential to develop a design that is unique. If the students have trouble, use the magazine photographs as a viable alternative. If using photographs, colors must be changed and details should be eliminated. Because the magazine or art reproduction is altered, it becomes more the child's own creation.

RETARDED. Older students should have few problems with the process. Be sure to emphasize the use of one of the child's own drawings as a design. It may help to seal sections with rug sealer as they are hooked so that the yarn will not pull out.

VISUALLY IMPAIRED. If highly contrasting colors are used, the intermediate or older visually impaired students should have few problems. It may help to seal sections with rug sealers as they are completed so that nothing will put out. The hand-tie process is preferred for the blind student.

PHYSICALLY HANDICAPPED. A more abstract torn paper picture could become the design for a rug hooking. In using such a design, those who really cannot draw would not be embarrassed. It may be best for students to work in teams of two. For the more involved students, other types of hooking machines (also available from any major mail order art supplier) may be easier to handle. Do this textile project as a large group activity. Each can then contribute in some way. For example, one or two can make the design and others can hold the frame while one or two do the hooking.

Evaluation

POTENTIAL OUTCOMES. The child has mastered the rug hooking process with 90 percent or more accuracy. He has chosen his design idea from a drawing he has done earlier or executed specifically for this project. The design has been altered so that there are large areas of colors and few (not over six) small details in it. The child has maintained interest and persisted in the project and completed it without a lot of prompting.

CLOSURE. The completed rug hooking can be displayed. It can be made into a wall hanging by adding dowel rods at top and bottom. It can become a pillow cover by being stitched onto an existing pillow or pillow cover. Such completed items can be a source of income if they are sold at local fairs or bazaars.

RESOURCE BIBLIOGRAPHY

Art Principles and Processes

A few basic references have been selected and annotated. They have been chosen for their clear, uncomplicated coverage of the topics. The list is consciously selective to underscore the principles of quality and brevity.

GENERAL

Barger, B. *Nature as designer*. New York: Reinhold, 1966.

This book is a sensitive photographic essay on artistic forms, colors, and textures occurring in nature. In its illustrations there is a wealth of design inspiration for crafts activities, especially textiles and ceramics.

Bevlin, M. E. *Design through discovery* (2nd ed.). New York: Holt, Rinehart & Winston, 1970.

This book discusses basic design elements and principles as they occur in many parts of life. Some of the areas covered are design in textiles, ceramics, architecture, interior design, and painting.

Feldman, E. B. *Varieties of visual experience* (basic ed.). New York: Abrams & Prentice-Hall, 1967 & 1972.

This book presents a basic art history overview in layman's language. There are some good illustrations and a brief discussion of design as it relates to works of art.

Horn, G. *The crayon*. Worcester, Mass.: Davis, 1969.

This book discusses many different methods of drawing using crayons. It includes, among others, sections on crayon rubbings and encaustic.

Lacey, J. C. *Young art nature and seeing, a fundamental program for teachers*. New York: Van Nostrand Reinhold, n.d.

A fundamental presentation of design using the natural environment. These design concepts are specifically related to the young student to increase his awareness of the environs and art.

Linderman, E. W., & Linderman, M. M. *Crafts for the classroom*. New York: Macmillan, 1977.

This book is a comprehensive coverage of many, many basic and more complex art and crafts processes. It is a valuable resource.

Timmons, V. G. *Painting in the school program*. Worcester, Mass.: Davis, 1968.

This book is a good basic presentation of the many different painting techniques and materials appropriate for the public school art program.

CLAY

Ball, F. C. & Lovoos, J. *Making pottery without a wheel: Texture and form in clay*. New York: Reinhold, 1965.

This book is a classic layman's guide to fundamental off-the-wheel ceramic processes. Among other processes, slab, coil, and sling construction are covered.

Nelson, G. C. *Ceramics*. (3rd ed.). New York: Holt, Rinehart & Winston, 1971.

This book includes some historical information and a more advanced discussion of ceramics, including information about glazes. It is a classic resource.

PHOTOGRAPHY

Anderson, Y. *Teaching film animation to children.* New York: Van Nostrand Reinhold, 1971.

> This book covers many basic ways of making motion pictures without expensive hardware. The focus is on elementary children and includes illustrations of their work.

Davis, P. *Photography.* Dubuque: William C. Brown, 1972.

> This book is a comprehensive overview of photographic fundamentals appropriate for the intermediate or secondary student. Terminology, processes, and equipment are carefully explained.

Holter, P. *Photography without a camera.* New York: Van Nostrand Reinhold, 1972.

> A host of approaches to photography that do not require a commercially made camera are covered. Several simple designs for homemade cameras are fully explained.

PRINTMAKING

Brommer, G. F. *Relief printmaking.* Worcester, Mass.: Davis, 1970.

> This book covers many of the basic printmaking processes appropriate for elementary school children.

LaLiberté, N., & Mogelon, A. *The art of monoprints: History and modern techniques.* New York: Van Nostrand Rinehold, 1974.

> This book includes some good visual examples of historical and contemporary monoprints. Many ways of enhancing this simple artistic process are covered in this small book.

PUPPETRY

Anderson, B. E. *Let's start a puppet theatre.* New York: Van Nostrand Reinhold, 1973.

> In addition to discussing various kinds of puppets, the book covers the construction of different types of stages and theatres.

Kampmann, L. *Creating with puppets.* New York: Van Nostrand Reinhold, 1969.

> This book is a good overview of many different ways of making all kinds of puppets.

WEAVING, HOOKING, AND DYEING

Alexander, M. *Weaving handicraft; fifteen simple ways of weaving.* Bloomington, Ill.: McKnight & McKnight, 1954.

> This small pamphlet provides all the instructions for simple looms that anyone can make without special equipment.

Helps and hints, Service Committee, Handweavers Guild of America, Inc., West Hartford, Conn., n.d.

This pamphlet gives some basic patterns and ideas for the beginner. It also includes hints for teaching weaving to impaired students.

Hollander, A. *Decorative papers and fabrics.* New York: Van Nostrand Reinhold, 1971.

This book includes some good illustrations and instructions on many fold-and-dye processes. Marbled paper, block printing, and other textile dyeing processes are included.

Rainey, S. R. *Weaving without a loom.* Worcester, Mass.: Davis, 1966.

A good basic discussion of many weaving processes. There are some fine illustrations in this fairly comprehensive book.

Wiseman, A. *Rug tapestries and wool mosiacs.* New York: Van Nostrand Reinhold, 1969.

This book covers rug hooking and other simple rugmaking processes. Sources of equipment and suppliers are included.

JUST FOR FUN

These four books cover basic art and art-related ideas and games and toys that can be made with children. They are included to point out that art ideas and inspiration are not always found in "art" books.

Caney, S. *Steven Caney's playbook.* New York: Workman, 1975.

Caney, S. *Steven Caney's toybook.* New York: Workman, 1972.

Dolan, E. F. *The complete beginner's guide to making and flying kites.* New York: Doubleday, 1977.

Fiarotta, P. *Sticks and stones and ice cream cones, the craftbook for children.* New York: Workman, 1973.

Art/Special Education and Art Therapy

These are a few of the books available in art/special education and art therapy. Periodical literature has not been included.

Fukurai, Shiro. *How can I make what I cannot see?* New York: Van Nostrand Reinhold, 1974.

This book is a personal narrative of a Japanese teacher's experiences in teaching art to blind children. Through its prose and illustrations, a sensitive understanding of the artistic efforts of the visually impaired is communicated.

Kramer, E. *Art as therapy with children.* New York: Shocken, 1971.

This book, written by one of the pioneers in the art therapy field, explains the art as therapy approach in the treatment of handicapped and disturbed children. The author uses illustrations and case material from her extensive clinical experience in her discussion of this therapeutic approach.

Hollander, H. C. *Creative opportunities for the retarded child at home and at school.* Booklets 1-6. New York: Doubleday, 1971.

This series, written for parents and laymen, documents art activities that can be (and were) done by retarded children and their parents. Each booklet covers a different art media including painting, printmaking, clay, woodworking, and stitchery.

Lindsay, Z. *Art and the handicapped child.* New York: Van Nostrand Reinhold, 1972.

This book includes a descriptive section on various handicaps and an illustrated section on art activities and ways they can be adapted for special impairments. Drawing, painting, printing, placing, puppetry, and modeling activities are discussed.

Lowenfeld, V. *Creative and mental growth* (3rd ed.), New York: Macmillan, 1957.

The section of this book titled "Therapeutic Aspects of Art Education" continues to be a definitive and comprehensive statement on the uses of art with a variety of handicapped children. Unfortunately, this chapter has been deleted in later editions of the book.

Naumburg, M. *An introduction to art therapy: Studies of the "free" art expression of behavioral problem children and adolescents as a means of diagnosis and therapy.* New York: Teachers College Press, Columbia University, 1973.

This book is a revised edition of the initial 1947 publication which was (and continues to be) a classic documentation of psychoanalytic approaches to art therapy. Six case studies of behaviorally disordered children ages 4.5 to 17 are discussed.

Uno, A. Q. *Aesthetic activities for handicapped children.* Texas Education Agency, Division of Special Education: Federal Assistance for the Education of Handicapped Children, P.L. 89-313 Amendment to Title 1, Part B EHA. State Project No. 4-660-00-31, n.d.

This is a resource guide for adults planning aesthetic activities for the intermediate (junior high school aged) handicapped student. Focus is on a multi-sensory approach incorporating all the senses for motivation in art activities. Also included are a short discussion of design concepts and basic definitions of special education and art education terminology

Rhynlle, J. *The gestalt art experience.* Monterey, Calif.: Brooks/Cole, 1973.

This book is an accounting of gestalt psychology, therapy and art. The author's personal reflections and the case studies illuminate the gestalt approach to art therapy with insightful sensitivity.

Rubin, J. *Child art therapy: Understanding and helping children grow through art.* New York: Van Nostrand Reinhold, 1977.

This book is an overview of one person's therapeutic work with impaired and typical children. The uses of art for diagnosis and treatment of children and families in a variety of settings are discussed and illumined through case studies and illustrations.

REFERENCES

Anderson, W. *Art learning situations for elementary education.* Belmont, Calif.: Wadsworth, 1965.

Hubbard, G. A., & Rouse, M. J. *Art: Meaning, method and media, grades 1-6.* Westchester, Ill.: Benefic, 1972 & 1975.

Lansing, K. *Art, artists and art education.* New York: McGraw-Hill, 1969.

Kramer, E. *Art as therapy with children.* New York: Schocken, 1971.

Kramer, E. *Art therapy in a children's community.* Springfield: Thomas, 1958.

Rhyne, J. *The gestalt art experience.* Monterey, Calif.: Brooks/Cole, 1973.

Chapter VII

GETTING IT ALL TOGETHER

ART MATERIALS AND WHERE TO FIND THEM

Look at a pile of discarded building materials, a stack of flattened cardboard boxes, a sack of clothing scraps, or a bundle of old newspapers. *Is* there anything more to see in this assortment of trash? Absolutely, if the spectator is thinking art. All those items are potential art materials. They are all free and can all be recycled into art. Therefore, the building materials can become wood sculpture; the cardboard, free-standing life-size figures; the newspapers, valuable artproofing media. It is this kind of art perception and flexibility that is necessary if there is to be any substantial art program, given the shoestring budgets that are a reality today in the schools.

Ferreting art materials requires an entrepreneur's wisdom, energy, and selectivity. Recycling these materials into art necessitates a touch of the Master Artist. Using discarded materials can easily result in a hodgepodge of junk art unless some care is exerted to transform the discard so completely that no one recognizes its original form or source. Therefore, an ice cream carton mask is so transfigured by paint and paper that anyone seeing the mask would never suspect its origins. A cardboard model of a town is so executed that the buildings are buildings and not a chaotic mix of film and toothpaste boxes. These boxes have been so disguised that they can only be perceived as the bricks and mortar of a town.

In recycling materials, it also helps to rely on their own harmony and relatedness. Therefore, boxes belong with other boxes, papers with other papers, and nature objects with other nature objects. These innate commonalities can then be incorporated into art activities which may *only* use different kinds of recycled boxes, different kinds of wood scraps, or different kinds of scrap papers.

To help trigger the entrepreneur and his scrounging instincts further, the sections that follow briefly enumerate local school and community resources. A short list of mail order suppliers is also included. Finally, an art survival kit is described to insure that all the very special children have art.

Local Resources

There are many, many local resources for art materials. Each community has its own unique character and thus differs in possible opportunities for various art items. Before doing any purchasing, investigate and explore all other potential free local sources. Realize also that recycling and scrounging materials require storage space. The classroom may not have such space, so other areas must be located.

A list of possible sources for all items discussed in the art activities in this sourcebook has been compiled. It is presented in three areas: School Sources, Community Resources, and Mail Order Suppliers. Such a list can only be a beginning. Hopefully, it will trigger thought toward other potential places where art materials can be obtained.

A CALL FOR HELP

Before purchasing or scrounging any items on the three lists, put out an S.O.S. to local church groups and on the local radio station. Ask for those items that cannot be easily located, as well as the following:

Buttons	Mirrors, especially a large one
Cloth scraps	Paint shirts and smocks
Costumes and props such as different types of hats	Socks
	Yarn and yarn scraps
Needles and thread	

Collaborate with other teachers on the requested list. Organize a pick-up point and storage areas. Some boxes will be needed for sorting your collection.

SCHOOL SOURCES

The school can be a fertile field for art media. Once sensitized to the needs of the art program, the school staff can become key factors in obtaining art materials. Probably the most valuable persons are the custodial staff and the kitchen personnel. School sources have been broken down into four parts: the custodian and his closet, the main office, the school kitchen, and other departments.

THE CUSTODIAN & HIS CLOSET

Bleach	Paper towels
Boxes	Pliers
Buckets	Razor blades, single edge
Cardboard	Soap, liquid and bar
Disinfectant	Sponges
Hammers	Synthetic foam packing pieces
Nails	Toilet paper cardboard rolls

The custodian may also be the source of many discarded items that can be recycled.

THE MAIN OFFICE

Brown wrapping paper
Carbon paper
Cardboard, especially thin grey tablet backs
Chalk
Ditto paper
File folders
Hole puncher
Index cards
Paper clips, including large ones

Paper cutter
Pencils
Rubber bands
Rulers
Scissors
Straight pins
Stapler
String
Synthetic foam packing pieces
Tape, cellophane and masking

There may be other potential materials. A secretary can be a powerful ally in scrounging and recycling office discards for the art program.

THE SCHOOL KITCHEN

Aluminum, foil sheets and pie tins
Bleach
Boxes in various sizes
Buckets
Cardboard
Coffee cans and lids
Containers; tin cans, dishpans, etc.
Cookie sheets
Disinfectant
Egg cartons
Electric frying pan
Flour
Food coloring
Ice cream cartons, round 5 or 10 gallon (20 or 40 l) size
Jars, including gallon size (4 l) size for mixing tempera paint
Knives, flatware and sharp pointed ones

Meat trays, beadboard type
Mixing bowls
Muffin tins
Paper sacks in all sizes
Paper towels
Paper towel cardboard rolls
Pasta
Plastic bags, small and large garbage size
Plastic bottles
Pie tins
Salt
Soap, liquid and bar
Seeds
Tin cans
Tubs
Vegetable shredder
Warming tray
Wax paper

Take a tour of the kitchen. There may be other things that can be used. If the school kitchen does not have a particular item, someone else's kitchen can provide it. If kitchen resources are exhausted, the grocery store can supply the item, probably at a price.

OTHER SCHOOL DEPARTMENTS

Athletic Department
Used 16 mm film

Home Economics Department
Bleach
Cloth scraps
Fabric cement
Dye
Iron
Needles and thread
Scissors
Yarn

Industrial Arts Department
Hammers
Nails
Metal nuts, washers, etc.
Pliers
Sand
Sandpaper
Sawdust
Sheet metal
Tubing
Wood scraps
Wood shavings

Playground
Drawing surface
Nature objects: bark, leaves, tree
    branches, seeds, stones, and weeds

COMMUNITY RESOURCES

Local merchants are often very willing to donate items for the art program. The following list includes materials that are usually discarded by local businesses but that can be saved and recycled into art.

COMMERCIAL RECYCLING SOURCES

Appliance, Bicycle, and Furniture Stores
Cardboard, large and small boxes
Carpet scraps
Cloth scraps
Metal nuts and washers
Outdated pattern books
Synthetic foam packing pieces

Make personal contact with store owners. They may have other potential art items and will save these for the class on a regular basis.

Camera Store
Slide mounts
Used film

Probably slide mounts will have to be purchased.

Businesses with Computer Operations
I.B.M. cards

Paper computer tape
Used computer printout paper

The computer paper and cards will be clean on one side. The paper can be used for most drawing activities.

Lumberyard, Hardware, or Paint Store
Carpet scraps
Cloth scraps
Metal screen roll ends and scraps
Paint in discontinued lots
Wallboard rolls, discontinued and outdated
Wallboard scraps
Wood scraps

Ask at the store for other discarded items that can be recycled for the art program.

Newspaper
Ends of newsprint rolls
Other papers

Newsprint at the very end of the roll cannot be printed and is usually discarded. This newsprint and other paper scraps are good sources for drawing paper.

Printing Firms
Boxes
Scrap papers

Many kinds of novel paper scraps can be scrounged for use in any art activities requiring construction and assorted paper scraps.

Restaurants and Food Chains
Beadboard meat trays
Boxes
Cardboard circles from pizza parlors
Containers for water and paint
Ice cream cartons, round 5 or 10 gallon (20 l or 40 l) size

LOCAL SOURCES FOR PURCHASING ART ITEMS

Some art materials just cannot be scrounged and have to be purchased. A list of local sources for such items follows. In some instances, these firms may donate art materials. Ask!

ART MATERIALS LOCALLY AVAILABLE

Lumberyard, Hardware Store, or Paint Store

Brushes	Metal nuts and washers
C clamps	Plaster of Paris
Carpet tacks	Pliers
Hammers	Sand
Nails	Shellac and shellac solvent (alcohol)
Matt knife or utility knife	Wheat paste

Variety, Discount, or Ten-Cent Store

Brushes	Markers, watercolor and permanent
Bulldog metal clips	(alcohol base)
Burlap	Needle and thread
Cellophane	Newsprint
Chalk	Pattern books
Clay, oil base	Shoe polish
Cloth	String for warp
Clothespins, pinch kind	Tissue paper
Clothing dye	Tempera paint
Construction paper	White glue
Crayons	Wooden spoons
Drawing paper	Yarn
Fabric cement	

Ask for outdated pattern books. They are a good source for starter sheets. The tempera paint, drawing paper, construction paper, and newsprint may not come in large enough quantities to be economically purchased for the whole class. The school district central warehouse or a mail order supplier may be a better source.

Local Art or Hobby Store
Brayers
Glazes
Rug backing
Rug hooking machine or needle
Water base (earth) clay
Water base printer's ink

Generally, these items are cheaper when ordered through a mail order arts and crafts supplier. Check with the art supervisor before ordering glazes.

Mail Order Suppliers

Sometimes it is desirable to mail order supplies. In ordering, it helps to team up with other teachers because quantity orders are cheaper. For example, papers are cheapest in large sizes. However, a paper cutter will be needed to cut paper into usable sizes.

It is always sensible to window shop and compare catalogue prices. A list of some major suppliers follows. They will send free catalogues on request. Many items may be available through the school district's central warehouse. Check there first before ordering through the mail.

In ordering, remember to include freight charges. Many suppliers feature their own labels on items. These items are usually comparable in quality and cheaper in cost. The local art supervisor or art teacher can provide more specific consumer advice.

LIST OF MAIL ORDER SUPPLIERS

General Suppliers
Dick Blick
P. O. Box 1261
Galesburg, IL 61401

Creative Materials, Inc.
5377 Michigan Ave.
Rosemont, IL 60018
(Supplier for 4-Hole Training
  Scissors)

Nasco Arts and Crafts
901 Janesville Ave.
Fort Atkinson, WI 53538

Pyramid Artist Materials
Box 27
Urbana, IL 61801
  or
Pyramid Artist Materials
6510 North 54th Street
Tampa, FL 33610

Triarco Arts and Crafts
Delco Craft Division
1001 Troy Court
Troy, MI 48084

(Triarco has several regional locations; ask for nearest one.)

Arts and Activities Magazine
150 N. Central Park Ave.
Skokie, IL 60076
  (Includes a comprehensive list of
  suppliers annually, usually in its
  February issue.)

Clay Supplies
American Art Clay, Inc.
47717 West 16th Street
Indianapolis, IN 46222

Sax Arts and Crafts
P. O. Box 2002
Milwaukee, WI 53201

Hobby Craft Division
Westwood Ceramic Supply Co.
14400 Lomitas Avenue
City of Industry, CA 91744

Leather Supplies
Tandy Leather Company
A Tandy Corporation Company
Ft. Worth, TX 76107

Printing Supplies
Hunt Manufacturing Company
1405 Locust Street
Philadelphia, PA 19101

J. L. Hammett Company
10 Hammett Place
Braintree, MA 02184

Weaving
Belding Lily Company
Shelby, NC 28150

THE ART SURVIVAL KIT

How are art materials ordered? How does one plan and order materials for a whole year? Where does one start? What is absolutely essential? To answer these questions, especially for the beginning teacher who has little idea about how many and what kind of art supplies are essential for a year-long art program, the art survival kit has been compiled.

The kit is just that, a survival kit. It represents a bare-bones list of materials which will be necessary to an art program's survival. The kit is not absolute, and the teacher may amend some parts of it for special needs of a particular class. The kit is built around the needs of a group of twelve primary special education children. If a larger group needs the survival kit, then multiply the amounts by the appropriate factor. For a smaller group, subtract by the appropriate factor.

Before doing any ordering of materials consider what, if any, materials are provided by parents and/or the school district. Often, crayons and scissors will not have to come out of the art budget. Also consider what can be recycled and scrounged locally and what can be provided through the school district's central warehouse.

If ordering is to be done in large amounts or with another teacher, be sure there is sufficient storage space for the supplies. Also consider the trade-off between saving money by ordering dry paint and dry clay and the time necessary to add water and mix these materials.

It might make sense to only order part of the materials and wait for class reactions and class needs before spending all the monies. It may also help to have a discretionary fund for some special art items. In this way, much more flexibility and spontaneity will be incorporated into the art program because an immediate need for an art item can be met.

In determining the specific amounts of materials outlined in the art survival kit, a "guesstimate" was made based on several factors. There may be other factors in operation which others might wish to consider. This is a purely individual matter. Here is the formula for this "guesstimate" of art materials needed.

Based on 180 school days and 100 minutes per week for art, there are 72 art days (art twice a week). About two thirds of these art days are spent on two-dimensional art work requiring paper (50 days). Allow five pieces of paper per child per art class (5 times 12 times 50). The result is 3000 pieces of paper and insures enough for use at other times in each week. One fourth of the amount should be construction paper and the rest various drawing papers.

The other amounts were determined based on personal research and other sources (Hoover, 1961; Salome, n.d.). Above all, it must be underscored that these are *suggested* amounts and the individual's own experience with a particular class will be the ultimate judge.

Finally, in presenting the art survival kit, it must be noted that some art activities discussed in the sourcebook have been eliminated because the kit is for basic *survival*. If the teacher is truly resourceful and fortunate in having a larger budget, then activities such as sandcasting, slide- and filmmaking, meat tray printing, rug hooking, hand tying, dyeing activities, and creating with papier-mâché can also be included. The kit is summarized in two charts: a purchase list and a scrounge list.

THE ART SURVIVAL KIT: PURCHASE LIST

Based on Needs of Primary Class of 12 Children for Entire Year
(Metric equivalents are indicated in parentheses)

It is *crucial* that all art materials be nontoxic. Materials will have their nontoxicity stated on the label. If there is no such statement, check with the manufacturer.

Item	Amount	Comment	Source
Brushes	16, ½ inch (c. 1 cm), flat with short handles. 4, ¼ inch (c. ½ cm) wide. No. 6 watercolor can also be used. All should have short handles.	There is no need to invest in expensive brushes. They wear out too quickly. Handles can be cut off if too long. Hold back some for later in the year.	Local discount stores.
Clay	25 pounds (c. 11 kg) of water base (earth) clay.	Check school for kiln. If using kiln, need to order 4 pints (c. 1840 g) of glaze. Check with art supervisor on recommended type. Water base clay can be ordered and mixed by class. Cheaper but more time consuming.	School district local central warehouse may stock, or mail order house.
	Or 10 pounds (c. 4.5 kg) flour and 10 pounds (c. 4.5 kg) salt.	Cannot be used for making windchimes or liquid-holding containers.	School kitchen may provide, or local grocery store.
Construction Paper	8 packages of 50 sheets each, assorted colors, 12 by 18 inches (c. 30 by 4.5 cm).	Can be cut in half for smaller sheets. If paper cutter available, can order in larger sizes and save some money. Cheapest source will probably be central warehouse or mail order house.	School district central warehouse Or Mail order house Or Local variety and/or art store.

Crayons	1 box per child in boxes of 8 assorted colors, plus 4 extra boxes for refills.	Older children can use thinner crayons. Some classes may bring their own.	Same.
Drawing Paper	12 packages, 50 sheets each, 12 by 18 inches (*c.* 30 by 45 cm). Cream manila or white paper, 60 pound (*c.* 27 kg) weight.	Can be cut in half for smaller projects. If paper cutter available order in larger sizes and save money. Drawing paper is also used for painting. Cheapest source will probably be central warehouse or mail order house.	Same.
Glue	½ gallon (*c.* 2 1), white, nontoxic. Or 12, 1¾ oz. (*c.* 350 g) containers for the children, and 3 larger 16 oz. (*c.* 450 g) containers.	Can share with another teacher and buy 1 gallon of glue (*c.* 4 1). Smaller containers can be refilled from larger ones.	Same. Local hardware stores also supply white glue.
Markers	12 sets of 8 assorted colors.	Best to have 1 set per child. May order 2 or 3 larger sets and share.	Local discount store Or School district central warehouse Or Mail order supplier.
Masking Tape	3 rolls, ¾ inch (*c.* 1.5 cm) wide, 60 yard (60 m) roll.	Need for displaying art work, taping papers to work surface, etc.	Local discount stores often cheapest. School districts may provide as part of office supplies.
Newsprint	500 sheets of 12 by 18 inch (*c.* 30 by 45 cm).	Local newspaper may donate. Computer printout paper can be substituted. Local firms will donate used printout paper. Newsprint used for many drawing and some printing activities.	School district central warehouse Or Mail order house Or Local art store.
Scissors	12 pair, 4 inch (*c.* 10 cm), blunt; 2 pair pointed; 1 pair large desk type.	May need to order some left-handed pairs. May need 4-holed training scissors. Some children provide their own.	School district central warehouse Or Mail order house Or Local variety or discount store.
Tempera Paint	Dry 1 pound (450 g) cans. 4 each: red, blue, yellow. 2 each: black, white, orange, green, violet (purple), brown.	Dry paint is cheaper but must be mixed and stored. (Mix with liquid soap for easier cleaning.) If ordering liquid, increase amount of each color unit by 1.	School district central warehouse Or Mail order house. Local discount stores may have in smaller amounts. Local art stores may carry.
Wrapping Paper	1 roll, 36 inch (*c.* 3m) wide.	Can share with other classes. Often front office has wrapping paper. Scrap cardboard can be substituted in many of the activities. Makes a good large painting surface. White is more expensive than brown.	School district central warehouse Or Mail order house.

THE ART SURVIVAL KIT: SCROUNGE LIST
Based on Needs of Primary Class of 12 Children for Entire Year

Item	*Comment*
Cardboard	Can be used as a painting surface for all kinds of construction.
Cloth Scraps	Test to be sure children can cut or tear.
Containers	Need pot pie tins, butter tubs, tin cans, coffee cans for water, glue, paint, etc.
Knife	A sharp kitchen knife or single-edge razor blade needed to cut cardboard.
Mixing Bowls and Spoons	Needed for clay mixing. Probably can be borrowed.
Old Newspapers	Necessary to artproof work areas.
Paint Shirts or	Necessary for most art sessions.
Smocks	Each child should have his own.
Paper	Ditto paper, computer printout paper; other types might be scrounged.
Paper towels	
Pencils	School provides or child brings.
Plastic Bags	Dry cleaning bags can be used. Smaller bags can be recycled. The school lunchroom or local grocery store may donate.
Sacks	School kitchen, local grocery stores can provide. Children themselves can collect and donate all sizes of paper sacks.
Soap	School provides.
Sponges	Custodian may provide.
Stapler	School office supplies.
Straight pins	School office supplies.
Water	Either via sink or via 2 or 3 buckets (1 for dirty water and brushes).
Wood scraps	Lumberyard, construction sites provide free.

Amounts have not been specified in the scrounge list. These would depend on the individual lesson planned, materials immediately available, the needs of the teacher, and the children and available storage space.

REFERENCES

Hoover, F. L. *Art activities for the very young.* Worcester, Mass.: Davis, 1961.

Salome, R. A. *Suggested amounts of several basic materials for elementary art.* Unpublished manuscript, Normal, Ill.: Illinois State University, n.d.

AUTHOR INDEX

A

Absen, A., ix, xi
Ain, E., 48
Alexander, M., 238
Anderson, B. E., 238
Anderson, W., 180, 241
Anderson, Y., 238
Art Therapy Training, 97, 177

B

Ball, F. C., 237
Barger, B., 237
Barnfield, Larry S., 72 fnt., 85 fnt., 91 fnt., 92 fnt., 164 fnt.
Berlyne, D. E., 152, 178
Bevlin, M. E., 237
Blackwood, P. E., 124 fnt., 178
Brandwein, P. F., 124 fnt., 178
Brittain, W. L., 22, 26, 28-29, 41, 49, 180
Brommer, G. F., 238
Brumfiel, C. F., 178
Buktenica, N. A., 116, 178
Burke, T., 178

C

Calder, Alexander, 115
Campbell, D. T., 49
Caney, S., 239
Castanesa, A., 99, 178
Castrup, J., 24, 26, 48
Cooper, E. K., 124 fnt., 178
Cratty, B. J., 24, 26, 48
Cruickshank, W. M., 19

D

Davis, P., 238
deKooning, Willem, 142, 197
Dienez, Z. P., 178
Dolan, E. F., 239
Duckworth, E., 125 fnt., 178

E

Educational Development Center, 125 fnt., 127, 178
Effland, A., 44, 49
Eicholz, R. E., 98, 178
Eisner, E., 44, 49
Ennever, L., 124 fnt., 125 fnt., 126-127, 178

F

Feldman, E. B., 237
Fiarotta, P., 239
Fitts, W. H., 94
Fleenor, C. R., 98, 178
Ford, F., 18
Fraser, T. P., 124 fnt., 178
Fukurai, Shiro, 15, 18, 239

G

Gibb, G., 99, 178
Golomb, C., 22, 49
Good, R. G., 179
Goodwin, P., 191, 192 fnt.

H

Hamacheck, D. E., 94
Hanks, C., 95, 179
Harlen, W., 124 fnt., 125 fnt., 126-127, 178
Harms, J., 25, 49
Harris, D. B., 4, 18, 22, 26, 49
Hashman, H., 178-179
Herman, W. L., Jr., 179
Herrera, S., 127, 178
Hollander, A., 239
Hollander, H. C., 239-240
Holter, P., 238
Hoover, F. L., 250, 252
Horn, G., 237
Horne, Bruce, 190 fnt., 191
Horne, E. B., 124 fnt., 178
Hubbard, G. A., 180, 241

J

Johnson, G. O., 19

K

Kaltsouns, T., 179
Kampmann, L., 238
Karplus, R., 124 fnt., 125 fnt., 126-127, 178
Kellogg, R., 21-22, 24, 49
Kirk, S. A., 3, 9, 18
Kirkpatrik, J., 98, 179
Kline, Franz, 142, 193, 197
Klineman, J., 15, 19
Kramer, E., ix, xi, 180, 239, 241
Krasner, L. P., 6, 19

253

L

Lacey, J. C., 237
LaLiberté, N., 238
Langer, S., ix, xi
Lansing, K. M., 22, 49, 97, 179, 180, 241
Lavatelli, C. S., 152, 179
Lawson, C. A., 124 fnt., 125 fnt., 126-127, 178
Lerner, J. W., 4-5, 18
Lewis, H. P., 49
Linderman, E. W., 237
Linderman, M. M., 237
Lindsay, Z., 240
Lindstrom, M., 22, 49
Long, N. C., 7, 18
Lord, 3
Lovoos, J., 237
Lowenfeld, Viktor, ix, xi, 22-23, 26, 28-29, 41, 49, 180, 240

M

Maestas Y Moores, J., 49
Mager, R. F., 44, 49
Marcus, I. D., Jr., 10, 19
Martin, E., 178
McAshan, H. H., 43, 49
McFee, J. K., 5, 49
McKinley, Gary, 190 fnt., 191
Mitchel, L. S., 152, 179
Mogelon, A., 238
Moore, W. J., 179
Morreau, L., 46, 49
Morse, W. C., 8, 18, 19

N

Naumburg, M., 240
Nelson, D., 98, 179
Nelson, G. C., 237
Newman, R. G., 7, 18
Nuffield Mathematics Project, 99, 179

O

O'Daffer, P., 98, 178

P

Payne, J., 178, 179
Piaget, 125, 152
Pollock, Jackson, 142, 197

Q

Quinn, T., 95, 179

R

Rainey, S. R., 239
Randle, J. C., 127, 178, 179
Rhyne, J., 240-241
Rogers, R. E., 126, 179
Romney, W., 179
Rouse, M. J., 180, 241
Rubin, J. A., 15, 19, 20, 49, 240

S

Salome, R. A., 250, 252
Sarason, I. G., 19
Saunders, R. J., 22, 28, 49, 51, 59
Sawrey, J. M., 9, 11, 14, 19
Schein, J. D., 10, 19
Schwartz, R. D., 49
Scott, R., 48
Sechrest, L., 49
Shanks, M. E., 178
Sigel, I. E., 152, 179
Silver, R. A., 9-10, 19
Smith, David, 115
Spodek, B., 152, 179
Spurgeon, J., 191, 192 fnt.
Stake, R., 44, 49
Stolnitz, J., ix, xi

T

Telford, C. W., 9, 11, 14, 19
Thier, H. D., 127, 178, 179
Timmons, V. G., 237
Trafton, P., 98, 179

U

Ullman, L., 6, 19
Uno, A. Q., 240

V

Voelker, A. M., 126, 179

W

Wayne, H. L., Jr., 178
Webb, E. J., 43, 49
Wells, D., 178-179
Wills, J., 191, 192 fnt.
Wiseman, A., 239
Woodson, B., 191, 192 fnt.
Wylie, R., 94

Y

Young, E., 25, 49, 51, 59

SUBJECT INDEX

255